SHARE THIS TOO

More Social Media Solutions For PR Professionals

Chartered Institute of Public Relations (CIPR)

Edited by Rob Brown and Stephen Waddington

WILEY

Registered office

John Wiley and Sons Ltd, The Atrium, Southern Gate, Chichester, West Sussex, PO19 8SQ, United Kingdom

For details of our global editorial offices, for customer services and for information about how to apply for permission to reuse the copyright material in this book please see our website at www.wiley.com.

Wiley publishes in a variety of print and electronic formats and by print-on-demand. Some material included with standard print versions of this book may not be included in e-books or in print-on-demand. If this book refers to media such as a CD or DVD that is not included in the version you purchased, you may download this material at http://booksupport.wiley.com. For more information about Wiley products, visit www.wiley.com.

Designations used by companies to distinguish their products are often claimed as trademarks. All brand names and product names used in this book and on its cover are trade names, service marks, trademarks or registered trademarks of their respective owners. The publisher and the book are not associated with any product or vendor mentioned in this book. None of the companies referenced within the book have endorsed the book.

Limit of Liability/Disclaimer of Warranty: While the publisher and author have used their best efforts in preparing this book, they make no representations or warranties with respect to the accuracy or completeness of the contents of this book and specifically disclaim any implied warranties of merchantability or fitness for a particular purpose. It is sold on the understanding that the publisher is not engaged in rendering professional services and neither the publisher nor the author shall be liable for damages arising herefrom. If professional advice or other expert assistance is required, the services of a competent professional should be sought.

Library of Congress Cataloging-in-Publication Data

Share this too : more social media solutions for PR professionals / Chartered Institute of Public Relations (CIPR) ; edited by Rob Brown and Stephen Waddington.

    pages cm

  Includes index.

  ISBN 978-1-118-67693-6 (cloth)

1. Public relations. 2. Social media. I. Brown, Rob, 1962 December 17– II. Waddington, Stephen. III. Chartered Institute of Public Relations.

  HD59.S451563 2013

  659.20285'4678–dc23

2013024673

A catalogue record for this book is available from the British Library.

ISBN 978-1-118-67693-6 (hbk) ISBN 978-1-118-67692-9 (ebk)
ISBN 978-1-118-67686-8 (ebk)

Cover design: Salad Creative Ltd

Set in 10/14.5 pt FF Scala Pro by Toppan Best-set Premedia Limited
Printed in Great Britain by TJ International Ltd, Padstow, Cornwall, UK

CONTENTS

LIST OF CONTRIBUTORS

Brian Solis	Principal, Altimeter Group
Rob Brown	Managing Partner, Rule 5
Stephen Waddington	European Digital & Social Media Director, Ketchum
Dom Burch	Head of Social Media, ASDA
Robin Wilson	Social Media Director, McCann Erickson
Ged Carroll	Digital Director, Burson-Marsteller
Kate Matlock	Digital Strategist, Ketchum
Adam Parker	CEO, Realwire
Dr Mark Pack	Head of Digital, Blue Rubicon
Sharon O'Dea	Senior Manager, Online Communications, Standard Chartered Bank
Paul Fabretti	Head of Social Media, Telefónica UK
Michael Litman	Senior Social Strategist, AnalogFolk
Russell Goldsmith	Digital & Social Media Director, markettiers4dc & How To TV
Stephen Davies	Senior Consultant, 33 Digital
Scott Seaborn	Executive Creative Director, XS2
Dan Tyte	Executive Director, Working Word Public Relations
Matt Appleby	Managing Director, Golley Slater PR Wales
Kevin Ruck	Co-founder, PR Academy
Hanna Basha	Partner, PSB Law LLP
Chris Norton	Director, Dinosaur PR
Becky McMichael	Head of strategy and innovation, Ruder Finn UK
Rachel Miller	Director, All Things IC
Stuart Bruce	Founder, Stuart Bruce Associates

Richard Bailey	Lecturer in Public Relations, Leeds Metropolitan University
Jane Wilson	CEO, CIPR
Julio Romo	Founder, twofourseven
Jed Hallam	Social Director, VCCP
Katy Howell	Managing Director, immediate future
Gemma Griffiths	Managing Director, The Crowd & I
Philip Sheldrake	Managing Partner, Euler Partners
Richard Bagnall	Director of Insight and Analysis, Gorkana
Drew Benvie	Founder, Battenhall
Andrew Bruce Smith	Director, escherman
Simon Collister	Senior lecturer in digital communications at University of Arts, London

FOREWORD

Brian Solis, Principal, Altimeter Group

Do you realize just how much is changing right now? I promise you that it's bigger than you think. And your role in this is also much grander than you know or believe. See, disruptive technology, social networks, new influencers, they're levelling the media hierarchy. The ado of crafting messages, pushing them upon targets, and propagating while attempting to control your story is not only the old way, it's the very thinking that's at the forefront of new communications.

This isn't about the new tools that are before you.

This isn't about social media or popular social networks.

This isn't about bloggers and blogging.

Nor is this about tablets, smartphones, and the app economy.

This is about putting the public back in public relations and social in social media and that has nothing to do with tools or technology we overly celebrate today. Slow down. Take a breath. While there's an abundance of change there isn't a wealth of innovation in processes or methodologies.

The truth is that in a time when we could change everything, we're running without clarity of direction or vision. We're not necessarily talking about a revolution as much as we're conforming revolutionary opportunities into familiar packages. We're merely taking what we know and applying it to what's new. In many ways, we're working against ourselves. But, what's happening right now is both revolutionary and evolutionary. And in the face of the unknown it is courage that carries us forward and creativity that will open new doors.

This is a time to rethink the value proposition of marketing and communications and your role within it.

Why is what you do important? Stop. Try that answer again. There's a reason that your friends and family have a hard time understanding what you do for a living. It's because the value you think you provide and the opportunity that is presenting itself to you are in fact two very different things. Essentially, your experience carried you this far but it is your vision and ambition that will carry you forward. Think again about the value you offer and the value that others say you deliver.

Allow me to share a slice of my life with you . . .

I've fond memories of surfing. I would grab my board and wetsuit, play great music, and head for the beaches of Southern California. The ocean was my sanctuary as I would surf for recreation, therapy, and also tranquillity. There was just something about the smell of the ocean, the sound of the waves, and the ability to dance with Mother Nature in a way where she *let* you lead and you appreciated the momentary gesture.

When snowboarding grew in popularity, I immediately embraced it. I did so because I saw it as an art form that was easy to categorize against something familiar. In fact I thought of it as winter surfing and I was wrong to do so. I brought to something new my previous experience and expected it to carry me forward into new territory in a very different environment. What I didn't bring along was a new and open mindset. I overconfidently got on my board, leaned back as you do in surfing and set out to surf that mountain the way I thought I should. I learned, quite painfully, that I did the very thing that you're not supposed to do. See, in surfing, and skateboarding, your back foot is essentially the rudder. You steer by leaning back and using your back foot to steer your course. In snowboarding, it's the exact opposite. You lean forward.

All it took was someone to point out that there was a different philosophy to the approach. Once they did, I was as soulful on a snowboard as I was surfing. It just took an open mind, perseverance, and several ice packs.

Today, in what is nothing less than an emergent moment for marketing and communications, I see even the best of them leaning back instead of leaning forward. It takes a different philosophy. It takes a different approach. If you take a moment to think about it, everything is different about what's taking place now and its direction and future is unwritten.

Again I ask. What is the value of what you do? What's in it for you, your business, and those with whom you engage? This time, think about it beyond the company you represent. Think about it from the perspective of the people you're hoping to reach . . . every step of the way. People are part of everything you do now and you are also among them.

Value is not boundless. Value is in the eye of the beholder and it varies based on the context of the relationship and your desired outcomes. It is relationships, after all, that form the foundation of business. Marketing and communications are merely enablers for conveying value while also investing in and reinforcing relationships.

What you do and how you do it now serves a higher purpose. This is why I believe that your role in this is much grander than you may realize or believe. Lean forward.

Brian Solis, digital analyst and author of What's the Future of Business (WTF)
www.briansolis.com
@briansolis

INTRODUCTION

This isn't a book about a specialist area of PR, it is about how current practice is evolving and where industry as a whole will be in the immediate future.

Share This: The Social Media Handbook for PR Professionals published by Wiley in 2012 was conceived as a practical handbook for PR people interested in changes taking place in the media and the impact that this was having on the practice of PR. It was written by 24 public relations practitioners, receiving critical acclaim and quickly establishing itself as a number one bestseller in the PR book chart.

Share This Too is even more ambitious. It is a pragmatic guide for anyone that works in communication or public relations. It is a larger book than the original with more than 30 contributors, each of whom is acknowledged as an expert in their field.

The group has been assembled from the CIPR Social Media Panel and associates, many of whom contributed to *Share This*. It includes academic, in-house, and agency practitioners from a mix of business, public sector, and third-sector.

Six of the contributors are published authors in their own right.

This isn't by any means a second edition. The content complements the first book by probing deeply into what is current in the theory, delivery, and evaluation of 21st century public relations and organizational communication.

The editorial process for *Share This Too* followed that developed for *Share This*. Contributors worked to rigorous editorial guidelines, submitting their draft text to a Google Document. Each chapter was peer reviewed by the other contributors.

Our thanks go to each of the authors for investing their time and energy in this project and the team at the CIPR for supporting this project, in particular Phil Morgan, Kim Roberts and Andrew Ross.

Rob Brown and Stephen Waddington

2013

Part I

The Future of Public Relations

Chapter 1

Rob Brown

The distinction between digital and "mainstream" or "conventional" channels is at best unhelpful. The term "new media" is archaic and the line between new and old is impossible to draw.

Audiences are changing: every graduate entering the workplace now and forever was born after the arrival of the web. Print won't disappear in a single generation, whilst there is an aging population more at home with dead wood and ink, but it will be consumed by an ever decreasing demographic. The binary idea that something is digital or not is no longer very useful. Are radio and TV digital or analogue? The answer is that they are both, or possibly neither.

It appears likely that social networks passed the 50% adoption threshold in the middle of 2011. They are no longer niche channels accessed primarily by young people. According to website monitoring company Pingdom, the average age of Facebook users is now over forty.

It is often argued by those that decry social networks that they are somehow marginal channels simply because they don't like them or manage perfectly well without them. Universal adoption is seldom achieved by any technology. It doesn't matter that some people, perhaps even a significant proportion, will never use Twitter; some people don't own a television. The fact is that social channels now play a significant part in communications and for many they have become their first preference for news consumption. We must call time on the notion that digital or online PR is somehow a specialization or a separate discipline. Digital PR is dead.

The continuing evolution of the media

There was a time, not so very long ago, when our concept of the media was a simple one. Printed newspapers were divided neatly into national, regional and local. There were trade and consumer magazines. We had national and local radio stations and television channels that you could count using your fingers. There was also a time, a bit further back, when we just had cave paintings.

Newspapers have re-invented themselves as multi-platform media brands operating across lots of different delivery systems. Print newspapers exist primarily for the convenience of their older readers. Never mind the quality of the papers, feel the width. Not quite as bulky as they used to be are they? Every print newspaper has an online edition and for most there are apps for phones and tablets. We now expect online newspapers to carry video.

Recognizing the trend towards tablet computers, the *Financial Times* launched a promotion at the end of 2012 offering a Google Nexus 7 tablet free to any subscriber in the US taking out a one-year subscription to the digital edition. That's more than just a promotion given that the Nexus 7 retails at $199, which is almost half the value of an annual subscription. Barnes & Noble have also heavily discounted the Nook Colour tablet along with a yearly digital subscription to the *New York Times*.

The way we watch television has changed. Sky+, BBC iPlayer, YouView and a plethora of other systems have handed the schedule to the viewer. Commuters watch their favourite programmes on their phones on the way to work. Content from broadcasters and from other sources including brands is converging. Does it matter whether we listen to radio on a dedicated box in the car or kitchen or through the headphones of a laptop? The line between digital and analogue has faded to the point where it is barely identifiable.

The blurring of channels

Is the *Huffington Post* a newspaper? The title undoubtedly owes something to the history of print. Most of the content, however, is produced by non journalists. That is not intended to be pejorative. It is a simple fact that the majority of contributors do not meet the commonly understood definition of journalism as a paid job or profession. The other obvious observation is that the *Huffington Post* isn't printed on paper.

If you listen to both BBC Radio 4's media show and the *Guardian's* Media Talk on your iPod, is one a radio show and the other a podcast?

If you compare the websites of *USA Today* – the biggest selling newspaper in America – and CNN – the main all news channel on US television – they are pretty similar. In fact the video content is more prominent on the newspaper site than on the TV site. Google has been a news aggregator for more than a decade and Twitter now links to news stories via its "top news" feature.

Talking to friends and colleagues, most of us often don't register where we get our breaking news; it may be via a link on Twitter or the car radio. What really matters is the story.

The impact of social media and networks

Social networks at their inception didn't have much to do with news. As the name implies they were largely social, helping us to connect with old or current school friends. Now many of these social channels are at the core of both the gathering and dissemination of news.

The world woke up to Twitter's capacity to deliver news almost instantly, during the Mumbai terrorist attacks of November 2008. Since then its role has become far more pervasive. Twitter delivers news but it can also influence the agenda. Debates often take place in the social space before they are elevated to the pages of newspapers or broadcast channels. Journalists recognize the importance of building their follower numbers in order to promote traffic to their stories.

In 2012 Google made some significant changes to its news search which included greater integration with Google+. Google+ comments appear on news search pages and in real-time coverage pages. Google+ members are also able to see comments from people in their circles on the news pages. Scott Zuccarino, the Google News product manager, said at launch: "many news stories inspire vibrant discussions on Google+, and today we're starting to add this content to both the news homepage and the real-time coverage pages."

The growth of social media adoption

In recent years delivering communications programmes using social networks as delivery channels was a specialist activity. When the networks were new, adoption was low and they were niche channels. Social networks are now a mainstream phenomenon. Facebook claimed in October 2012 that it had passed the billion user mark with more than 50% of the US population signed up, and Australasia, Latin America and Europe all have similar adoption levels.[1]

NM Incite, a joint venture between research firm Nielsen and management consultants McKinsey, took a comprehensive look at social media adoption in 2012. They found that the total time spent on PCs and mobile devices grew by 21% over the previous year, with time spent on mobile apps more than doubling.[2]

According to a Pew report published in December 2012 people in developing countries are joining social networks at a higher rate than the populations of Europe, North America and Australasia. The global report looked at 21 nations and found that the majority of internet users in Brazil, Mexico, Tunisia, Jordan, Egypt, Turkey, India and Russia use social media.[3]

The report also indicates that the adoption of mobile phones has led growth. In fact the way people access the internet is perhaps a more important question for PR people than whether they access the news via digital or analogue platforms.

Digital is part of every programme

The most powerful argument for the absence of a division between traditional and digital PR is that it is difficult to conceive of a PR campaign that is entirely without a digital dimension.

---

[1]Report: Social network demographics in 2012: http://cipr.co/Wsb2vE
[2]The Social Media Report 2012: http://cipr.co/XiuBpJ
[3]Social Networking Popular Across Globe: http://cipr.co/WrWaPH

Print publications without any form of digital outlet are a rarity, so even if you think you are sending a press release to a print title you are putting it online too. That alone makes it essential for a PR person to understand the dynamics of the web.

Many journalists were amongst the earliest adopters on Twitter. Many appear to be more inclined to respond to an engaging tweet than they are to a phone call or email. If it is possible to build a relationship with a journalist via that route why would any PR person choose not to do so?

Evolution and the opportunity for PR

I believe that the discipline of PR is in a process of rapid evolution, where the knowledge, skills and practice of public relations are changing. It would be complacent to say that this doesn't present us with some real challenges. It also provides the PR function with some real opportunities.

The evolution of the media and communications in general is reshaping the nature and the relationships between different types of marketing communications operations. PR people face increased competition from advertising agencies, search engine optimization (SEO) specialists, digital agencies and others. However, public relations practitioners are uniquely placed to take advantage of a world where conversation and dialogue have largely supplanted top-down, one-way messaging. Our skills are firmly rooted in debate, discussion and the art of persuasion. We have always operated through intermediaries when delivering news and information. The intermediaries may have changed and broadened but those skills are as valuable as ever.

There are new skills to learn too, many of them were covered in *Share This. Share This Too* explores the knowledge and skills base still further.

One of these skills is the ability to read and interpret web analytics. I've encountered PR people who visibly freeze when the subject of analytics is raised and yet we've always used analytics. Combined circulation figures, key message scores and the discredited practice of advertising value equivalents were all analytics. The data may be more complex – "getting information off the Internet is like taking a drink from a fire hydrant" said Mitchell Kapor, pioneer of the PC industry – but it's increasingly easy to access and gain insight from. Many web services and social networks have easy-to-use built-in in analytics. Every PR person should have at least a working knowledge of how to gather insight and information this way.

Opportunities we should seize

The socialization and democratization of the web have redrawn communications and in doing so they have blurred boundaries. With the challenges this brings there are also new opportunities.

Video content

Video content will become increasingly evident in PR campaigns. The growth in video consumption is astronomical. YouTube statistics are eye-watering. Psy's Gangnam Style has racked up a billion views and on YouTube as a whole there are approaching 5 billion views a day. Platforms like Apple TV are bringing down the walls between web TV and current broadcast platforms. Cost of production is in freefall. Producing engaging video content should become a serious consideration for many PR campaigns.

PR-led SEO

> "Google is not a search engine. Google is a reputation-management system . . . online, your rep is quantifiable, findable, and totally unavoidable. In other words, radical transparency is a double-edged sword, but once you know the new rules, you can use it to control your image in ways you never could before."

Clive Thompson said this in *Wired* in 2007.[4] PR has always been about reputation management and a key determinant of reputation is the content on page one of a Google Search. The most important tool that search engine optimization specialists have at their disposal is now the "press release". If

---

[4]Wired: http://cipr.co/WXwpmN

we educate ourselves about the value of good editorial combined with link strategies as part of PR, we can greatly elevate the power of PR. The search engine companies are actually working in our favour, since they are engaged in a constant struggle to promote natural search elevating real news and information. This is where the enlightened PR person comes in.

Redefining our relationships with journalists

The hugely insightful journalist and blogger Tom Foremski has said "PR people . . . are pitching stories to journalists who have very much smaller pageviews on the stories they write, and far smaller Twitter/Facebook communities to which to distribute their stories, than the PR people." PR people need to build their own communities both to deliver news directly but also so that we are able to direct a relevant audience to stories that have been written with the independent perspectives of journalists.

Digital PR is dead because all PR is digital.

Biography

Rob Brown (@robbrown) has worked in PR for over 20 years and for over 15 years held senior PR positions within three major global advertising networks: Euro RSCG, McCann Erickson and TBWA. He launched his own business "Rule 5" in MediaCityUK, Manchester in November 2012. Rob is the author of *Public Relations and the Social Web* (2009), blogs for *The Huffington Post* and has written chapters for *Public Relations Cases: International Perspectives* (2010), *Public Relations: A Managerial Perspective* (2011) and *Share This: The Social Media Handbook for PR Professionals* (2012). He is founding chair of the Chartered Institute of Public Relations Social Media Panel.

Chapter 2

THE SHIFT TO CONVERSATION: CONTENT, CONTEXT AND AVOIDING CHEAP TALK

Dom Burch

In the race to be liked on Facebook or followed on Twitter, brands must focus on creating engaging content that resonates with their customers or stakeholders. Social media content should always be relevant to who you are and what you do. The most authentic brands resist the temptation to follow the buzz and always strive to look and feel the same on the outside as they do on the inside. Traditional media relations, as we know, are gradually being eclipsed by the rise in social media relations. The days of PR departments endlessly issuing press releases to generate news and capture column inches are in decline. What's more, traditional print coverage is becoming less relevant to brands, many of whom are now significant media owners in their own right (Nike, Red Bull, Audi).

With access to large groups via social networks, brands are beginning to engage significant numbers of customers or stakeholders in regular conversation and, when managed carefully, positively influence their perception. In that context, generating engaging and relevant content (or news as it was once known) continues to be one of the most important disciplines for strategic communication professionals.

While the means of communication are shifting from traditional media to social media, the need to focus on creating engaging content that resonates with a brand's publics, be they customers or stakeholders, has never been more important. Yet some brands have placed too much emphasis on reaching scale quickly at all costs, without due care and attention towards the quality of the connections being established.

Unlike press releases of old that often jumped straight to the big sell, social media requires brands to be less direct and more willing to engage in conversation.

Getting started

The best content-led engagement strategies are built on a simple three-pronged approach: listen first, engage second, and seek to influence or persuade last. Sequential in order, but not necessarily equal in terms of time needed to master each phase, it is essential before getting started to gain insight into what people are saying about your brand.

Case study: Asda

Asda followed a methodical five-year plan when first approaching social media in 2009. The first year was almost entirely dedicated to listening and monitoring. Year two led to trials of Twitter handles and the introduction of a new interactive corporate blog/website called Your Asda. The monitoring and listening continued, leading to insight that enabled Asda to focus on engagement in year three. In year four, armed with three years' worth of insight, two years of trialling things and a year of outreach and engagement, Asda was able to accelerate its efforts and significantly grow its presence on social media. Year five sees the introduction of tightly managed programmes that seek to influence customers by sending large numbers of them towards specific activity, be that online or in store.

Asda's five-year strategic social media model
Monitoring and listening
Social networks like Twitter have become relatively free, real-time focus groups, where increasing numbers of people openly discuss a brand's advertising, pricing, products and services, members of staff or customers. As a result, savvy marketing and PR professionals have quickly

learned the importance of listening closely to what is being said. The old adage that your reputation is what people say about you when you leave the room is still true, but social media monitoring now gives brands unrivalled access and insight into those conversations outside the room.

Brands in traditional sectors like financial services have taken longer than most to get started, dwelling on stage one. There are notable exceptions like First Direct, which led the way in trialling social media on its core website. However, many others have at best been listening without much engagement – perhaps fearful of regulators, or amplifying customer service issues, or because internal structures cause inertia.

Other sectors like retail and travel have recognized the opportunity, and have worked hard to avoid reputational issues by listening closely to what people are saying about them, and moving quickly to intervene, taking problems offline to resolve them swiftly.

Knowing when to join in
Blindly following the social buzz each day can take brands into uncomfortable territory, and can leave customers – be they followers or fans – questioning the validity of their relationship.

Just because everyone else is talking about something doesn't mean a brand should too. For example, when the Duchess of Cambridge announced she was pregnant, brand after brand clamoured to celebrate the imminent new arrival. Many fell into the trap of making tenuous connections.

When approaching social media, it is absolutely key to have a clear content strategy. It forces brands to consider who they really are and what they stand for. The risk of not having a strategic approach is that some brands try too hard to be popular by blindly following the crowd or buzz of the day, inserting themselves into conversations without a clear reason or purpose. Even sponsoring non-related but popular hashtags on Twitter can be met with a muted response at best or a negative reaction at worst. Asda Deals sponsored a Ricky Gervais trending hashtag to recruit new followers. Many reacted angrily to Asda Deals appearing in their timeline.

Content and context

Natural and meaningful conversations in social media reflect conversations in real life. They are two-way dialogues, not one-way broadcasts, where open-ended questions are posed to seek out opinions.

Conversations in the real world become more meaningful as the relationship develops, and don't tend to jump immediately into a justification of a particular viewpoint or into an aggressive sales pitch.

So when brands adopt this style in social media, with an audience that it hasn't harnessed and built trust with, the reaction can be either negative or disengaging.

Context therefore dictates a brand's tone of voice. Red Bull has a clear brand proposition, giving it the licence to associate itself with a breadth of hair-raising events and activities. Most brands, however, are more restricted in what they can legitimately be interested in. If you are a shop that sells baked beans, always bear in mind that's how others will view you.

Social media content should always have a clear purpose, be that to inform, entertain or inspire. Before embarking on a social media programme, brands should consider carefully what outcomes they are seeking to achieve. Are they attempting to gain insight, elicit a response, or drive traffic, whether online or in-store? By being explicit about what their social media content is trying to achieve, they are better placed to set clear, measurable goals that can act as a benchmark for future activity.

Building the right relationships

The biggest mistake a brand can make on social media is prioritizing the rapid acquisition of new fans or followers above the quality of the relationships they are building. At Asda there is a mantra when it comes to measuring the success of social media – "fans are for vanity, engagement is sanity".

Some of the most successful brands currently harnessing social media have taken an organic approach to building their communities. That's not to say that organic necessarily means slow. From a standing start it is possible to build large communities and reach scale quickly, but the tactics used are important and will dictate who joins the community, how actively engaged they are, and how relevant a connection has been made.

When handled well, social media lets brands recruit ambassadors and cheerleaders, who once engaged have the ability to turbo-charge natural word of mouth and act as the first line of defence when things go wrong. Stefan Olander, VP of Digital Sport at Nike, famously said: "Once you have established a direct relationship with a consumer, you don't need to advertise to them." That's how powerful social media can be.

One size doesn't fit all

While the mass market appeal of Facebook gives brands the opportunity to reach large numbers of their customers through their newsfeeds, other social networks can create opportunities to reach different customer segments or interest groups.

The key is understanding the unique benefits each social network might bring to your brand – and then, if you decide it's worth investing the time and effort, identifying the type of content or conversations that are appropriate in each context. Simply copying posts designed to generate fan engagement on Facebook and pasting them into Google+ or Twitter is missing the point. Content strategies need to be in a continual state of review as the social media landscape shifts and changes.

Tailored content that fits distinct social platforms and meets the needs of the specific audience is likely to develop in the same way as it did for traditional PR professionals who once had to write different releases for different sectors – be that trade, consumer, local or national.

A case study of using social media at the heart of an organization – Hope and Social

Hope and Social is a six-piece rock band based in Leeds, Yorkshire. Formed in 2008 the band is characterized by its "Pay What You Want" approach to music. Nobody really "manages" them as such, but they work hard to ensure their fans feel every bit as much a part of the band as the musicians themselves.

They have released four albums in less than four years, all under the banner of Alamo Music, the first ever fan-funded, fan-owned record label.

(*Continued*)

This is how they describe themselves on the home page of their website www.hopeandsocial.com:

> "We make timeless music and give it away, like our brand new album All Our Dancing Days. We involve people in everything we do, and they never fail to amaze us. We have fun and make art. We create events to remember. We talk about what we do and stuff we care about. We hail from Yorkshire in the north of England, where we have an enigmatic studio called The Crypt. We share what we learn from the mistakes that we make. Fingers crossed, we will die with our hearts out in bloom. We are Hope and Social. Lovely to meet you."

Ben Denison "helps out" with the band, and has had a huge influence on how they have adopted social media, making it an integral part of how the brand operates and functions. Ben says:

> "Content and context is king. Putting your products within a story is absolutely key. They become more valuable objects that way. People buy into the story and the product. As the two become intertwined you lose track of which is the story and which is the product. The barriers are removed.
>
> Organisations used to be characterised by how they saw themselves from the inside and how others viewed them from the outside. When the two were different, something would inevitably leak. Social media now means the two must be the same as you tell your story to the outside world.
>
> Social at its best is small; it is telephone not megaphone. Brands therefore should think of social media like being in a country pub. You wouldn't walk in and start shouting about how great a person you are or handing out cash. You'd sidle up to the bar, pull up a stool and listen in to the conversations going on around you. You'd join in when you had something interesting to say, and it wouldn't be about you, it'd be about something you know that you want to share to spark the interest of others. Social media is no more complicated than that.

Wherever possible you should celebrate the values of the organisation that you are in. Have a common belief that everyone aligns themselves to, a higher purpose that connects with people, and moves your content away from the functional to the emotional.

More and more forms of corporate communication are moving towards conversational style harnessing the personality of the brand. Emails sent from organisations are more likely to be opened if they are interesting, not just shouting calls to action at you. You can't preach or direct people to go here or go there all the time.

Cleverly devised content is a person to person experience with the ambition of creating "vibrating" advocates as I call them. Cheerleaders who have been positively infected by who you are, what you stand for, and what you do – but in that order not the other way round.

Thinking person to person means every post, every tweet, every email, every interaction has to be as good, if not better than the last – otherwise the people who you are engaging with will slowly begin to lose interest. And winning them back round is really hard to do.

As social media develops and grows it will be important for brands to create sub-groups and smaller clans of people who are passionate about certain things. You can't expect everyone to love everything about you, so remind yourself you are in the country pub and striking up conversations.

Building friendship is based on equality and genuine interest in others. Then if you're really smart you can tell them about your little country pub down the road and when you leave, they may just follow for a nightcap, and if you're really lucky they'll bring one or two friends with them."

Danny Blackburn is head of content at IMP Media Ltd, a social media agency based in Leeds with clients including Everything Everywhere, Hobbycraft and Asda. He says a lot of companies admit they

(Continued)

focus on engaging content without really understanding what it actually means: "In a nutshell it's about having a clear strategy to begin with (we're saying X to Y in order to achieve Z), knowing your audience, giving them what they actually want, and doing it in a way that encourages them to respond, get involved or tell others." He points to a number of examples of brands getting it right.

Intrepid travel: Genuinely inspiring, high-quality content. They really understand the motivation of the people they're conversing with. They use social media in a way that manages to promote the brand without actually feeling like it's promoting the brand. I look forward to their posts popping up in my newsfeed: www.facebook.com/intrepidtravel.

Rapha Racing: Yes, I know it's cycling (snore), but it's a cracking example of brand extension. Rapha clothing is expensive, exclusive, boutique gear for people who "appreciate quality" (or "with more money than sense"). The Facebook Page exudes the same feeling which makes people want to spend so much cash. It's aspirational, reeks of quality, and makes you feel like you're part of a club. The fanbase is small, but that's fine for a brand like this: www.facebook.com/rapharacing.

Red Bull: It's an obvious one, but you can't argue with 'em. They're essentially a media company now – massively high production values, producing content that's perfect for the people they're trying to reach and to convey the image they want to put out there. They have a massive fanbase and engage them online by covering the subjects the fans care about and (generally) the subjects that aren't covered anywhere else. Great use of sponsorship too, amplifying the very best stuff they produce far and wide: www.facebook.co.uk/redbull.

Danny adds: "It's all about really understanding who you're talking to and producing relevant content – that takes investment of time, money and creativity. You look forward to, enjoy and welcome the most engaging Facebook content appearing in your newsfeed.

I guess it's easier to stay relevant when your target demographic is focused and narrow. If Red Bull suddenly diversified into nappies and baby wipes they'd struggle to talk to their existing Facebook audience in an engaging way – the same is true for Asda if it tried to talk to its audience about action sports. Although babies riding freestyle motocross bikes would be quite cool . . ."

Biography

Dom Burch (@domburch) works for Asda. He studied PR at Leeds Metropolitan University back in 1994, graduating with a BA Hons degree in the
summer of 1998. His first (unpaid) job was with Cause Connection, a CSR
unit within Saatchi & Saatchi, before being properly employed by Green Flag
in Leeds as a PR assistant. Following a two-year stint at Direct Line in Croydon
Dom joined Asda in 2002, working his way up from PR manager to head of
PR and social media. He is the architect of Asda's social media strategy, and
looks forward to the day when he never has to speak to a journalist.

Chapter 3

CONTENT FRAMEWORKS: USING CONTENT TO ACHIEVE MARKETING COMMUNICATIONS GOALS

Robin Wilson

Content is probably the most powerful asset in current marketing communications campaigns and will only become more important. In terms of engaging audiences, and driving business goals, creating a compelling content strategy is perhaps one of the most critical factors facing businesses today. What follows is an overview and a simple methodology for planning content strategies with practical tips for producing content frameworks.

Rise of content marketing

In the age of shareable "always on" communications, brands are being urged to become publishers and use content more effectively to deliver business benefit. More and more companies are creating and publishing content across their owned media platforms, sharing content through earned media channels and displaying content in paid media. This has led to the rise of a new discipline called Content Marketing.

According to the Content Marketing Institute (CMI):

> "Content marketing is a marketing technique of creating and distributing relevant and valuable content to attract, acquire and engage a clearly defined and understood target audience – with the objective of driving profitable customer action."[5]

---

[5]Content Marketing Institute: http://cipr.co/TXKvb5

Research suggests that content marketing is set to grow in importance. In 2012 Econsultancy published research in conjunction with Outbrain[6] that revealed that 90% of digital marketing executives believe content marketing will become more important in the next 12 months.

However, the move to becoming a publisher is not a simple one. Brands are used to selling products whereas publishers sell advertising space. It's a different way of thinking. The Econsultancy research reported that only 38% of digital marketers have a defined content strategy.

Acting like a media company and producing content that people want to read, watch or listen to, is very different from producing content you want people to read – the difference between publishing and advertising.

Some companies have adopted this way of thinking. Red Bull[7] is probably the best example of a brand acting like a publisher as it produces content that people want to watch while integrating the brand messages. The trick is having a content strategy at the heart of your marketing strategy.

Developing content strategies

Like any marketing communications or public relations strategy, a content marketing strategy should be part of the wider marketing strategy. It should take the organization from point A, where you are now, to point B, where you want to be and deliver against business objectives.

The following process for developing a content strategy is pretty straight-forward and a good starting point.

1. Marketing objectives

What marketing objectives can you contribute to or influence with content? Some of the marketing objectives that content can impact on are:

- **Brand health:** the right kind of content used in the right context can affect positive sentiment, favourability and goodwill towards the brand.

---

[6]Econsultancy report and blog post: http://cipr.co/YzXDC3
[7]Red Bull Facebook Page: http://cipr.co/yeOP9N

- **Brand recognition and recall:** highly shareable, compelling content can spread far and wide and help raise awareness of a brand, product or service.
- **Education:** highly visual content in particular can really help educate an audience on a complex or emotive issue. The NHS in Leicester produced a very powerful social marketing campaign on teen pregnancy[8] that showed a young girl giving birth in a playground from the point of view of a schoolmate, capturing the moment on a mobile phone. (Unfortunately, the video was subsequently banned by YouTube.)
- **Purchase consideration and loyalty:** content, particularly that which creates repeat interaction, can be used to keep the brand front of mind, which supports consideration and repeat purchase.

Maybe it's stating the obvious, but the starting point should be to think about how content can be used to contribute to the organization's marketing objectives.

2. Content objectives

What do you want the content to do? Thinking about the marketing objectives you want to affect, work out content-specific goals. It's worth thinking about the specific actions or reactions you want content to generate. For example:

MARCOMMS OBJECTIVES	CONTENT OBJECTIVES	CONTENT KPIS
Brand Recognition	Awareness	Views
Brand Loyalty	Engagement	Shares, comments, Likes, Retweets, repins.
Education	Awareness	Views
	Engagement	Shares, comments, Likes
Sales	Leads, enquiries	Click throughs

Types of content objectives and how they can impact marketing communications objectives

---

[8]Teen pregnancy video: http://cipr.co/11mTmr7

The specific content objectives and associated KPIs will be bespoke to an organization's marketing plan and business goals.

3. Audience behaviour

What type of content does your audience read, watch, share and interact with?

It's important to work out early on in the process what content is going to appeal to your audience and, perhaps more importantly, what content will drive the action you desire. Usually, a range of content will appeal to your audience and drive several actions. Things to look at are:

- **Subject matter:** areas of interest that are relevant to the brand. Everyone has shared a cute animal photo at some point, but often this type of content is not highly relevant to the brand or product.
- **Organization expertise:** the expert content an organization can provide that will help or be useful to the target audience.
- **Content format:** does the audience watch large amounts of video content, or mainly photos and text?
- **Online behaviour:** what does the audience do online? Do they just watch content or do they create content and comment on others' content? It is worth looking at the channels they use and how they use them. Forrester's social technographic behaviour research[9] is a good place to start.

In an ideal world, primary research, such as that gained from focus groups and quantitative surveys, would provide the best insight into an audience's content habits. However, in the real world, looking at how your target audience currently interacts with content on yours and your competitors' online properties can generate useful insights into what will work and what won't.

Thinking through the three points above provides a good foundation for developing a content production framework that will deliver against your organization's objectives.

---

[9]Forrester technographics: http://cipr.co/VPm9hZ

Content production framework

While it is likely to vary from organization to organization, it's worth thinking about the sources of content. A simple methodology that provides some structure to content production is the 3Cs.

Created content

This is content created and owned by the organization. A good starting point is to review all the content that has already been created. For example:

- Presentations used for sales, conferences and internal comms.
- Marketing collateral.
- Event photos and videos.
- Customer service communications.

The next step is to look at simple ways of creating the required content. There is usually lots of good stuff in the heads of senior management and other knowledgeable people in the organization that can be simply downloaded into video interviews, blog posts or articles.

Then, to ensure a steady stream of content, build content creation into as many of the organization's activities as possible. A good motto is "everything counts" as it's better to have too much content than too little. Record and snap exhibitions and events where the organization has a presence and ensure that things like visual PR stories are captured. Ideally, an organization should start creating activities that will produce the content required.

As noted earlier, Red Bull is probably the best at this, as the organization has content creation at the heart of all of its marketing. The drinks company has a media unit dedicated to producing content and all of its sponsorship activities are captured and shared across its owned media channels.

Curated content

Curating content from trusted third parties can add elements to a content programme that are not easily created by the organization. For example, sharing content from expert sources, such as specialist blogs, can add expertise that doesn't exist within the company. Sharing content from news organizations and other companies related to their sector can broaden the appeal of an organization's content marketing.

For curated content to have the most impact, it's important for the organization to add something to it. This isn't about changing the content, but adding some context as to why it is relevant to that organization's audience. Posting a link to an interesting article on Mashable with a comment saying "hey, check this out" doesn't really add any value – it's more appealing to an audience if the organization explains why it will be interesting and perhaps adds its own opinion or take on the topics discussed in the article.

Also, creating content is resource intensive, so having a strategy that involves curating others' content ensures there can always be sufficient volume of content.

Organizations should be diligent in making transparent what content is curated and what is created. It may be stating the obvious, but there should be no hint of claiming someone else's content as your own. All curated content should be credited and, where appropriate, permission to share from the content's owner obtained.

Commissioned content

Commissioned content is, perhaps, a misleading term as it is not necessarily just about organizations paying producers to make content on their behalf: it also includes traditional influencer relations, where an organization builds relationships with bloggers, journalists and other influencers and works with them to supply information that the influencer then turns into content, then shares that content on the influencer's owned media. Blogger relations, media relations and other forms of influencer relations, which do not involve any financial payment to the influencer, fall into this category.

In addition, organizations should source content producers to create bespoke content, e.g. commissioning a famous director to produce a short film on behalf of the organization. The Prada[10] film directed by Roman Polan-

---

[10]Prada film: http://cipr.co/YAh9ıh

ski and featuring Helena Bonham Carter is a good example. Here, the film has credibility due to the reputation of the director and people will want to watch the film in its own right. The film will be shown on broader channels than just those owned by the organization. The same principle applies to working with photographers, writers, videographers – any situation where the commissioned content relies upon the credibility of the producer.

This activity blurs the lines with created content. The main difference between created and commissioned content is that a great deal of the commissioned content's value comes from the producer. The audience knows that the producer has made the content for the organization and that is part of the content's appeal.

Getting the balance right

The 3Cs is a good starting point for developing a content framework. Getting the balance of created, curated and commissioned right will depend on the organization's marketing strategy and resources. As a general rule, the most successful content frameworks tend to have more created content than both commissioned and curated. However, success depends on the quality of content produced – the days of getting an intern to take some snaps on their iPhone are long gone.

Below are a few tips that often prove useful:

- **Be interesting:** try and produce content that is compelling to the specific audience that also contributes to the brand objectives.
- **Don't hard sell:** while the content strategy should contribute to a business objective, don't make it all about "buy it now!" People will switch off and go elsewhere.
- **Add value:** try and think about what the audience would find useful that they can't easily get elsewhere and how you can help the audience.
- **Create trust:** use your organization's knowledge to talk with expertise about your field. Ensure that you keep any promises you make.
- **Talk with, not at:** respond sensibly to interactions generated by your content. Don't just "Like" every comment on your Facebook Page. People respond better when they talk with another human being.

Content matrices

When planning how to execute a content strategy, it is often useful to draw up a content matrix that shows what content is going to be used where and when. It's good to ensure there is a balance of:

- **Topics:** you don't want to be talking about the same thing over and over.
- **Formats:** a mixture of text, photos videos, graphics, games, contests, quizzes, will keep the audience's interest.
- **Organization v subject:** balance content about the organization, brand and products with content on non-brand subjects that are still relevant but appeal to the audience.
- **Interactions:** ensure there is something for the audience to do, i.e. there are calls to action, things they will want to share, contests and quizzes to enter or just information that they will find useful. Naturally, common sense should be applied and not every Facebook status should be "Like this now . . .".

Then it's a question of timing. It is good practice to define your content cycle, i.e. the time period for a particular batch of content to run before it is refreshed. By having a content cycle, you can create regular events or activities that people look forward to, e.g. Friday giveaways. Often two to four-week cycles are used – the example in the table below is a two-week cycle.

However, as we are working in a world of "real-time" and "always on" communications, it is essential to build flexibility into the content matrix to enable the organization to respond to topical events and news.

Conclusion

When developing a content strategy, many of the typical communications planning practices apply, e.g. thinking about what you want to achieve, your audience habits and how you want the audience to react. Like any marketing communications activity, thinking things through and applying common sense are highly important. It's important to get the balance right between the different types of content that will appeal to the audience. No one really wants to enjoy the silence of content being ignored.

CONTENT TYPE	Objective	day 1	2	3	4	5	6	7	8	9	10	11	12	13	14
Brand/organization	Awareness	X								X		X			
Product, feature, attribute	Sales		X												
Calendar event	Awareness			X										X	
Topic of interest	Education				X										
Engagement tactic, quiz, contest	Engagement					X					X				
Useful fact	Engagement						X	X					X		
Offer	Sales								X						X

Content matrix example

Biography

Robin Wilson (@robin1966), social media director at McCann Erickson Manchester has over 20 years' PR and social media experience representing brands including Apple, Durex, Facebook, Motorola, MTV, Symantec and Yahoo!. Robin was lucky enough to launch the iPhone in the UK, head up Facebook agency's corporate comms team in the UK and launch Yahoo!'s social search engine, Yahoo! Answers. At McCann Erickson, one of the world's largest marketing communications networks, Robin has devised and directed campaigns for Crabbies Ginger Beer, Lambrini, Holiday Inn, Wickes and Durex – which won several awards including the CIPR Best UK Digital Campaign in 2009.

Part II

Audiences and Online Habits

Chapter 4

Ged Carroll

Digital has been painted both as the future and as a threat to the role of the public relations practitioner. However, digital tools provide techniques to enhance campaign planning and messaging for both on- and offline PR. This chapter provides new ways for the PR practitioner to plan and introduces some of the online tools available to facilitate this process.

Where we've come from

Public relations as a profession arose with the industrial age and mass media. A founding father of the industry, Edward Bernays, is known as the pioneer of publicity; he used principles of the emerging discipline of psychology to help mould audience attitudes. Publicity is a one-way message process that mirrored the command-and-control structures that appeared in early mass production.

Many of Bernays' techniques would be familiar to the PR practitioner:

- Stunts
- Third-party advocacy or endorsement
- Surveys
- Press releases.

Bernays himself described his work:

> This is an age of mass production. In the mass production of materials
> a broad technique has been developed and applied to their distribution.
> In this age, too, there must be a technique for the mass distribution of
> ideas. (Heath 2004 p. 78)[11]

Bernays' planning, whilst taking into account psychological effects, had a limited insight into the consumer audience he was trying to reach because marketing research as we know it was in its infancy.

Public relations up until recently hadn't moved its understanding of audiences on much further than in Bernays' day. The focus on media relations was on relationships with intermediaries; journalists, industry analysts, editors, broadcasters, producers and DJs. Prior to the internet, during the golden age of the mass media, this made a lot of sense. Television programmes like the British soap opera *Coronation Street* could capture up to half the available audience during the late 1960s and early 1970s, which gives you an idea on the relative power of intermediaries at that time. PR, with its focus on media relations through intermediaries, hasn't involved planning in the same way as other marketing disciplines.

Now, a number of factors are changing things dramatically. The media industry on which media relations depend is going through dramatic change. By September 2012, taking into account inflation, the US newspaper industry was found to have had a precipitous drop in print advertising revenues from a high of $63.5 billion to $19 billion – below the level in 1950.[12] Taking into account online revenues, the combined revenue was still less than that spent on print advertising in 1953.

It is perhaps no coincidence that the peak revenue in 2000 occurred soon after Pyra Labs launched one of the first easy-to-use weblog publishing services – Blogspot. These are US numbers, but they show a trend reflected in many developed countries.

---

[11]R.L. Heath, *Encyclopedia of Public Relations, Volume 1*, Thousand Oaks, 2004, ISBN 076191286X, 9780761912866

[12]"Free-fall: Adjusted for Inflation, Print Newspaper Advertising Will be Lower This Year Than in 1950", CARPE DIEM, Professor Mark J. Perry's Blog for Economics and Finance blog: http://cipr.co/XejU7v

Many mainstream media brands have struggled to build businesses based on news content. At the time of writing News Corporation closed *The Daily*, an electronically published newspaper designed to be read on tablet devices like the Apple iPad. *The Times* announced a digital subscription with a subsidized Android tablet as a business model that closely mirrored how UK mobile phone companies sell their post-paid contracts.

Into this changing landscape arrived a new set of influential writers:

- Beauty bloggers
- Gadget bloggers
- Bloggers who blogged about the process of blogging.

Former FT journalist Nick Denton set up one of the most profitable blog companies, Gawker Media, in 2002; by 2009 its annual revenue was estimated to be $60 million.[13] Denton is running a successful if smaller media business because of the creative destruction that is happening in the news media industry.

Where we're at

PR is a more complex process than previously and the landscape of potential influencers you will have to engage with has become more complex. The place to start and address this challenge is through rethinking how we do planning. This has been broken down into three sections:

- **Insights** – to better understand audience behaviour and opinions.
- **Influence** – to understand who are the most powerful conversationalists on social platforms.
- **Messaging** – to sense check the language that an organization uses in its communications.

---

[13]The Twenty-Five Most Valuable Blogs In America. 24/7 Wall St blog: http://cipr.co/TEApM3

Insights

For years advertising agencies have had research teams that have helped prove the case as to why a campaign should be run and provided evidence of effectiveness. Part of the reason why this hadn't been a large-scale phenomenon in PR companies is one of scale and budget. In more recent times, insights have become the starting point of campaigns as they provide knowledge of the consumer and the campaign becomes a conversation opener.

The changes online put some more cost-effective tools in the hands of organizations.

Google Trends provides a visual indicator of level of search interest over time, shows hot spots of interest in a given country and allows comparisons against competitors to be run. It is a very good proxy to understand relative brand awareness and interest and how it has developed or ebbed over time. You can even get a rough idea of whether news stories have stimulated brand interest.

This works well for consumer brands, but is less beneficial for business-to-business orientated brands where the search volume and hence quality of the insights obtained is likely to be lower.

Both *Google Trends* and Google's *Keyword Tool* are different from most of the other tools available because the data is much more democratic.

Most tools look at what is being said in online conversations which, despite the social web, is still only a small sub-set of existing and prospective consumers for a product or service.

Whilst he was at Yahoo! Bradley Horowitz[14] came up with a model of the relationship between consumption of social content and conversations using audience segmentation based around three segments: creators, synthesizers and consumers.

- Creators were 1% of the user base – these were the people that wrote blog posts or started threads in forums.
- Synthesizers were 10% of the user population – these were people who may retweet content or like a post.

---

[14]Creators, Synthesizers, and Consumers, Elatable, Bradley Horowitz blog: http://cipr.co/YQLXP7

- All of the user population would consume at least some content some of the time rather than be an originator.

Google Trends[15] gives some insight into the last content consumer segment. This model generally holds true in terms of its proportions; the only exception would be social properties of luxury brands with a large aspirational fanbase like Burberry, which, by 2012, had a Facebook Page with over 14.5 million likes.[16]

There are a number of tools that help get an impression of online conversations. The three free ones I would recommend are *Addict-o-matic*,[17] *Social Mention*,[18] and *WhosTalkin*.[19]

Addict-o-matic provides a snapshot of blogs, Twitter posts, YouTube videos, Flickr and the latest news. It is useful to find out what is happening in near real time. Facebook and forums are two major gaps in the content snapshot that it provides.

Social Mention looks at similar channels to *Addict-o-matic*, but provides a bit more depth in terms of the content that it surfaces rather than just a snapshot. It provides metrics on how often the brand has been mentioned and the identity of the people who have discussed it most often recently. Probably the biggest advantage of *Social Mention* over *Addict-o-matic* is the ability to download this information as a CSV file which can be opened in a spreadsheet.

WhosTalkin manages to consolidate similar content but includes public Facebook posts and some content from forums; this is presented as a stream and has no analysis.

There are a number of paid-for tools that provide a greater depth of search for insights, different ways of segmenting the conversation and a greater level of analysis. Econsultancy reviews 15 vendors alone in its buyer's guide.[20] I have used and recommend *Sysomos MAP*[21] because its fee is transparent and

---

[15]Google Trends: http://cipr.co/1220tD4
[16]Burberry Facebook Page: http://cipr.co/XTHVip
[17]Addict-o-matic: http://cipr.co/WRpEWR
[18]SocialMention: http://cipr.co/w62bwR
[19]WhosTalkin: http://cipr.co/11XUr7W
[20]A. Zaidi, Online Reputation and Buzz Monitoring Buyer's Guide 2012, Econsultancy, 2011
[21]SysomosMAP: http://cipr.co/TQos2P

predictable, it trawls a large amount of online data and is able to provide access to data more than 30 days old.

Most of the major suppliers will provide a free trial and comprehensive demonstrations to allow you to see the power of their products. Test-drive a few to see what works for you.

Influence

Finding influencers for a PR campaign used to be relatively easy; there were a number of database services that listed out publications and their editorial teams. Their information was usually updated once a year or so, so the contacts were sometimes out of date, but it was easy to obtain replacement information.

Influence is now a bit different; influence can be more contextual although major media brands are still referenced and trusted. There are three broad measures that tend to be considered:

- Popularity – how many followers, Facebook likes or readers that a content creator has on their Twitter account, Facebook Page or website.
- Propagation – how much content is shared or retweeted.
- Mentions – how much a person or brand is mentioned by others.

Cha *et al.* (2010)[22] found in their study of Twitter audiences that propagation was the most important attribute to influence.

There are a number of tools that look at measures of influence. Here are some of the ones that tend to rely more on propagation rather than popularity as a measure.

Edelman's *TweetLevel*[23] is a particularly good way of surfacing Twitter accounts that are influential around a subject over time, or assessing how relatively influential an account is with propagation being a major factor. *Tweet-Level* is unique in terms of the way Edelman has been transparent with its algorithms' composition. *Twitalyzer*[24] provides more of a rounded view on a

---

[22]Cha *et al.*, Visualising Media Bias through Twitter, 2010: http://cipr.co/XvovCk
[23]TweetLevel: http://cipr.co/XSFLBw
[24]Twitalyzer: http://cipr.co/XXDbZ3

given Twitter account. The service is available both as a seven-day free trial and a paid-for version.

Sysomos MAP turns out similar results to *TweetLevel* for the authority of tweets, with the additional advantage that the results can be downloaded as a file that can be opened in a spreadsheet program.

For blogs, the best analogue of propagation would be backlinks from other sites. Backlinks are the basis for a lot of search engine optimization (SEO) work; consequently there are a wide range of good quality tools out there to use.

Google has a specific command

```
link:insertyourdomainname
```

But, like most things that are free, it is limited in its utility. The results provided aren't exhaustive and the information can't be pulled into a spreadsheet easily.

A second Google command that provides a more holistic view is

```
link:insertyourdomainname
info:yourdomainname
```

This provides access to:

- Google's cache of the domain.
- A list of sites that Google considers similar to the domain mentioned in the link command.
- Where the domain links out too, which can provide a better guide to the blog's community than an author-curated blog roll.
- A means of containing the domain name as a term on page, to capture non-hyperlinked mentions.

Moz *Open Site Explorer*[25] provides a paid-for solution that is ideal for analyzing backlink data. Factors that are important include:

- The authority of the site domains.
- The variety of the site domains linking back.

Pulling this data into a spreadsheet allows these factors to be looked at more easily.

---

[25]SEOMOZ Open Site Explorer: http://cipr.co/XXDe7e

Whilst the current Facebook obsession is with likes, a better measure of propagation is shares of posts as a metric. Facebook's newsfeed algorithm governs how many people see those shares in their news feed, but despite this, shares are still the best analogue for propagation.

Messaging

Messaging is something that PRs generally work on with key decision-makers within an organization to reflect an image internally. As salespeople have long known, mirroring a recipient's language is a key way of building rapport.

With this in mind, Google's *Keyword Tool*[26] allows PRs to put some science into the process. By looking at local monthly search volume for key phrases within the messaging, Google can provide data to back up choices or suggest higher volume alternatives.

This won't prevent some PR faux-pas phrases like "leading end-to-end solutions provider", or "best-of-breed solutions" appearing in the messages created but does put the PR on a stronger footing to provide a data-based rationale for choices made.

Biography

Based in Hong Kong, Ged Carroll (@r_c) is Greater China digital director at Burson-Marsteller (B-M). Prior to B-M, he spent 15 years in London, setting up successful digital practices working with blue-chip brands. He started marketing as a rave DJ/promoter. Ged co-authored *The Social Media MBA* and is an Econsultancy training faculty member. Find out more at: renaissancechambara.jp/about.

---

[26]Google keyword tool: http://cipr.co/WXxaMP

Chapter 5

Kate Matlock

Digital anthropology, simply defined, is the study of how internet-mediated com-munication via computer or mobile is impacting our culture and behaviour. This chapter looks at how social media and digital technology is changing us – for better or worse.

Over the past few years, as use of social media channels and the technology with which people access them have evolved, many practitioners have dis-cussed the changes we have seen among ourselves, our workplaces, and our friends and families. As someone who works in social PR, I am not an anthro-pologist. An anthropologist undertakes significant, documented ethnographic research before commenting on cultural change.

Fortunately, many of these research reports are published and while the results are subjective they are useful. However, I would be doing the entire field of anthropology a disservice if I did not state my research methodology upfront with a hefty caveat. My commentary is based on extensive reading in this subject as well as observational, and in some instances practical, research to qualify my statements.

There are many areas where we have seen cultural shifts and will continue to see them, as our homes become smarter, technology fills the classroom, and our information and communication channels evolve. A whole book could be dedicated to discussing these changes; I will focus on the impact these changes are having on etiquette and relationships.

Etiquette – a definition

Etiquette, as defined by Wikipedia,[27] "is a code of behaviour that delineates expectations for social behaviour according to contemporary conventional norms within a society, social class, or group"; whereas manners "involve a wide range of social interactions within cultural norms". Let's restate this. Having good etiquette means meeting a certain social expectation where your manners fit the normal, accepted interactions within that society.

Growing up, perhaps you were taught how to be polite by saying please and thank you, placing a hand on your parent's shoulder to signal you are waiting for your turn to speak, opening doors for a lady, not disturbing others during the dinner hour or after 8pm, and giving your undivided attention when in the company of others. Of course, you may have grown up in a time that either pre-dated or saw the rollout of call waiting, dial-up, personal cellular devices and computers, and broadband internet. As technology advanced, many of the etiquette issues we see in society today can be linked to mobile use, social networking, FOMO (fear of missing out) and the need to always be on and connected.

Table manners – family, friends and business

If you were like me growing up, a typical family dinner was held at the kitchen/dining room table with the occasional night in front of the television together. There would be the discussion of the day, and you would wait until it was appropriate to ask to be excused. It would not have been acceptable to take a phone call during dinner and to talk at the table. Mum would frown at dad if work called. Dad would frown at child if a friend rang. "I'm sorry, I can't talk right now. I'll call you back after dinner" may have been the standard response.

Today, the statistics[28] for mobile ownership could indicate that many families have one phone per family member. Those phones may even be allowed at the table during dinner in some families. Look around you the next

---

[27]Etiquette: http://cipr.co/Wslɪks
[28]Pew Internet: Mobile: http://cipr.co/YAtJNZ

time you are in a restaurant and look at families with children. Many under the age of 15 likely have either an iPod or borrowed mobile and are playing games. This is today's busy activity for children at the table. Teens may be texting friends or playing games. Mum and dad may even grab their phones to settle an argument (apparently 27% of adults have done this, according to the Pew Internet Mobile Report). At home, are families unplugging and having family time or are we all so wrapped up with our work, school and social lives that the place setting is now fork > plate > knife > spoon > phone?

Certainly, among friends, more often than not you will have someone taking a call or messaging at some point during your lunch gathering. Again, look around the restaurant. Scan for a couple awkwardly looking at their phones, rather than each other; or find a group of friends and see how many have their phones in their hands. It has become the norm to have your mobile out on the table, face up, to ensure you see or hear each notification. It is nearly Pavlovian. We have been trained by the sound of chimes and crickets whirring, or the flash of light or pop-up window, to immediately look at the resulting message – despite the company we are in.

Even in business settings, when dining with clients or colleagues, has it become acceptable to use a mobile phone at the table? According to *The Little Book of Etiquette*,[29] when conducting business meals:

> "Your cellular telephone should only be used away from the dining table and only in an absolute emergency. Often viewed as a power game, using your personal telephone during the meal insults your dining companions. Excuse yourself to make calls only if the call cannot possibly wait."

This piece of advice may have been true at the time of publishing (1996) when people had brick-sized Motorola StarTAKs, but truly, should our behaviour be any different now? Take this simple test by responding "yes" or "no" to each:

---

[29]S. Long, *The Little Book of Etiquette: Tips on Socially Correct Dining*, Sterling Publishing, 2000, ISBN 9780760720196

1. I keep my mobile phone on during meetings so that others can have continued access to me.
2. I usually answer the phone when I am in a restaurant.
3. I tend to talk louder on a mobile phone than I do when I am using a landline phone.
4. As a rule, I instantly answer my mobile phone in public places regardless of how much physical distance there is between me and other people around me[30]

Now, before reading the answers, go back and look at questions 1, 2 and 4 and insert the idea of texting, tweeting or messaging in lieu of calling. Now, according to Sabath's key in her book *Business Etiquette*, if you answered "yes" to all four, you are "telecredible" and are likely perceived as rude by those around you. Three yeses and you annoy others. One or two, you are more civil than most. None, you are completely civil. Interestingly, the response to number four has a suggested personal distance of "at least two arms' lengths away from those around you".

For those of you who responded with yeses to talking or messaging n the phone during business situations, think back to when you've been with your family or on a date or with your friends and see if your answers are the same. In my experience, more often than not mobile phones were visibly present at the [dinner] table; more often than not people who took calls in a public area were speaking loudly (more loudly than they probably realized); and of those I saw take a call at the table, none excused themselves.

Outside of business dinners where a certain amount of restraint and decorum are observed, how is it that these rules seem not to apply to family meals or friendly gatherings? This need to not miss anything, in addition to the need to document each moment (location check-in, mentioning who you're with on Twitter, posting a group photo to Facebook; foodspotting on Instagram, etc.) further demonstrates this shift in etiquette at the table, or out

---

[30]A.-M. Sabbath, *Business Etiquette: 101 Ways to Conduct Business with Charm and Savvy*, Falls River Press, 2006, ISBN 9780760776087

and about more generally with others. It has become acceptable to split our attention between those in the room and those we are communicating with digitally as our "time is not spent with others, [rather] it is spent for others".[31]

Attention span and absentee attendance

Think back to the last event you attended where there was a special speaker. Did you have a pen and paper, or were you using a mobile/tablet/laptop to take notes? Did you also have your email open? How about Twitter? Facebook? How tuned in to the speaker were you?

With the addition of hashtags and tweet-walls that show the online conversation during events, do we find that it enhances participation and listening for that clever, tweetable sound-bite? Or are we distracted by it, and all the other open connections we have going? Can we not just pay attention to the person on the floor anymore?

Certainly, parents, you would want your child paying attention in class. After all, you want them to have an education and put away their phone. Facebooking and texting during class are today's doodling and passing notes.

Put yourself in the speaker's shoes for a moment. Time and thought has gone into preparing a presentation, which people are presumably interested in hearing. You take the stage and click the mouse as you narrate each slide. As you speak, you survey the audience and try to count the eyeballs you can actually see. If you were the first speaker, you might have been lucky, but after lunch, you're lucky if 1/3 of the room is still actively listening.

In a profession that preaches active listening, we seem to suck at it IRL. We listen with our eyes online and our ears offline, but not with the same kind of care and attention we once demonstrated. Now, speakers have to build better stories, have flashier graphics and get interactive with their audience (even if you must bribe with cupcakes as I may have done before). Those tactics aren't a bad thing, but if your bum is filling a seat, why is it so hard to focus?

---

[31]Jones, Steve, ed. *Virtual Culture: Identity and Communication in Cybersociety*. Chicago: Sage Publications, 1997.

Having a connected device spreads our attention. Many social media types would like to think they can listen, tweet, like, RT, reply to an email, look up and clap on cue and still walk away from an event having gotten what they paid for with that one golden nugget of awesome. Perhaps it's true, but have wifi and mobile technology turned us into multitaskers with short attention spans? I'd say yes, and not only at the professional level but at the school/ university level as well where "some instructors see the availability of wireless in the classroom as a challenge to teaching and learning; students with mobile devices may not be giving their full attention to the class activities . . .".[32] Are our online lives more important than the offline moment we are experiencing?

Etiquette – breaking up

My final point about the changes in etiquette due to technology and social media brings us to that sad and uncomfortable discussion starting with the seemingly innocent phrase "I think we need to talk". Breaking up is hard to do, no matter what the situation. It involves confrontation, a myriad of feelings, likely some tears, and many people would rather avoid it altogether if they could.

Most of us would still say that, despite the difficulties, it's respectful to do it in person. Perhaps that's because the idea of what's right has been passed down by generations before, when people didn't have phones or a "Dear John" letter was as good as it got for those who couldn't do the deed in person. Today, texting is the modern-day version, and it's not considered any better now than a "Dear John" letter was then.

Even more cowardly is passively informing your partner it's over by changing your relationship status on Facebook. Our children may never know what it's like to be looked in the eye while telling or being told by someone that things aren't working out. People are texting, tweeting, changing statuses, unfriending, unfollowing, blocking and deleting to break up. In fact, if you want to take the public way out and you're not sure what to say or how to

---

[32]Wireless in the Classroom: http://cipr.co/Xf2bNk

share your break-up feelings, you can search online for a bank of tweets and posts to reference.[33]

If this tendency for online cowardice and humiliation isn't enough, there is another issue in break-up protocol and it's not just whether to break up online or offline, but rather which online medium is best. There is a growing trend in break-ups – one that I claim more research from online and "I have a friend who . . ." stories rather than personal experience – where whole dramas are aired online for all to see. It could be a long thread on Facebook or watching two social media darlings trade remarks before issuing statements of their singlehood and mutual respect. Pro-tip: don't change your relationship status on Facebook to announce you're single post-break, but instead hide that status completely.

If 1 in 5 relationships are started online,[34] it doesn't mean they should be ended in the same way. According to a MSNBC Survey[35] in 2012, 48% of break-ups in online relationships happen by email. That allows for a significantly longer message than Berger's Twitter-length Post-it note message that causes cringing among *Sex in the City* watchers. "I'm sorry. I can't. Don't hate me." Breaking up is just one of the many relationship areas where communicating via social media or digital device is changing our behaviour and rewriting the rules of what is seen as acceptable etiquette.

With the changes in table manners, attention spans and relationships, one can already see the big shifts in etiquette in our culture. The very devices and communication platforms with so much promise for bonding and sharing information are actually altering our behaviour and making us forget our manners. As Miller and Horst say, ". . . perhaps the most astonishing feature of digital culture is not this speed of technical innovation but rather the speed by which society takes all of these for granted and creates normative conditions for their use."[36] We just have to decide whether we will continue to accept it and re-write the rules of etiquette.

[33]Break-up tweets: http://cipr.co/YAIgJy
[34]Stay Up to Date: Introducing the Official Match.com Blog: http://cipr.co/YAwten
[35]Dating/Relationship Statistics: http://cipr.co/Ws2O8p
[36]H. Horst and D. Miller eds, *Digital Anthropology*, Berg, 2012, ISBN 0857852906

Biography

Kate Matlock (@katematlock) is a digital strategist at Ketchum in London working with consumer and corporate clients providing social content, consultation and education. Prior to joining the world of social PR, Kate completed her MA at Central Saint Martins where she studied whether trust can be enhanced through better design of online profiles. Kate is an advisory board member for *Social Media Week London* and regularly speaks about online dating, identity and personas.

Chapter 6

Adam Parker

Platforms such as Klout, Kred and PeerIndex seek to provide a measure of social capital based on social media data and are a novel addition to effective influencer relations. However, these relatively new tools require human, real-world awareness and an understanding of the limitations of an algorithmic approach.

What is social capital?

Social capital is not new, nor is it something that relates specifically to social media; it has been the subject of academic study and debate for decades. There are two key perspectives on social capital; one is that it is attached to an individual and the other that it is attached to society as a whole. The UK Office for National Statistics, for example, considers social capital a measure of society's collective "health".[37] A noted collective definition is by Robert Putnam, Professor of Public Policy at Harvard University:

> "Social capital refers to the collective value of all 'social networks' [who people know] and the inclinations that arise from these networks to do things for each other ['norms of reciprocity']"[38]

---

[37]ONS Guide to Social Capital: http://cipr.co/YR65AP
[38]R. Putnam, *Bowling Alone: The Collapse and Revival of American Community*, Simon & Schuster, 2002, ISBN 0743203046

An individual view, as described by Nan Lin, Family Professor of Sociology at Trinity College, Duke University, defines social capital as:

> ". . .investment in social relations by individuals through which they gain access to embedded resources to enhance expected returns of instrumental or expressive actions."[39]

What Lin calls "embedded resources" are the amount and variety of wealth, status and power of those with whom an individual has direct or indirect ties. "Instrumental actions" here mean actions taken in order to make economic, political or social gains, and "expressive actions" are actions taken to preserve an individual's resources.

In an influencer relations context, it is this individual perspective that is perhaps most useful.

Influence and social media capital

Influence is "the capacity or power of persons or things to be a compelling force on or produce effects on the actions, behavior, opinions, etc., of others".[40] The term is often overused or misused, but it is everywhere, and was even described by Michael Conroy of Temporo[41] as the social media industry's "white whale".[42]

The potential to exert influence is purported to be a key element of social capital. Lin wrote that it could also produce benefits such as access to information, greater "social credentials" or authority, and a feeling of wellbeing created by public recognition of an individual's claim to these resources.

Influence is an inherently difficult thing to observe, and even more difficult to measure. To do so, we need to isolate the element exerting influence and the resulting "action, behaviour, opinions etc." caused by it.

Given its relationship to social networks, there has been a drive to measure social capital and its resulting influence within social media. There are many

---

[39]N. Lin, Building a Network Theory of Social Capital: http://cipr.co/XlDtc9
[40]Influence definition: http://cipr.co/11PNbq5
[41]Michael Conroy, Mapping Social Media Influence: http://cipr.co/VGK3ja
[42]White Whale definition: http://cipr.co/XJYnmY

tools and platforms that claim to do this, and three of the best known at the time of writing are Klout, Kred and PeerIndex.

All three talk about measuring influence. Klout's strapline is "The Standard for Influence" but, as we have already noted, influence is not easily measured. What they attempt to measure is arguably closer to *social capital*, highlighted by Brian Solis in his report *The Rise of Digital Influence*,[43] and as they mainly focus on signals and measurements from social media; "social *media* capital" might be a more accurate description.

Relevance is King

In his report, Solis highlights what he describes as "the Pillars of [Digital] Influence", reach, resonance and relevance. Reach is a function of popularity and goodwill, but also physical proximity. Resonance is the frequency of a message or object, how long it appears and the engagement it generates. Relevance is the authority that a person has on a subject, the trust placed in them, and their underlying social relationships.

Solis suggests that it is the combination of reach and relevance that is measured by any of these scores. What this highlights is that *relevance* is a necessary condition: reach, or popularity, is worthless without relevance. Therefore, the relevance of those that can be reached is also important, and vital to understanding the value of scoring approaches to social media capital.

Social media capital scoring approaches

The scoring approaches of three popular platforms are summarized below.

Klout: Scoring (out of 100)

The Klout Score incorporates more than 400 signals from seven different networks. We process this data on a daily basis to generate updates to your Klout Score.[44]

---

[43]Altimeter Group, The Rise of Digital Influence: http://cipr.co/WXxHhK
[44]Klout score: http://cipr.co/YMiN9X

These "signals" include comments, retweets, mentions, followers and subscribers. Some signals are only available when Klout has access to networks other than Twitter, e.g. LinkedIn and Facebook.

Klout: Relevance

Accounts are allocated topics about which Klout thinks they achieve influence. You can use these topics to see the accounts that Klout ranks most highly for each. At the time of writing, I am apparently most influential on recessions, Facebook and apps, about none of which I'm especially knowledgeable or vocal.

Kred: Scoring

Kred has two scores:

Influence is the ability to inspire action. It is scored on a 1,000 point scale. We measure Influence by assessing how frequently you are Retweeted, Replied, Mentioned and Followed on Twitter.

Outreach reflects generosity in engaging with others and helping them spread their message. We measure Outreach on Twitter by your Retweets, Replies and Mentions of others.[45]

Outreach is a cumulative score that has no maximum, although the highest score at the time of writing is 12.

Kred also takes into account similar data from Facebook if you have given it access. Kred is the most transparent of the three, letting you see an audit trail of where your Kred points have come from.

Kred: Relevance

Accounts have Global scores, but they also have Community scores based on Kred's assessment of their relevance to particular areas. I rank as most relevant on Advertising, which is at least a little more accurate than Klout.

---

[45]Kred rules: http://cipr.co/VMogGU

PeerIndex: Scoring (out of 100)

PeerIndex is the most opaque in terms of its scoring methodology.

The PeerIndex algorithm recognizes the speed and quantity by which users spot, share (and thus endorse) content on any specific topic. Our content recommendation decisions can thus be used as a proxy to measure our knowledge and authority in a specific subject area. Your authority on a subject is affirmed when the content you share is approved, i.e. Retweeted, Facebook Shared, +1'ed or commented on, by someone else with authority on the subject.[46]

PeerIndex: Relevance

PeerIndex is in the process of adding support for topics. It currently gives an account a score for the topics it judges relevant. These topics are very broad, e.g. "News, Politics and Society".

Comparing Klout, Kred and PeerIndex

An argument can be made that PeerIndex's opacity is an asset, as the more an individual knows about their score, the more they can take action to try to increase it. For instance, the knowledge that linking other social media platforms to your profile can boost your score may encourage people to do so. The more the score can be gamed, arguably the less valuable it is.

When we understand how each scoring system works, we then need to understand the scale that applies to the scores. Both Klout and PeerIndex use logarithmic scales, while Kred takes a normalized approach.[47] A logarithmic scale means that as you ascend it becomes more and more difficult to increase your score, so there will be proportionally fewer accounts ranked between 20 and 29 than there were between 10 and 19, and so on. A rough estimate suggests Klout may have a logarithmic "base" of around 3–4 in relation to these bands. The more transparent Kred publishes its influence scoring distribution online, and their data shows that on 11 November 2011, accounts with scores

---

[46]PeerIndex FAQ: http://cipr.co/W6RHjH
[47]Sean Carlos, Can Social Influence Be Distilled Into A Score? Part 2 – Potential Pitfalls: http://cipr.co/WAxcxs

of greater than 850 only made up approximately 0.02% of the total, while accounts with scores between 501 and 550 accounted for 12.5%.

This is important when considering outreach since, despite what the numbers might suggest, logarithmic scoring means someone with a Klout score of 90 is likely to have considerably more than 50% more social media capital than someone with a score of 60. It seems likely that relatively few users fully understand the nature of a logarithmic scale, or are even aware of the difference that scale makes to scoring, which is potentially problematic and could make the scores less intuitive than they appear to be.

Clout v. Klout

A fundamental issue with all of these approaches is that they base their scores predominantly on social media interactions and data, while much of a person's social capital is more likely to be based on their actions and relationships in the real world. Not considering real-world reach might mean that someone's influence score seems laughably high, or indeed unreasonably low. For example, a journalist writing for the *Financial Times* might personally have relatively little social media capital, but has the potential to exert greater influence in their role with an authoritative media outlet.

In response to criticism on ignoring the effects of real-world influence, the platforms have tried to include elements of real-world social capital by allowing people to award others extra Kred or Klout, though these are necessarily limited in their impact to prevent the scores being "gamed" too easily.

In an innovative approach to including real-world data, in August 2012 Klout began incorporating an individual's Wikipedia page, its page rank and the ratio of inbound to outbound links in their scores. The more popular their page, the higher the score. This resulted in Barack Obama's score rising, and Justin Bieber's falling. This inventive proxy for potential real-world social capital seems intuitively effective, if the President of the United States now ranks higher than a teen pop sensation.

Other wild-card accounts whose true social capital is probably marginal at best were also downgraded significantly. Astrology/horology mouthpiece @Xstrology, ranked at 95 in June 2012, had fallen to 81 by the end of the year and @uberfacts, which broadcasts interesting trivia, fell from 94 to 83 in the same period. By this measure, Klout and PeerIndex (which rank these particular accounts much lower, at 69 and 74 respectively) certainly appear to have a potential advantage over Kred, with Kred ranking both of these accounts at its maximum Global Ranking of 1,000.

Including Wikipedia as part of the score will only adjust the score of individuals who have Wikipedia pages and most people or organizations won't. For example, in the UK PR community, only five of the top 10 in *PRWeek*'s UK *Power Book 500* 2012 have Wikipedia pages, despite their considerable social capital within the industry. These tools are trying to get better at taking real-world status into account, but it is an enormous task and they are still in the early stages.

The data

To gain an understanding of which individuals score the highest, I looked at all tweets from English-language Twitter accounts with Klout scores of 80+ during a 24-hour period.[48] Klout was only selected due to the ease of accessibility of this data via the DataSift platform.[49] The 55,000 tweets identified came from 4,301 different accounts, and analysis of a random sample of 100 of them showed that 87 were "Verified" by Twitter. Verification is used by Twitter to establish the authenticity of accounts and is generally applied to well-known individuals and organizations. Of the remaining thirteen, ten were relatively well-known individuals, brands and outlets, including Elvis Costello, audio brand Dolby and *Metal Hammer* magazine.

So, to state the obvious, the people and organizations ranked as having more social media capital were mostly those who are likely to have more social capital in the real world. Unsurprising, but it doesn't mean that their scores are without meaning, as they do provide evidence of who is investing most successfully in engaging with their publics on social media.

As social media develops, it seems likely that almost every notable person or organization will have to become part of the online community. After all, recent additions to Twitter include UK Prime Minister David Cameron and the Pope. This could mean that ultimately the online world will mirror the offline one, with differences reflecting relative levels of investment and tactical

---

[48]Period analyzed was 15:00 17 December 2012 – 15:00 18 December 2012
[49]DataSift: http://cipr.co/XhEEwW

advantage. When this happens, the scores will tell us who is using social media best to interact and engage and, possibly, who is managing to stay ahead of social rankings and game the system. However, as we all become more Twitter-literate and social online there may come a time when there will be a limited amount of this distinction left for social media scoring to illuminate.

Social capital for PR

So, can these scores be useful to public relations professionals? To my mind the answer is a "yes", albeit a very cautious one. They can provide you with some helpful data for influencer outreach and community development, using the scores and their assessment of relevant influencers on a topic to help start and/or refine an influencer list. They could also prove valuable in crisis communications and reputation management, to help identify members of the online community who talk about you and who may have the most potential to damage or enhance your brand's reputation within social media.

Another more recent development is the use of such scores and analysis in an internal communications context. Here such measures of relevant social capital could be used to identify the people within an organization who have expertise in a particular area, who are most likely to engage on a topic in internal discussions or have the widest internal networks.

In all these situations, social ranking tools can be useful. However, they are relatively new and require, like much new technology, consistent analysis and sense-checking. For example, when using the scores to assess levels of social media capital within your team, don't overlook less active but well-connected individuals. When building lists for influencer outreach, keep in mind that relevance is everything: throw out wild-cards, only compare scores across individuals who are broadly similar, and remember the importance of assessing an individual's real-world social capital.

The value of social capital

Social capital is purported to be a measure of an individual's potential to exert influence. Assessment of an individual's social capital can be a powerful tool to help PR professionals identify relevant people or organizations with whom to connect.

Online social capital ranking tools are far from perfect; they are still very young, filling a niche created by the growth of social media, in itself relatively new. Social capital scoring is useful: it can enrich and expedite the process of finding and ranking relevant influencers for outreach and reputation management. We should use them, but we should do so with an active awareness of their limitations, and a healthy degree of human judgement regarding each individual's real-world "clout".

Biography

Adam Parker MCIPR (@AdParker) is chief executive of RealWire, the UK media intelligence company, and is the architect of its Lissted application – a tool for discovering influencers on Twitter. Adam also contributed the chapter "Media Relations Modernised" to *Share This*, on the importance of putting Twitter at the heart of influencer relations. He is a chartered accountant and previously spent nine years with PwC in its audit, corporate finance and consulting practices. He occasionally blogs at www.showmenumbers.com.

Chapter 7

Dr Mark Pack

Social media can appear a very unfriendly and rude place at times. However, with a mix of common sense, preparation and careful management you can steer around the unsociable corners and bask in the benefits of the social ones.

Only a few years ago the simple news that someone was joining Twitter was often newsworthy. Now it is commonplace and only newsworthy when it involves the most prominent of people.[50] But Twitter still hits the mainstream news far more regularly than that – particularly with stories of people being questioned by the police for what they have tweeted.

Beneath all the debate over how far the law should circumscribe what people can say on Twitter, there is widespread agreement that social media contains all sorts of unsociable, rude, drunk or threatening comments at times. No surprise either – for social media is made up of humans and humanity has always had its unsociable edge.

Just as the rest of our lives does not have to be over-run with such behaviour, nor does our slice of social media. It is a matter of choice. Not a matter of easy, neat, perfect choice but choice nonetheless. We have control over where we go, what we do and how we interact with others. Just as avoiding walking past a downmarket pub at chucking out time is a sensible way to avoid problems on a Friday night, so too we decide where we go and what we do online.

---

[50]For example, the Pope in late 2012

Offline this can seem a chore, unreasonably cramping our freedom. Online, it is easier to make those choices, exert that influence – and not feel our freedom has been nearly as cramped. Easier, that is, if you understand how to make the choices and which ones matter most.

The three problems to avoid

For those acting at the intersection of public relations and social media, there are usually three related problems to avoid. First, saying something that either gets you or your firm the sack or has the police come calling, makes you an instant inductee into the "How not to do social media" Hall of Fame.

Second, having a social media presence over-run with hostile or – even worse – mocking comments and feedback.

The third is often forgotten, but is one to cling to dearly as you navigate round the first two. That is to become so scared of the results of interaction that you close your ears to the negative comments out there (and stick your hands over your clients' ears too). It is a danger because sometimes the critics are right. There might actually be something useful or even urgent to learn amid the hyper-ventilating angst.

It is also worth remembering that the exceptionally rude person throwing invective your way may be more deserving of sympathy than ire. For all the warnings about the modern habit of prescribing a medical explanation to everyone's behaviour, there are people with mental health issues and they do use social media. I am pretty sure, for example, that the one case I have directly experienced where online abuse turned into a series of seriously unpleasant phone calls was due to someone who needed medical help.

Even such exceptional cases aside, listening is good. A while back I found myself surrounded by litter as a firm's cleaners had failed to do their job properly. I took to social media to let them know. The result? Silence. What could have been an opportunity to identify someone who wasn't doing their job properly – or was being asked to do too much and so couldn't do their job properly – was instead consigned to the internet dustbin. My frustration but their loss.

This is why Walmart took so enthusiastically to social media. For a firm often at the centre of public controversy, it may seem surprising they were so keen to embrace a medium through which people could readily knock them. What Walmart's senior managers appreciated, however, was that the easier it is for people to moan, the easier it is for them to pick up just the sorts of problems – a faulty product, a badly run store – which might otherwise slip through their management systems or only percolate upwards slowly. Listening to complaints is a vital safety net to cover the inevitable slip-ups which occur in even the best managed systems. As with offline life, the skill is to manage and sort criticism, not hide hermit-like in electronic isolation ignoring everyone.

With that in mind, how best then to tackle the other two problems?

Staying out of trouble

The first – how to avoid saying something that causes trouble – is the most straightforward, at least in theory. Unless you deliberately wish to be edgy and court controversy (which can be a route to publicity and success, of course), simply avoid saying things online which you would not want either a job interviewer to have read just before you walk into the room or your mother to see just before you turn up for Christmas. (Substitute father/aunt/vicar/ Richard Dawkins depending on your own family and faith setup.)

In theory, privacy settings can be your friend and ally – you simply carve out space for offending comments without them ever being seen, in theory. The practice is somewhat harder.

Mistakes are easy to make, especially as privacy settings become increasingly complicated and span multiple services supplied by the same firm. In fairness to those writing the accompanying text, these days they are often in fairly plain English but even simple sounding phrases can be tricky to fully fathom. A multitude of simple choices itself often ends up being confusing.

Whilst writing this, I took a look at all the privacy settings Facebook offers me. I got up to 86 different options before getting bored with counting. Even with each of them being apparently simple choices to make, the odds of me getting one wrong out of the 86 plus are non-trivial. Then there is the problem of keeping up with changes to the privacy settings, not to mention changes in who you want to see your "private" content as your life and career evolve.

What that all means is that privacy settings are a handy tool for refinement but a pretty poor safety net. More like a safety colander. The real protection comes from not putting content online in the first place.

How to manage feedback and responses

Turning then to the second problem: that of how to manage the quality of user feedback and user-generated content on the social media presences of clients.

Handling and minimizing anti-social behaviour online has some similarities with doing so offline, and these similarities make the "broken windows theory" of criminologists a useful starting point for planning your online approach.

In the offline world, there is good evidence that allowing low-level problems (such as graffiti and broken windows) to fester in a community ends up encouraging more criminal behaviour. Tackling the low-level problems, by contrast, helps to prevent more serious problems too, as otherwise seeing the fruits of other people's bad behaviour encourages more and worse bad behaviour.

As one writer put it, applying this to the online world:[51]

> "Much of the tone of discourse online is governed by the level of moderation and to what extent people are encouraged to 'own' their words. When forums, message boards, and blog comment threads with more than a handful of participants are unmoderated, bad behavior follows. The appearance of one troll encourages others. Undeleted hateful or ad hominem comments are an indication that that sort of thing is allowable behavior and encourages more of the same. Those commenters who are normally respectable participants are emboldened by the uptick in bad behavior and misbehave themselves. More likely, they're discouraged from helping with the community moderation process of keeping their peers in line with social pressure. Or they stop visiting the site altogether . . .

---

[51]Does the broken windows theory hold online?, Kottke.org: http://cipr.co/WOwf14

Very quickly, the situation is out of control and your message board is the online equivalent of South Central Los Angeles in the 1980s, inhabited by roving gangs armed with hate speech, fueled by the need for attention, making things difficult for those who wish to carry on useful conversations."

Search engines also kick in an extra problem. If you have spam comments appearing on a site or page, it makes it look less trustworthy and reputable in the eyes not only of your readers but also search engine algorithms, hitting your search engine prominence.

Therefore, the first step is to make sure you select platforms for your online activities which provide appropriate environments to encourage good behaviour and allow you to moderate. This can require quite subtle technological knowledge and experience at times. For example, Facebook generally has a better tone of conversation than many other platforms because nearly everyone on it uses their real name, with their comments closely associated with who they really are. However, the Facebook comments feature on third-party websites offers only relatively crude moderation options, which can more than cancel out the other Facebook benefits.

Take a look at existing users of a platform to see what sort of comments tend to appear. YouTube, for example, is well known for the less than salubrious nature of many of its comment threads. That may not be a reason to avoid it, but it means going in with your eyes open.

Then, based on this background knowledge, make sure you go through all the moderation and discussion options. For example, on YouTube many people now choose to disable all comments – avoiding the non-salubrious problem whilst still allowing interaction by embedding the videos on their own sites.

It is important to decide whether or not to take the option, where offered, of "pre-moderating" everything: that is only letting comments appear after they have been approved. This provides a sure quality control but comes at a cost. It means the pace of online conversation is slowed. It also can come with a legal risk. If you pre-moderate everything and then publish a libellous comment, your legal defences are much weaker than if you automatically publish everything and only moderate after the event.

Whichever approach you take, alongside the technical decisions you should have a transparent (and sensible!) moderation policy, both as a guide for your work and also as an answer to public questions about what is being done and why.

Often a good starting point is the BBC's rules, though bear in mind that they are perhaps a little more prescriptive and a little longer than you might need:[52]

- We reserve the right to fail comments which . . .
- Are considered likely to disrupt, provoke, attack or offend others.
- Are racist, sexist, homophobic, sexually explicit, abusive or otherwise objectionable.
- Contain swear words or other language likely to offend.
- Break the law or condone or encourage unlawful activity. This includes breach of copyright, defamation and contempt of court.
- Advertise products or services for profit or gain.
- Are seen to impersonate someone else.
- Include contact details such as phone numbers, postal or email addresses.
- Are written in anything other than English – Welsh and Gaelic may be used where expressly stated.
- Contain links to other websites which break our Editorial Guidelines.
- Describe or encourage activities which could endanger the safety or wellbeing of others.
- Are considered to be "spam", that is posts containing the same, or similar, content posted multiple times.
- Are considered to be off-topic for the blog discussion.

What the BBC also has, and you should too, is an escalation policy so everyone knows how to deal with something which appears more serious – such as an allegedly libellous comment or something which gives out personal information about someone that is inappropriate. Make sure you know where the

---

[52]BBC Blog Network, House Rules: http://cipr.co/TFt5jh

relevant expert advice will come from and who makes the decisions if such an event were to happen on your site.

Alongside this, you should have an effective spam filter (or be using a platform that has one built in). The volume of spam comments posted up on even low-traffic blogs can be eye-watering. There is good and free or cheap software that saves you from having to manually handle such voluminous crud.

Think about how you might want to structure feedback to help the quality rise. Should you have options to let people vote on it or options to let particular pieces of feedback be highlighted as star contributions? Letting readers vote comments up or down, for example, can encourage group think and the dominance of the majority view rather than debate and diversity. Think how rare it is to see someone say, "I think your view is totally wrong but it is an interesting contribution to the debate so thank you for making it." Instead, they just hit the thumbs down button.

Consider how you plan to respond. Just as a good meeting chair can bring out the best of an audience or pander to its worst, so interaction can encourage or discourage the non-window breakers. Respond positively, thank people, answer questions and follow up complaints. That encourages better interaction and helps drive the bad aside.

When doing so, ignore – yes, ignore – the advice "don't feed the trolls". You should feed them – once. There are many reasons why people may appear to be trolling but are actually redeemable. One polite attempt at giving them a second chance is worthwhile. It will not always work, yet is worth trying.[53]

Conclusion

Remember you cannot control other people's behaviour on the internet, but you can set the environment and you can influence it. Get that right and the unsociable side of social networking becomes an occasional annoyance rather than a serious problem.

---

[53]Why you should feed the trolls, Mark Pack: http://cipr.co/UtJzfV

Biography

Dr Mark Pack (@markpack) works at Blue Rubicon, *PR Week*'s Consultancy of the Year. He is also a Visiting Lecturer at City University on its journalism programme and ran the Liberal Democrats' 2001 and 2005 internet general election campaigns.

This is the 23rd book he has contributed to as an editor or author, including *101 Ways To Win An Election*, co-authored with Ed Maxfield.

Part III

Conversations

Chapter 8

Sharon O'Dea

Gamification – the use of game thinking and mechanics to engage audiences – has been one of the most talked about trends in digital communications over the past two years. Used well, game techniques can be powerful tools to engage employees, customers and the public to change behaviours, develop skills and drive innovation.

First coined in the 1990s, the term has emerged in recent years as a way to describe interactive online design that plays on people's competitive instincts. It uses rewards to drive action, including virtual prizes such as points or badges; status indicators such as friend counts or leaderboards; and experience points such as achievement data and progress bars.

Using game mechanics to create incentives is nothing new. Creating competition by offering rewards and recognition is a motivational technique that's been employed for centuries – there are even examples in ancient Greek mythology. It's argued games tap directly into the cognitive and psychological predispositions of humans to engage in game-like behaviour that they find interesting, rewarding and engaging.

But for recent generations, games are big business, generating $78 billion in revenue in 2011.[54] Each week, 3 billion hours are spent playing games.

Those in their 40s and under have grown up with gaming as a common form of entertainment. Games are now mainstream and highly sophisticated; current game thinking is the product of three generations' worth of rapidly-evolving

---

[54]"Factbox: a look at the $78 billion video games industry", *Reuters*: http://cipr.co/TJPQ5N

design. It's no surprise communicators are looking at how they can use the success of games to engage with audiences.

It's a technique that's rapidly gaining traction; research firm Gartner estimate 70% of the world's top 2,000 companies will have at least one gamified application by 2014.[55]

Fun is central to the success of gamification – the aim is to use the mechanics that make games fun and absorbing in non-game platforms and experiences to boost participation and engagement.

At heart the technique is simple; in the movie of the same name, Mary Poppins persuades her young charges to tidy up by gamifying the chore, telling them "in every thing that must be done, there is an element of fun. You find the fun, and oh, the job's a game!" The key is understanding what is fun, by looking at the things that motivate people to participate – autonomy, mastery and purpose – and incorporating these into your communications.

Gamifying participation at DevHub

Evo Media Group's DevHub enables users to create their own sites or blogs. In 2009, they found only 10% of DevHub users finished building their site, and few users spent money on any of the add-on special features.

Evo's Chief Executive, Geoff Nuval, looked to games to increase engagement, revamping the site to give users points, coins and badges for participation.[56] The relaunched site offers a step-by-step process where users progress to the next level on completion, like completing a mission in a game, in order to build their "online empire". Users receive virtual points for adding text or photos, or sharing with friends.

DevHub uses a handful of simple game techniques – breaking a process down into achievable tasks, providing feedback and recognition, and creating additional context – which are proven to encourage greater engagement.

Since turning the process of site-building into a game, DevHub has seen the number of users completing the process of building their site rise to over

---

[55]Gartner Predicts Over 70 Percent of Global 2000 Organisations Will Have at Least One Gamified Application by 2011, Gartner: http://cipr.co/TJPZG8
[56]Why gamify DevHub?, DevHub.com: http://cipr.co/TJPZG8

80%. In addition, more users are subscribing to paid features and the number of users keeps growing as people are interacting more frequently with the site.

Consumer loyalty: Samsung Nation

Loyalty programmes are one of the oldest forms of gamification around. They began when small shopkeepers would reward their regular shoppers with a free item or two for their continued custom. In the 1930s these tangible rewards for loyalty gave way to alternative, less tangible means of exchange with the introduction of Green Stamps. In the 1980s came the first loyalty points schemes, spearheaded by the airline industry. These broke the link between offering things of value in exchange for loyalty; while points could (theoretically) be exchanged for flights, such schemes grew in popularity because they realized the value of status and recognition to loyal users. This trend continued to evolve and in the last decade we've seen the emergence of virtual rewards, which break the link with real-world value entirely in favour of public recognition of status.

Korean electronics giant Samsung sought to bring its loyalty programme up to date with the launch of Samsung Nation,[57] which recognizes and rewards those who engage with the brand on its website and social media sites. Users earn badges for completing activities such as writing reviews, watching videos and participating in forums, rewarding users who engage, and particularly those who advocate for the brand, with higher status.

Samsung Nation has been described as the first gamified corporate website. Using game mechanics – in particular conferring status on regular users – they've turned customers into advocates on their own website and beyond, creating powerful word-of-mouth communications.

Science: FoldIt

While games are a powerful means by which people can engage with products or brands, many believe that games can be used for social good. Jane McGonigal,

---

[57]Samsung Nation: http://cipr.co/11VoHsv

author of *Reality is Broken: Why Games Make Us Better and How They Can Change the World*, believes games are essential to the survival of our species.

She asked how we can take some of the feelings people have when they're playing games – cooperation, commitment and problem-solving – into real-world situations. Collectively, players of World of Warcraft have spent 5.93 million years solving virtual problems in the game's world. What if, asks McGonigal, people applied that same level of commitment to solving real-world problems?

A group of scientists at the University of Washington sought to find out. They created FoldIt,[58] an online puzzle in which users participate in biochemical research by folding proteins using tools provided within the game, a process that helps us to understand their structures better.

FoldIt works because it already involved game-like elements (the puzzle solving of folding proteins) as well as intrinsic rewards (the feeling you've helped improve medicine). It was a huge success – in just 10 days game players solved a problem that had stumped scientists for 15 years. Turning the work or process into a game put complex challenges and rewards into a more approachable context, using gaming behaviour to solve a seemingly intractable puzzle.

How GiffGaff turns customer service into a game

One company which is highly successful in gamifying work is GiffGaff, the fastest-growing mobile phone company in the UK. The network, whose tagline is "the mobile network run by you", provides game rewards to its user community in order to incentivize peer-to-peer customer support and word-of-mouth marketing.[59] Points are awarded for recruiting new customers and providing helpful answers to questions.

GiffGaff uses both monetary reward – points can be converted into account credit – and recognition of status in order to encourage speedy and helpful responses to common customer queries. The results are extraordinary; in

[58]FoldIt: http://cipr.co/X3pcV8
[59]About Us, GiffGaff: http://cipr.co/XnSme8

2010 the user community provided 100,000 answers to 10,000 customer queries, with an average response time for questions of just 90 seconds.

The network employs less than 50 paid staff, relying on the user community and its growing pool of user-generated knowledge to power customer service instead. The customer loyalty this generates is remarkable; in a recent customer satisfaction survey, members rated service levels as 9 out of 10, and they had a Net Promoter Score of 73% – higher than that of both Apple and Google.

Snake Oil 2.0?

Industry researchers caution communicators to beware of overblown claims, warning that gamification is currently being driven by novelty and hype. Gartner predicts that by 2014, 80% of current gamified applications will fail to meet business objectives because they're badly designed.[60]

Game designers, in particular, have been scathing about the adoption of game techniques by communicators and marketers, with some calling the trend "snake oil 2.0".

Research vice president Brian Burke elaborates: "The focus is on the obvious game mechanics . . . rather than the more important game design elements, such as balancing competition and collaboration, or defining a meaningful game economy. Many organisations are simply counting points, slapping meaningless badges on activities and creating gamified applications that are not engaging for the audience."

Much of this criticism is fair. Adding the ability to gain points or badges – what some call "lameification" – can be a successful tactic in the short term, but unless it's intrinsically rewarding for the player, the behaviour it drives is rarely sustainable. A spike in engagement can result from even the most rudimentary "pointsification", but that spike will drop back to where you started if your audience realizes you've offered them nothing of value.

---

[60]Gartner says by 2014, 80% of current gamified applications will fail to meet business objectives due to poor design, Gartner: http://cipr.co/Wu9Tp2

It's healthy to be sceptical about a technique that promises to solve a problem as complex as motivating people. Making a success of gamification means thinking beyond the buzzword and using game features to reward desired behaviour, create more intensively participative processes, track group progress and establish feedback loops that reinforce and accelerate desired outcomes.

How should communicators use gamification?

When designing game-based communications, it's essential to think about why someone would be motivated to engage or participate, and how the game can increase motivation.

Traditional thinking on motivation assumes people are driven by money and reward. But a number of studies – most notably those pulled together by Dan Pink in his book *Drive*[61] – reach a different conclusion; people are motivated to participate in play or discretionary work by autonomy, mastery and purpose.

1. Autonomy

People enjoy things they choose to do more than those which they are coerced into. Games are a voluntary activity, and it's this which makes them appealing. This autonomy, the sense of being able to explore opportunity as you choose to, is what makes people satisfied with a task.

Successful games allow users to choose their own path. They set an end goal, but many possible ways to achieve that goal, and the ability to explore. Provide the information people need to complete a game without too heavily directing play in a way that reduces a user's sense of control.

The sense of autonomy is easily damaged if you link extrinsic reward – such as a prize – with participation. These rewards can curb a sense of self-direction and reduce the feeling of control.

---

[61]Drive, DanPink.com: http://cipr.co/YD4FpG

Unexpected rewards – what game designers call Easter Eggs – generate a greater sense of autonomy as they reward game play without linking activity and prize. Location-based game Foursquare provides these unexpected rewards through special offers, encouraging participation while giving users that sense of autonomy.

2. Mastery

People love to learn and master new skills, games and environments, so successful game experiences give the user a sense of progress and achievement.

"Fun is just another word for learning," says Ralph Koster, author of *A Theory of Fun for Game Design.* "Fun from games arises from mastery. It arises out of comprehension. It is the act of solving puzzles that makes games fun."

Video games provide optimum conditions for learning, by providing interesting but achievable challenges, and setting goals and rules. We feel best when we are neither over- nor under-challenged, so you should provide a series of smaller but progressively stretching goals.

Varied pacing provides both experiences of failure (from which you can learn), but also more rewarding moments of success, giving a sense of achievement. This could be through having structured, visually present goals or breaking a story down into stages or tasks that vary in style and complexity.

Rewarding games also give experiences of mastery by providing regular positive feedback that gives the player a sense of achievement as they play.

3. Purpose

A game or activity needs to connect with the user in a meaningful way. This could be through creating a strong back story, connecting to a community of interest, or by linking with a user's own goals or passions.

On personal finance site Mint.com, users can set their own financial goals and work towards them by saving or paying off debts. By using customizable goals, which the user can tailor to their own circumstances, the game has real meaning for the player.

Mint.com founder, Aaron Patzer, says: "What we have learned is that any game aspect has to be more oriented toward a specific thing that you are working toward . . . otherwise you have no system of points with no levels or no end game."

It's this real-world connection and the ability to gamify one's own personal goals which makes fitness and health apps such as Nike+ so successful.

Games might also create meaning if they connect in some way to an interest or passion that the user already has, for example an interest in science. FoldIt appealed to users who already had an interest in biology; the game created a prosocial context in which playing contributed to the corpus of scientific knowledge, providing a strong motivation to play.

Video games rarely provide meaning which relates to a real-world context. Instead, they create meaning by wrapping the game in a good story, such as saving the world from impending doom. This overarching narrative gives meaning to all the tasks and games played within it.

To create an appealing story you need good-quality supporting visuals and copy. Be sure to design the context and back story as carefully as the game mechanic to make it appealing to users.

The future of gamification

Some argue gamification is a fad. And they might be right; adding points and badges as a means of making boring things interesting is a trend that's unlikely to succeed, or to last very long. On the other hand, incorporating game mechanics into campaigns so that those engaging with them find them more intrinsically rewarding – that's a trend that's as old as the hills, and likely to be around for good.

In a world where distinctions between work and leisure time are increasingly blurred, creating rich game experiences has enormous potential to build engagement between organizations and audiences. But for this to be successful, these need to be well designed.

As shallow engagement gives way to well-designed game-like experiences, we may well see the term (an ugly neologism) replaced with the core of the technique: designing for motivation. Gamification is not a single strategy or toolbox, but rather taking inspiration from successful game design in order to create campaigns which invite greater participation and engagement.

Biography

Sharon O'Dea (@sharonodea) is Senior Online Communications Manager at Standard Chartered, a global bank headquartered in London, where she advises on web and social media strategy. Before moving into financial services she worked in communications for a host of well-known public sector organizations, most recently the Houses of Parliament.

An early adopter, prolific blogger and longtime geek, she's been using social media in one form or another for nearly 20 years. In 2007 she was a contributing author to the *Independent Guide to Facebook*, a consumer-facing guide to the then-new platform.

Chapter 9

Paul Fabretti

Posting to social media channels is an everyday activity that most brands and agencies do but is rarely as structured and accountable as other communications activities. This chapter explores the many challenges of managing multiple social media channels and offers some simple solutions to get things done more effectively.

What *is* community management?

Before we can explore the challenges around community management, it's probably worth defining what we actually mean by community management. As with much social media terminology, it can mean different things to different people and if we professionals can't work to a consistent definition, what chance do we have of communicating clearly to consumers?

For the purposes of this chapter:

> Community management is simply the nurturing of an audience, all of whom share a common interest.

That common interest could be a celebrity or a sportsperson but is frequently formed around products and brands. Typically, the person doing the nurturing is called a community manager and is responsible for a variety of things like:

- The creation of visual content (to stimulate discussion)
- Providing customer service or advice

- Broadcasting (brand) messages
- Managing (super) users or influencers
- Moderation (naughty words)
- Directing business change (feeding back within the business).

So whilst the role is relatively new in the spectrum of communications jobs, it certainly shouldn't be underestimated. Few people will have as much direct contact with customers as a community manager, nor face as wide a range of communications and reputational challenges.

All of which points further to the need for good structure and robust processes to meet the needs of the community.

1. Why is there a problem around community management?

Tough economic times call for tough action. Valuing the customers you already have has never been more important than in this hyper-competitive, recession-stifled world. Yet it seems that despite the importance that careful relationship management plays, few businesses have any kind of formal structure to adapt to the increasingly dynamic and viral aspects of the worlds that customers now inhabit.

Except that managing and nurturing relationships is nothing new. CRM programmes have been around for decades with the sole purpose of helping to understand and, ultimately, better serve the customer. The only problem with these systems is that they are designed for largely one-way, static communications. Direct mail, text, email – all are communications tools, which, by and large, are designed to say one thing at one time and hopefully generate a response.

(a) Recession PR – more for less

If you're reading this as a member of a PR agency (or in-house PR), the chances are that you're working longer and harder than you have done for a long time and perhaps for less. Budgets shrink, deadlines shorten and successful sell-ins become crucial as campaigns are created last-minute to respond to a sales push . . . oh, and you've just had a mini-crisis on your Facebook Page that needs dealing with before it goes viral . . . but it's about a missing delivery and you're just in PR . . .

In these time-pressed times, allocating the time needed to nurture an online community can easily become an afterthought, yet properly planned and structured beforehand can mean that your communities can become self-serving, self-advocating and responded-to in the timely fashion the customer expects, whatever their issue – when it's often needed most.

(b) Who owns it?

One of the other key problems with community management (or lack thereof) is the confusion around which area of the business actually owns social media. Many businesses just don't have a dedicated social media resource and aren't structured to deal with the dynamic nature of modern customer behaviours. As a result, community managers often sit within whichever department sees the most commercial benefit.

Sit your community manager too close to any one department and they invariably become drawn by the desire to focus on "their" department. They either sell (marketing), crisis manage (PR) or just help (customer service). Combined, these areas work very well, but keep them in silos and they become restrictive both for customers and the business.

This is where the external pressure of consumer demand can be a great corporate leveller. Customer demands for answers, inspiration and a timely response force businesses to break down existing barriers, resulting in internal teams having to communicate more to do the right thing at the right time.

(c) It's frequently inefficient

There's no getting away from it – social media can be an enormous drain on time. Planning content can take days, even for a few tweets. New content creation can take weeks. Whilst content creation can always be carried out in a controlled, organized fashion, the other inefficiency problem is rooted in the always-on nature of interactions on social channels. Whether you're allocating client work by the day, or even hour, there is no predicting what or when issues will need handling. As guardians of the brand's reputation you may need to deal with them in real time. Few agencies have got this time/money equation right.

2. Consumer behaviours are changing

Understanding the shift in consumer behaviour on any level will go some way to helping you recognize how you need to adapt your own community management processes. Consider the behaviours listed below when building your team structure or planning a campaign and ask yourself if you are resourced to handle them:

- Always-on – the consumer now operates at often unconventional hours. How will you handle the "out of conventional hours" interactions?
- Shares – consumers share experiences, good and bad, raising two key points: what are you doing to give them a positive experience worth sharing and how will you handle the feedback?
- Collaboration – consumers are working together to make things happen. Whether it is petitions or group-sourced purchasing decisions, are you ready for consumers working together?
- Creativity – the modern consumer has many more tools and a desire to be creative than ever before. Even simple applications like Instagram can unleash the creative flair of a customer. Are you allowing customers to be creative in a positive way and what is your contingency plan for when creativity works against you?

What should be on your community management checklist

As with any good social media strategy, community management starts with understanding your customer, where they are and what they are saying.

Fortunately, conversation monitoring tools provide powerful insights to allow you to plan and resource accordingly. You can categorize these insights into two broad areas and we'll now look at what this means for your planning:

1. Audience
2. Channels and Timing
3. Influencers
4. Content Planning and Performance
5. Moderation and Triage.

1. Audience

Community managers, through their daily interactions with consumers, instinctively know what topics drive most conversations. As a result, they are likely to have already prepared statements and responses that help resolve the most common issues.

Use a monitoring tool to continually find out which topics your customers are talking about in relation to you and your brand. It's also good sense to look outside of just your brand name. Look to see what people are saying about specific products, your competitors (and their products). Often, great insights (and opportunity) can come from seeing consumers' frustrations about rivals and their products.

All of these foresights allow the community manager to be ready for inbound complaints as well as prepare content to enthuse and delight your community.

2. Channels and timing

Again, coming out of the social media research comes an understanding of the places where customers are talking about you. From a community management point of view, this is crucial in knowing where you need to spend most of your time.

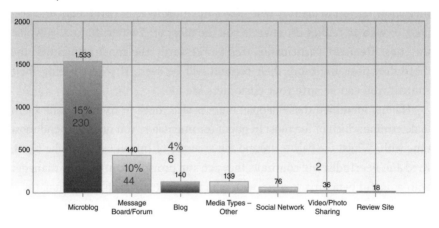

Charts like the above (from a monitoring tool called SM2) give a detailed breakdown of where the mentions of Brand X are. If there are, say, 2,300 mentions of Brand X per week, we can instantly see which channels we need to assign more time to.

By volume (1,533 mentions), we can see that in theory 65% of our time needs to be spent on Microblogs (Twitter) but the reality is that we perhaps only need to respond to, say, 15% of these comments (230 tweets).

Having broadly understood how much resource we need to handle the volume, we now have to understand when we need our community managers to be active and available to help. Most modern monitoring tools will indicate when, during the week and day, the majority of volume is created. This helps create a much more flexible but structured approach to your community management and enables you to understand whether a split-shift pattern works best versus a normal working hours approach.

Having understood where mentions are taking place (channels), we've been able to understand what is being said in each channel, the quantity of mentions we actually have to deal with and, finally, when these mentions take place.

3. Influencers

It is often the case that a small minority of users contribute the most noise in any given channel or community. It is the role of the community manager to identify these people and be able to develop a meaningful relationship with them.

Tools like Socialbakers (a popular analysis tool) go some way to achieving this, allowing you to identify who leaves the most likes or comments on Facebook or who @ replies or retweets you the most on Twitter. Naturally, whilst the most frequent participants aren't necessarily the most influential, the more they post, the more their content will be seen. If you're seeing their content, you can be sure your customers are too.

Having identified these people, there is also merit in trying to rank them to determine which of the most frequent commentators you need to spend most time with. Whilst the debate around the accuracy of Influencer tools like Klout, Kred and PeerIndex will continue, they can still provide a community manager with a useful benchmark score with which to evaluate each individual.

4. Content planning and performance

Albert Einstein famously stated that "insanity was doing the same thing over and over again and expecting different results" and in community management, this couldn't be more appropriate.

If you don't understand what content works, where it works and at what time, yet continue to post the same type of content day after day, your channels and community will remain flat and lifeless. Frustration will build both internally (your dreams of a world-beating Facebook Page are in tatters) and externally, as customers lose interest and go elsewhere to vent their frustrations. Or, worse still, they join and interact with a competitor.

Content planning may not be the most interesting part of the community manager's job, but it can be one of the most important. Without organized and relevant content, your channels are useless.

Use a content calendar rigidly (Google Drive shared documents are great) to filter down wider business plans into quarterly, monthly, weekly and/or daily themes. Divide up by business division and channel so you have an at-a-glance view of how your channels are serving the business. To this end, also consider inviting content ideas from around the business to contribute to the calendar so that there is a wealth of ideas from which to choose.

Take each theme and begin to craft your message. Be clear about when localization means changes need to be made, what multimedia assets need to be created or sourced (and their lead times) and what legal approval may be needed. If you already have a robust content creation process, get smarter by looking at content performance metrics to determine what type of message structure or media would work best and when.

Another important aspect of content planning is accounting for community "sentiment". Without understanding, or at the very least, considering, what mood your community is in, you run the risk of doing nothing more than pushing broadcast content out via a social media channel. A sales promotion post at a time when you have delivery problems is likely to antagonize and upset your community.

Good performance metrics are essential. Look closely at things like reach, visibility and the engagement of each post. Consider testing content. Does your latest post have more reach with a video or an image? What types of content get the most comments?

Also, consider "stress-testing" your channels. Understand the peak times for brand mentions, and the times of the day you get the most engagement. See how many posts you can fit into your day without spamming or losing fans. Each week, look at these content performance statistics to understand how you can continue to be relevant, visible and ultimately helpful to fans.

With the increasingly algorithmic nature of content visibility in social media, you need to understand what works, when it works and where it works.

5. Moderation and triage

Moderation can often take on a negative meaning, but is an essential part of managing and maintaining a healthy community. As an admin, you have a responsibility to ensure the wellbeing of the fans of your channel so that they aren't misled, bullied or otherwise abused. You also need to adhere to the rules and regulations of the channel you are using. Be clear in your social media guidelines about the expectations of the community. Be clear by creating a rule book (that may be shared externally too) about the kind of foul language, content and behaviour that will not be tolerated and explain how abuses of this will be dealt with, including the conditions of expulsion from the channel and/or reporting to the appropriate authorities.

Triage is the process of assessing an incident and evaluating its importance and what to do with it. The principle used in hospitals can equally be applied to community management.

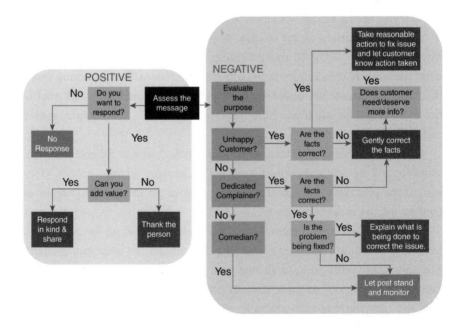

Create a workflow such as the one above to make sure you understand when and how to engage with any given issue, but most importantly, know who you need to go to for any given issue. Create an organizational chart based around the escalation topics and name individuals responsible for dealing with each issue.

The speed of response is as critical as the quality of the response.

Summary

Few people will have as much direct contact with customers as a community manager, or face as wide a range of communications and reputational challenges. This is why the management of social media channels requires such careful planning.

By using insights about your audience, their behaviours and locations, you can begin to frame a process which is both robust and scalable and which, more than anything else, serves your community in the way they want to be served.

Biography

Paul (@paulfabretti) is the Digital and Social Media Lead for Telefónica Europe. His role is to plan and deliver the Telefónica Europe social media vision and its initiatives, and to drive Global and European social media innovation and best practice. He was previously Head of the award-winning O2 UK social media team, which recently won the inaugural Twitter flock award for outstanding use of the Twitter platform. In 2009 he co-launched Manchester's first social media agency, gabba, which worked with brands like Dyson, Lexus, Microsoft and many police forces, including GMP and Merseyside.

Chapter 10

CURATION

Michael Litman

Content curation is billed by some as the future for brands in remaining relevant in an environment that changes daily. This chapter looks at the importance of content curation for brands, media, agencies and individuals: who's doing a great job of it and what can be learnt as a result.

"It's not information overload, it's filter failure"[62] a wise man once said. Digital culture is now a filter culture. We spend our daily online lives swamped with more information than we will ever have the time to digest. Whether we know we're doing it or not, we are filtering the haystack of information to get to the needle. We are all content curators.

But what does content curation really mean? It is defined as "the process of analysing and sorting Web content and presenting it in a meaningful and organized way around a specific theme".[63]

The job of a content curator sees them firstly deciding on a relevant niche or subject and then seeking out all available information which is then refined and arranged in a structured order. This is an order of importance and relevance, displayed in a hierarchy of resourcefulness.

However, content curation isn't just about collecting links and saving them, it is about providing context to the reasoning as to why one article is of higher importance than another. A content curator as a result becomes the knowledge source and the go-to person on that particular subject.

---

[62]Clay Shirky quote: http://cipr.co/XiEdR2
[63]Content Curation: Definition: http://cipr.co/14RArU5

The news now finds you

When it comes to news, social networks are the new front pages for breaking news. Do you remember how you first heard about Michael Jackson's sudden death? This world news event crashed Twitter, Google News, AOL, CBS, CNN, MSNBC and Yahoo, all at the same time.[64] When Twitter did come back up, nine out of the ten trending topics worldwide were related to Michael Jackson.[65]

Welcome to the era of Big Data

Because of the advent of high-speed broadband around the world, the barrier to people curating their lives online is considerably lower than it has been in the past. According to IBM, we are firmly in the era of "Big Data". Ninety percent of the data in the world today has been created in the last two years.[66] Take a moment to think about that and wonder how we ever find anything we're looking for on the web.

Searching for gold

Search engines increasingly help us to do just that. Google went on record in 2012 to say they are now answering 100 billion search results a month.[67] In a 2009 study on "Students use of researching content in teaching and learning" by The Centre for Research-Informed Teaching at University of Central Lancashire, they found that "a lot of students use Google but are bewildered by the amount of responses and will rarely look beyond the first couple of pages of search terms".[68]

---

[64]Michael Jackson's death grinds the internet to a halt: http://cipr.co/UXhdIL
[65]Michael Jackson Twitter Trending Topics: http://cipr.co/11Khm6G
[66]Big Data, IBM: http://cipr.co/VUoR2N
[67]Google Search Results, Search Engine Land: http://cipr.co/VI6418
[68]Research paper, University of Central Lancashire: http://cipr.co/XiFbNc

Why an organization would curate

Content curation is also an emerging trend for brands. They want to be part of culture, to be part of a broader message, which is not purely focused on their products, but also what value they are providing to the world.

"We need to stop interrupting what people are interested in and *be* what people are interested in" says Craig Davis, Chief Creative Officer, JWT.[69]

In January 2012, Josh Sternberg wrote how "Brands Want Content Curator Jobs"[70] for Digiday:

> "Publishing is a lot harder than it looks, or rather it's a lot harder to do it with the consistency, day after day, that's needed to build a long-term audience. That's leading some brands to hook onto the idea that their role lies more in the curation of content."

Neil Chase, SVP of Editing and Publishing at Federated Media, agrees:

> "If a brand is an expert in a certain topic, their reputation might make them a credible source of information. But if a company that makes toasters gives health advice, they might not be credible. If they're sending out recipes, that's a reason to trust them."

In 2013, curation of content by brands will move towards being the norm rather than a niche activity and it's getting easier to do. The web is also morphing into a much more visual landscape which supports the move to a more curation-led approach to content. In November 2012, blogging platform Tumblr had over 170 million monthly unique visitors and is one of the top 10 most visited sites in the US.[71] Some of the world's biggest brands are also on Pinterest, a rapidly exploding visual curation platform which helps brands engage with consumers in new ways.

---

[69]Purpose Made Everything: http://cipr.co/VU1sSc
[70]Brands Want Content Curator Jobs: http://cipr.co/VU1GsA
[71]Usage data on Tumblr; http://cipr.co/TJn0T1

What are the benefits?

- It helps with content discovery and drives traffic to your website (Pinterest for example now drives more referral traffic than Google+, YouTube and LinkedIn combined).[72]
- It helps build positive engagement around the brand, often without the consumer even knowing it because of the strength of the content.
- It helps create a competitive advantage and drives brand awareness. American Express is a leader in this space with the OPEN Forum platform, a hot-bed of content and experiences to help small businesses.
- It will never replace original branded content. Don't just do it for the sake of it. It will only magnify inadequacies. If there is no story to tell, share great ideas and find inspiration.

How to curate

There are a number of tools that make the curating of quality content a much more enjoyable experience than in previous years. The earliest example of this would be the advent of RSS, which dates back to 1995.[73] Google Alerts in 2003[74] allowed you to create, on a small scale, your own search engine. This was followed soon after by directory sites like Alltop.com which curated feeds on hundreds of interest areas. There are a vast number of social news curation apps today like Flipboard, Pulse and Google Currents.

Flipboard, probably one of the most well-known content curation apps, is a magazine-style social network and online news aggregator for Android and iOS. It became so popular and widely used that it was blocked in China on 15 May 2011 until Flipboard came out with a fully localized version on 6 December 2011 in collaboration with popular local social networks Sina Weibo and Ren Ren. As a result, the Chinese edition no longer includes Twitter or Facebook as social network options.[75]

---

[72]Pinterest driving referral traffic: http://cipr.co/TJnbxy
[73]History of RSS: http://cipr.co/WwG8C4
[74]History of Google Alerts: http://cipr.co/14DE6E1
[75]Flipboard China: http://cipr.co/11pg5CY

Some of the most popular applications used in content creation include:

- Twitter
- Pocket
- Buffer
- Delicious
- Storify.

Individuals who are leading the way in curation include:

1. Maria Popova, Brain Pickings (Sociology/Science)
2. Tina Roth Eisenberg, Swiss Miss (Design)
3. Eric Barker, Bakadesuyo (Human Behaviour)
4. Neil Perkin, Only Dead Fish (Culture/Trends)
5. Dan Calladine, Media Futures (Technology/Trends)
6. Daniel Roth, LinkedIn (General Business).

Case studies

A whole industry is effectively being created through brands that want to be part of a cultural, greater good. Red Bull didn't spend years developing the hugely ambitious Stratos project with the sole objective of selling more energy drinks; it was about the brand effectively creating the news itself. Brands are now media channels in their own right.

Pepsi

In April 2012, Pepsi created Pepsi Pulse[76] – an interactive, social media-driven dashboard for all things related to popular culture. Again, this was not purely about shifting soft drinks, but about becoming the destination for content. Pepsi Pulse consists of a mixture of original content (e.g. live streams of Pepsi sponsored events), crowd-sourced fan tweets

(Continued)

[76]Pepsi Pulse: http://cipr.co/11UuP02

and photos and articles from content partners like Hollywood.com and the Associated Press. They present the top 10 trending news items in real time on Pepsi Pulse through data collected by SocialFlow,[77] a social media optimization company.

Shiv Singh, global head of digital for PepsiCo Beverages, explained: "It's not enough anymore to have phenomenal TV ads – brands have to do more. Brand wars are being fought in news feeds and streams."[78] Users have the ability to share Pulse content easily on platforms like Facebook, Twitter and Pinterest to help Pepsi compete in a crowded market.

Does Pepsi now see itself as a credible source of news for people to keep coming back to? Singh answers: "In the last few years we've seen people in general care less about the source of an experience or who's creating the content, and more about the experience itself. People care less whether it's a TV network that's creating a really funny piece of video or whether a brand is."[79]

Intel

It can sometimes seem like there's a hot new start-up that's going to change the world sprouting up every minute and in-vogue companies like Twitter, Facebook, Instagram and Pinterest get all the attention. Traditional and established brands often get overlooked.

Intel, the $54 billion semiconductor chip company, sought to reverse this trend with the launch of iQ by Intel in 2012. It is a publishing platform curated by company researchers and engineers where Intel hopes to "connect with a younger audience and tell them the bigger story of who we are as a brand," according to editor-in-chief Bryan Rhoads. Beyond PCs and processors, Intel is seeking to be a more intrinsic part of popular culture.

The site, which looks similar to a Flipboard-style magazine, includes original content along with aggregated news from other sources like *The Guardian* paidContent and Mashable. Where iQ by Intel is ahead of

[77]Social Flow: http://cipr.co/Y9Srmq
[78]Mashable: http://cipr.co/14DEiTK
[79]Shiv Singh, Pepsi Pulse: http://cipr.co/TJnRD2

many of its competitors and counterparts is in its approach to curation. It puts curatorial content in the hands of its 100,000+ employees, giving them ownership of the company voice and telling impassioned stories from behind the scenes, by the people for the people.

Other notable mentions

It is worth mentioning a number of global brands using branded content at the core of their marketing strategies. Coca-Cola (Coca-Cola Journey), American Express (OPEN Forum), Qualcomm (Spark), Cisco (The Network), HSBC (Business Without Borders) and BCG (Perspectives) all do this. Coca-Cola in particular has a "Content 2020" strategy where the company is looking to "move from creative excellence to content excellence and gain a disproportional share of popular culture".[80]

On the flip side there are a number of start-ups like Percolate, Mass Relevance, CurationStation, Curata, PublishThis and Curalate who have created social curation products and services to help make it easier for marketers to make it part of their routine.

Summary

There is an old rule that in publishing, 90% of people will simply consume content, 9% will curate the content and 1% will create it.[81] We're getting to a point now where we are outgrowing the model. The Future Media department at the BBC agrees, in its "Online Briefing: The Participation Choice" where in 2012 it notes:

> "The model which has guided many people's thinking in this area, the 1/9/90 rule, is outmoded. The number of people participating online is significantly higher than 10%. Participation is now the rule rather than the exception: 77% of the UK online population is now active in some way. This has been driven by the rise of 'easy participation': activities which may have once required great effort but now are relatively

---

[80] *Marketing Week*, 2011: cipr.co/VU2Q7j
[81] 90/9/1 rule: http://cipr.co/YT3FS8

easy, expected and every day. 60% of the UK online population now participates in this way, from sharing photos to starting a discussion."[82]

Curation is growing up, fast, and in 2013 you will see significant investment from global brands putting it at the heart of their marketing strategies along with a multitude of tools and services that will take curation to the next level in terms of ease of use, processing and tracking. Are you going to join the curation nation?

Biography

Michael Litman (@mlitman) is a Senior Social Strategist at AnalogFolk, an independent global digital agency which uses digital to make the analog world better. BRANDSONVINE.COM. He has worked for some of the leading agencies in advertising and formerly PR, working for a wide range of global and start-up brands. Michael has spoken at numerous conferences and in his spare time enjoys writing for industry leading websites and magazines on trends in social media, technology and advertising. He was formerly the UK editor for Adverblog.com and in 2012, *Advertising Age* recognized him as one of most influential marketing bloggers in the world.

[82]BBC Briefing: http://cipr.co/11UvohA

Chapter 11

LIVE SOCIAL EVENTS

Russell Goldsmith

Live events, broadcast online on mobile and through social media, can help deliver true engagement within a community. Here, we explore opportunities created by Google+ Hangouts, whilst looking at what is required to keep audience retention beyond a few minutes.

When I rented a room at university, one of the other people in the house refused to contribute to the TV licence as he said that a television was "anti-social" and that "all people did was sit around a box in the corner of a room not talking to each other". His loss. All those quality hours spent in high-level discussion about *Neighbours* and *Home & Away* passed him by. Fast forward a few years and I wonder what his views would be on the fact that "social TV" has now become an exciting and challenging aspect for brands involved in content marketing, whether they are sponsoring or advertising around traditional TV programming, or producing their own videos online.

According to the TV Licensing Telescope Report 2012,[83] 26% of us say we have commented on a programme on a second screen, rising to 46% of those aged under 25 saying they have used a social media channel to comment on a TV programme. Most importantly for me though, is that 57% of the UK's social media users aged under 35 say social media buzz around a TV programme can affect whether they watch a programme live or not. Being involved in and following "chatterboxing", as the report calls the experience, in the build-up to and during a live programme, is actually becoming part of

---

[83]TeleScope, TV Licensing: http://cipr.co/TJxhP2

the viewing experience, and is encouraging people to watch a programme as it is shown on TV.

In another report published in September 2012 by BSkyB that includes a handy infographic,[84] they showed that 24% of us use social media for TV recommendations, with 12% saying they turn on the TV just because of something they've seen on social media. Imagine if we can get those social media users to recommend a live branded experience to their friends and followers. Brands must start to get on board with producing content to help build and engage their communities, especially within Facebook if the *Social Brands 100* report is anything to go by.[85] Published in May 2012, the report by Headstream showed that just 8% of all posts on Facebook by the top brands are video compared to 9% sharing links, 10% photos and 73% status updates, yet the report states that posts with videos are the most shared of all those types of updates.

There was possibly no better example of how people use social media, and in particular Twitter, whilst watching live TV than during the London 2012 Olympics and Paralympics. From the opening ceremony, where the @dannyboylefilm Twitter feed grew to hundreds of thousands of followers in just a couple of hours only for it to turn out to be just a fan's feed, and Sir Tim Berners-Lee tweeting "This is for everyone" from the middle of the event itself, throughout the rest of the games, Twitter and Facebook were key parts of the shared viewing experience. Twitter counted 9.66 million mentions of the opening ceremony between 8.00pm UK time, through to the end of the delayed US broadcast on NBC, which started more than three hours later.[86] Twitter, however, can also be a nightmare for programme producers and potentially the death of Sky+ for me. After all, how many of us have been out on a Saturday night, intending to catch up on a favourite programme after it was broadcast, only to check our social media feeds to find someone has revealed whodunnit, who won, or who was voted off? Even the stars of the shows themselves are having to learn how to get to grips with the whole

---

[84]How technology and social media are changing the way we watch TV, Sky: http://cipr.co/XiNXLp

[85]Social Brands 100: http://cipr.co/WtZtpq

[86]"Twitter: Olympics opening ceremony saw 9.66 million mentions", Cnet.com: http://cipr.co/XnIPUn

concept of social TV without ruining the experience for viewers. Fans of the singer Jessie J, for example, were furious after she revealed who she had picked for the semi-final of TV show *The Voice* on which she was a judge, two hours before the show aired on the BBC.[87]

Whatever your viewpoint on Social TV, the fact is that more video is being watched online than ever before, and as social media can drive engagement with the content, particularly in a live environment, it's more important than ever for PR to get involved.

Learn to walk before you jump

2012 saw live online brand-funded content grow stronger and stronger, culminating in October 2012 with the incredible jump from the edge of Space by Felix Baumgartner that, according to YouTube's blog,[88] was watched live by over 8 million people, myself and son included, on the Red Bull YouTube channel. Ben Sturner, of Leverage Agency said: "The value for Red Bull is in the tens of millions of dollars of global exposure, and Red Bull Stratos will continue to be talked about and passed along socially for a very long time."[89] However, we need to keep some perspective on what most of us are trying to achieve in terms of online broadcast, as not every PR executive has the millions of dollars required[90] to enable a man to jump from 128,100 feet. So keeping our own feet on terra firma, let's take a look at how we can engage our brand's social communities for a slightly smaller budget.

Hanging out with Google

Google+ Hangouts[91] is the latest technology to give organizations a very cost-effective way to bring members of their Google+ network together for a live

[87]"Jessie J Twitter Error", *The Mirror*: http://cipr.co/XVjj8Y

[88]YouTube Blog: http://cipr.co/WtZBp2

[89]"Red Bull Stratos Worth Tens Of Millions Of Dollars In Global Exposure For The Red Bull", *Forbes*: http://cipr.co/11Kr6Ol

[90]"Vertically Challenged", *Orlando Magazine*: http://cipr.co/UydHXE

[91]Google+ Hangout: http://cipr.co/14DItPB

video conference. However, the Hangouts On-Air feature, available to all Google+ users since May 2012,[92] means that, with the live feed being broadcast through YouTube, the stream can be embedded into other social networks too.

Cadbury's was an early adopter of Google+ and Hangouts and Jerry Daykin, their Social Media & Community Manager, says that he thinks brands should just "give it a try and think about a new way of connecting with your consumers and having a chat with them".[93]

The tool still has a long way to go before providing a perfect broadcast viewing experience, as you are still reliant on the broadband of those guests who are joining the Hangout. If using it for a brand-funded piece of content, it should still be professionally produced and as engaging and interactive as possible for the viewers. Time should be invested in the pre-production of the event, testing every participant's connection, their lighting, and ensuring they know the running order of the show you are producing so they do not end up speaking over one another, which could create a painful viewing experience.

There are so many opportunities for brands to use Hangouts to engage with their audience, aside from enabling spokespeople to join remotely which the CIPR has done as part of its CIPRTV series.[94] It can become an extension of a blogger engagement programme where bloggers can take part in a show themselves, or competition winners or fans can have the opportunity to ask questions to the Hangout guests, as in the example broadcast live by Google Play featuring Steven Spielberg[95] promoting his latest film, *Lincoln*, which was also streamed live on to a huge jumbotron in Times Square, New York.

From a B2B perspective, however, the fact that a YouTube feed can be embedded into a discussion thread on LinkedIn opens up huge opportunities. For example, a Hangout could enable viewers to watch a panel of key business opinion leaders debate a topic from their own desks anywhere around the world.

[92]Official Google Blog: http://cipr.co/YCTuNJ
[93]Google+ Hangout On Air With Cadbury UK: http://cipr.co/WwRohX
[94]CIPRTV, Google and public relations: http://cipr.co/TRsZix
[95]Google Play presents: Steven Spielberg and Joseph Gordon-Levitt: http://cipr.co/11pkVzW

Using LinkedIn for live broadcast becomes important given the fact that, according to the US-based Forbes *Video in the C-Suite* report from 2010,[96] 75% of executives surveyed said they watch work-related videos on business-related websites at least weekly, with more than 52% watching work-related videos on YouTube at least weekly. LinkedIn becomes important from a social networking perspective as, according to that same report, 54% of senior executives share work-related videos with colleagues at least weekly, and 47% said they post links to work-related videos to "networking" sites at the same rate. The figure jumps to 69% for those under the age of 40.

There's a first for everyone

Whilst live streaming is still relatively young, there remain plenty of opportunities to deliver that key PR hook of trying something new that, as well as engaging your own community, will also go a long way to generating coverage.

The Carphone Warehouse achieved this when it streamed the UK's first live gig on Facebook, featuring Eliza Doolittle performing from Ronnie Scott's in London to help promote the launch of the INQ Cloud Touch smartphone.[97] The choice of Facebook to launch the phone was due to the handset having a dedicated Facebook app which streams a live feed to the home-screen.[98] The PR angle was that there wasn't a physical audience watching Eliza perform in the club. Instead, the event, produced by markettiers4dc, working with Cake and Freud Communications, could only be viewed exclusively on The Carphone Warehouse Facebook Page which, as well as recording a huge increase in engagement, resulted in coverage in the national[99] and London press.[100]

In a similar manner, in July 2012, The Royal Albert Hall hosted what was billed as the first ever live Facebook science lesson, although in this instance,

---

[96]Video in the C-Suite, Forbes Insights: http://cipr.co/WOnBmd

[97]Eliza Doolittle performs Britain's first exclusive Facebook concert, markettiers4dc: http://cipr.co/VDwVGa

[98]The Carphone Warehouse Online Press Centre: http://cipr.co/UyeE22

[99]"Eliza Doolittle plays Facebook's first ever UK gig", *The Mirror*: http://cipr.co/XnJxB3

[100]"Eliza Doolittle plays to empty Ronnie Scott's in a Facebook first", *London Evening Standard*: http://cipr.co/14RHWud

there was an invited audience of schoolchildren too. Being a first, it again gained plenty of coverage outside of their own social network,[101] and can still be viewed on-demand.[102]

Producing live content

Understanding your audience, who they are (internal or external to the organization, business-to-business or consumer), where they will consume the content (home, office or on the move) and on what platform (desktop, tablet or mobile) will determine the style of live content produced, the production standards you work to and how to promote it to them to help encourage participation. For example, you can have a simple live webchat with one webcam focused on your spokesperson, but panning and changing camera angles, or using pre-recorded video inserts, slides and graphics can all help to keep your live broadcast interesting and your audiences engaged for longer. The pre-production process is therefore vitally important in briefing the team involved, creating a basic script and running order of your event and having a call sheet for live broadcast informing who needs to be where and when. Similarly, if sourcing a location to broadcast from, someone should always recce beforehand to check for everything from access, lighting and external noises to the important element of broadband connectivity. If there is insufficient broadband, usually around 4–6MB uncontended is required, then it's still possible to broadcast live via a mobile encoder or by hiring in a satellite truck, and so it's important to understand what is achievable within the available budget and timeframe.

When working with spokespeople or talent, you should brief them beforehand, letting them know how long they will be needed, what to wear, what questions they might be required to answer and, if presenting a live event, check as to whether they are used to wearing an ear-piece to listen to a producer or have read from an autocue before. There may also be various legal

---

[101]"Facebook to host science lesson live from the Albert Hall", *The Independent*: http://cipr.co/Y9YhnE
[102]"What Is Sound?", YouTube: http://cipr.co/WuorlF

forms to complete, such as health and safety risk assessments and talent release forms signing over rights to use the content beyond perhaps the live broadcast should you wish to make it available on-demand.

There are numerous types of live content that you can produce, from simply streaming a webcast of your event, like the Eliza Doolittle gig, to splitting the screen with slides if streaming a live conference presentation.

If producing a webchat, you could focus purely on the talent, as M&S did when Joanna Lumley answered questions from its 1 million+ fans on Facebook about its Shwopping campaign in June 2012,[103] or use a presenter to host the show and pose questions as they come through live via social media. Outside of the studio, you could look to produce more sophisticated web TV programming, as whisky brand Laphroaig has been doing for the past few years, its most recent Whisky Tasting event broadcasting live for almost an hour into its Facebook Page[104] from Germany in September 2012 during the Oktoberfest.

Finally, live events can also be linked directly to commercial opportunities. For example, etailer Littlewoods has begun to produce regular live TV shows exclusively for its Facebook fans featuring presenters such as Laurence Llewelyn-Bowen and Myleene Klass, the first of which they say stimulated record sales for featured products.[105]

Final thoughts

I didn't say how long ago I was renting that room at university, but let's just say I wasn't even on email at the time. It was many years before YouTube, Facebook or Twitter had even been thought of; it was even a few years before Netscape launched its first version of the web browser Mosaic in 1994.[106] It's therefore fair to say that no one could have predicted how the social experience of shared viewing would go so far beyond one room. What we also wouldn't have anticipated was the amount of content that people would watch that

---

[103]M&S Facebook: http://cipr.co/UyfbRG

[104]Laphroaig Facebook: http://cipr.co/VDxm3j

[105]"Littlewoods Facebook show prompts sales spike", *Retail Week*: http://cipr.co/11plr12

[106]Netscape Wikipedia page: http://cipr.co/11UI5ZC

wasn't scheduled on the TV itself, but could be viewed online, and in a branded community.

Biography

Russell Goldsmith (@russgoldsmith) has been involved in online marketing since 1995 and is now Digital and Social Media Director at markettiers4dc, a specialist broadcast communications consultancy which helps its clients to reach their audiences through traditional broadcast media relations in the UK and internationally and by creating branded content for aggregation online and streaming live events through social media. Russell sits on the CIPR Social Media Panel and is a presenter on CIPRTV.

Part IV

New Channels, New Connections

Chapter 12

MOBILE MEDIA

Stephen Davies

The mobile revolution is upon us. All day and each and every day we carry around with us powerful mobile computers that have more processing power than a desktop PC had only a few short years ago. Technology waits for no one and we have only skimmed the surface of the possibilities of this revolution as consumers rely on these increasingly powerful and ever-present devices. Today's smartphone is not primarily a phone and with its range of communication features has reduced the time we spend making actual calls. Tomorrow's smartphone will be like a third brain, with superior data-driven intelligence and more personalized and real-time information than we once thought imaginable.

Imagine yourself ten years ago with the mobile phone you owned at the time. You could talk, text and perhaps had the addictive Snake game on your Nokia. The more advanced may have owned a cameraphone producing low-quality pixelated images that seemed almost impossible to download.

Then again, in 2003 you may not have owned a mobile phone, as only 64% of the UK adult population did.[107] It's taken for granted now but at the time the mobile internet was unknown to most people and used only by those who could afford the high browsing fees. Even the once iconic Blackberry was still in its infancy and only used by a select group of people, mainly those of the suit-wearing corporate variety.

---

[107]Mobile phone ownership by sex and age 1999–00 to 2009–2010: http://cipr.co/VIh12N

Fast forward ten years. Blackberry came and almost went; mobile internet data costs have decreased tenfold; the introduction of the iPhone, iPad and subsequent launch of Google Android have revolutionized the ways in which we communicate and consume on the move; there are more mobile phones in the UK than there are people, and the new 4G network is providing, by today's standards, super-fast mobile internet.

This is just the beginning. On the horizon is a slew of technological and cultural advancements that will shape people's lives and how organizations interact with them.

The supercomputer in a smartphone

The growth in mobile technology is increasing at an exponential rate. The computing power of today's smartphone once had to be housed in a large room full of coolers to prevent it from over-heating. In the future the same processing power will be small enough to fit into a red blood cell. Future gazers predict that computing power will surpass human brain power by 2023 in what has been named Technological Singularity – the theoretical emergence of greater-than-human super-intelligence through technological means.

Think that this is merely speculation by over-enthusiastic *Star Wars* fans and you may think again. Technology and consulting company, IBM, built a supercomputer that can not only understand questions posed in natural language but can answer them using its databank of information with a superior degree of accuracy. When the supercomputer, Watson (named after IBM's first president), answers a question incorrectly it learns from its mistake, ensuring that if the same question is asked again it answers it correctly.

To prove its superior intelligence, and as a test of its abilities, Watson competed on the US TV quiz show *Jeopardy!* in 2011 against the show's two most successful players. The biggest all-time money winner and the record holder for the most consecutive games won both unsuccessfully competed against Watson in the special one-off show, vindicating the academic field of artificial intelligence and perhaps opening up the minds of the general public to such technological capabilities.

Finding additional uses for Watson is part of IBM's plan and mobility is being touted as a future feature. An article in US publication, *Businessweek*, titled, "IBM wants to put a Watson in your pocket"[108] outlined the company's plans to take Watson's technology and condense it to smartphone size, and caused excitement among the great and the good in mobile circles.

Whether it is IBM or another company that fits greater-than-human super-intelligence technology into a device the size of a smartphone remains to be seen. Though thanks to technology's exponential curve one thing seems certain and that is that a smartphone with Watson-like features will be available for consumer use in the near future.

Curated, personalized and highly mobile news

According to Ofcom the UK is the global leader in the mobile market, with Brits consuming more data on their mobile phones than any other country on a per head basis.[109] With one of the highest penetrations of smartphone and tablet ownership in the world, the social networking obsessive, high definition content consuming and information junkie Brit just can't get enough.

This trend is beginning to change how people find and consume news and is impacting on news organizations. *The Guardian*'s website is in the midst of change in terms of how people access it. In 2010 just 10% of visitors accessed it from a mobile device but by 2012 this had increased to 35%. The *Financial Times* has reported similar numbers, with 30% of online traffic coming from a mobile device. This growth is expected to continue for the foreseeable future.

These aren't isolated examples but an illustration of how news organizations around the world are experiencing a similar trend. Social networking sites like Facebook, Twitter and LinkedIn with their large communities and content-sharing features are playing a part in this shift but they themselves are facing similar challenges as their users increasingly use their mobiles to communicate and share with their friends.

Facebook in particular has seen a dramatic change in how people access the site, with over half of its one billion users coming via a mobile device.

---

[108]IBM Wants to Put a Watson in Your Pocket: http://cipr.co/11VcrLI
[109]UK leads world in mobile web use thanks to Facebook . . . and Gangnam: http://cipr.co/14DVetv

Facebook CEO Mark Zuckerberg anticipates the rate of growth in mobile usage will "exceed the growth in usage through personal computers for the foreseeable future".[110] A comScore research paper found that around 13% of all visits to UK national newspaper websites come from Facebook.[111]

After the introduction of its news app *The Guardian* saw a dramatic increase in referrals as 30% of all traffic to its news site came from Facebook. Changes to the Facebook platform have since seen the demise of the news app but nevertheless show the influence Facebook has over news publishers around the world.

While social sites make a big impact they are not the only mobile disrupter. News curation and social network aggregation apps pull in content from multiple sources to a single location to help the user consolidate multiple news sources and social networking profiles. They are changing the way in which consumers discover news. An example of this is Flipboard, a beautifully designed application for iPhone, iPad and Android which curates content from numerous social networking sites like Facebook, Twitter, Google+, LinkedIn and Instagram. It allows users to see, in a magazine-like format, what news stories and blog posts their friends, colleagues and influencers are linking to. Taking it one step further, Flipboard can create a magazine from Twitter searches (a specific hashtag keyword for example).

This kind of news consumption essentially takes the peer-to-peer recommendation model to another level. Whilst Flipboard isn't the only app that does this, it is certainly one of the most pioneering and forward thinking. It introduced a partner programme where publishers including big name ones such as *The Telegraph, New York Times, Esquire* and *Vanity Fair* and brands including Red Bull and Oprah allow Flipboard to aggregate their content and feed users advertisements along with it.

This type of news consumption is only the beginning, as users increasingly want to manage personalized news content on their terms. News consumption will be tailored in ways that previously seemed impossible. Personalized news and information will be delivered to the user based on

---

[110]Facebook anticipates growth in mobile usage rather than personal computers, Ken Yeung, The Next Web 2012

[111]UK leads world in mobile web use thanks to Facebook . . . and Gangnam: http://cipr.co/14DVetv

real-time factors including mood, location and current interests and will rely on intelligent separate devices that communicate and share data with one another.

The data-driven society with mobile at its core

The mobile device of the future will be a powerful device pulling in news, content and information; answering any question we may have in a matter of milliseconds and helping us make personal decisions based on its own logic, learning and, ultimately, inference. This efficient tool will become a dependable friend we can't live without.

It won't be the only device we carry around with us however, but will act as the central hub of an ecosystem of devices, clothing, jewellery, watches and loyalty cards all equipped with sensor technology to connect with, use and exchange information with one another.

This interoperability of technology is closely linked to the rise of both the Quantified Self movement and the Internet of Things and mobile will play a fundamental role in bridging the two. These sensors will create data that can be utilized by business.

Consider the following scenario.

It's 7.13am and Jon is woken by his mobile phone's alarm. The alarm will wake him anywhere between 6.45am and 7.15am depending on when he is in the lightest part of the sleep cycle. The phone is able to do this as Jon wears a sleep mask with sensors which track the three phases of sleep, REM, deep and light sleep so he can be woken at the appropriate time.

The mask sends sleep data to the phone and over time understands how much sleep Jon needs per night to feel fully awake during the day. On mornings when he hasn't had adequate sleep he will be served news articles on how to improve sleep and steps to take to feel fresh during the day after a bad night's sleep.

Jon's watch is not really a watch. Of course it tells the time but it is primarily used as a precise monitoring tool that analyzes his skin for his heart rate, heart rate variability, stress levels, blood pressure, blood glucose and fatigue. The watch is connected to his phone which collects the data and paints a picture of Jon's long-term health.

Any increase and ongoing fluctuation in the data and the phone makes an appointment with his doctor and shares the data with the doctor beforehand. On a day-by-day basis the health data is mapped to the calendar on Jon's phone, which allows him to pinpoint which parts of his day are causing his stress levels to increase. By addressing any issues Jon's health insurance premiums go down as a result because his health insurance company can see he is implementing positive changes to his lifestyle.

Part of these lifestyle changes may be in the foods Jon eats and he may move to purchasing a more healthy range. This kind of change will not go unnoticed at Jon's local supermarket, and by using his phone along with the store's loyalty app to pay for his weekly shopping he is a treasure trove of insight. His purchase of healthier food will prompt his phone to serve him health-related articles and features. When Jon suddenly starts buying only half of his usual weekly grocery shopping the supermarket may assume that he has split up with his partner and begin sending him discounts to dating sites. When months later his grocery shopping doubles it will be assumed that he has found and moved in with a new partner (or made up with the old one) and the phone will begin to serve him information on holidays for two.

This data of course is very personal and gaining access to it would require consent from Jon and people like him. There will be incentives for those who do so, however, and those that opt in to this data sharing will benefit from rewards, premium subscriptions, discounts and promotions.

The smartphone to multicorder

The "phone" in smartphone is an archaic reference to a bygone era of voice call only devices. Tomorrow's smartphone will be so far removed that a more relevant name for this device will be ushered in to aptly describe its functionality. The long-running sci-fi entertainment franchise, Star Trek, may have the answer with the Tricorder, a tri-functional handheld device used by the crew of the Starship Enterprise for scanning, data analysis and recording data.

The future smartphone could be called a tricorder, or perhaps, because of its multifunctional data analyzing, personal recommending, information consumption, self-learning and super-intelligence, the term "multicorder" may be a more appropriate name.

Regardless of the name, these devices will continue to alter our lives and our habits in new and powerful ways. Organizations of all kinds will need to embrace this change by creating freely available, up-to-date and relevant content; by creating partnerships with sensor technology companies and curation platforms; by understanding that decisions will increasingly be made on superior analysis rather than general instinct and by knowing that individuality has never been more important in this new and exciting age. Welcome to the next ten years of mobile.

Biography

Stephen Davies (@stedavies) is a digital communications consultant. He has worked in digital and social media since 2005 and has devised and implemented national and international digital strategies for a range of organizations in health, pharma, technology, consumer, media, government, not-for-profit and B2B. Stephen speaks on digital communications in the UK, Europe, Russia and the Gulf. His blog – since 2005 – has been recognized by industry professionals globally. He's been in *PR Week Power Book* twice, which claims to include the top 1% most "powerful and inspirational" UK PR people. He is a committee member of Forum Davos, an annual international conference held in Davos, Switzerland.

Chapter 13

Scott Seaborn

From smartphones to tablets to surface computers, here we give the lowdown on broad technology trends in the mobile marketing sector. Current technological advances are allowing mobile devices not only to talk to users, but to other machines too. Hyper-connected apps will create new opportunities for brands.

Technological advances are having implications for brands and marketers. There are five major technology-driven trends currently and the mobile device is at the centre of them.

1. Hyper-connected devices

Devices and other digital objects are becoming hyper-connected. Within a given radius from one another, devices are connecting and communicating at increasing speeds. Connected media devices are constantly emerging and they represent a wider spread of apparatus than the mobile telephone and tablet computer: internet fridges, interactive billboards, televisions, surface computers, vending machines, personal media devices, cars and even buildings are already talking to us via mobile phones and the internet. In the not-too-distant future they will be talking to each other as well, and talking fast. Hardware will be hyper-connected.

This area of mobile is developing fast. Seven major mobile operators from around the world recently agreed to work together to develop an international "machine-to-machine" platform that would help devices talk to each other.[112]

Implications for brand strategy

Creating useful device connections can help brands build "brand love". However, there are myriad ways to make the most of this insight. For example, the Project Re-Brief "Coke Vending Machine" is a very interesting use of mobile hyper-connectivity. It is a connected media reinterpretation of Coke's iconic "Hilltop" spot, featuring the song *I want to buy the world a Coke.* The mobile ad enables viewers to actually buy a Coke for someone, from their mobile, and deliver it in a city of their choice. As they watch the mobile ad, which ran on Google's Admob network, users can pick a city to send the Coke to, attach a text message and press a button that dispenses a drink through specially designed vending machines in that city. The viewer can even watch as their Coke is delivered.[113] The vending machine was connected to the mobile phone. But could ideas such as this also deliver ROI in wider areas than brand equity? Business solutions like creating operational efficiencies or cutting cost leakages will emerge from these kinds of brand ideas for connected devices.

A recent example of this embryonic practice would be Red Tomato Pizza's (Cannes Lions Winning) VIP Fridge Magnet from Dubai.[114] In this case the brand created a connected media object (a fridge magnet connected to the web) which acted like an "emergency call" button. When pushed, it used Bluetooth to connect with the consumer's mobile phone and set up an order for their favourite pizza. Again, a mobile phone connected campaign.

How can brands respond to this? We can think about which things to connect together and why. Which things are already connected today? There are going to be opportunities to run campaigns through connected devices that are not your own – as well as from your own packaging or in-store media

---

[112]"Seven Global Operators Form M2M Alliance", *Mobile Marketing Magazine*: http://cipr.co/11ViT5t

[113]Google: Project Re-Brief, "Coke Mobile Ad Demo, Cannes 2012 Mobile Grand Prix": http://cipr.co/xDKhLG

[114]Search http://cipr.co/xDKhLG for "Red Tomato pizza magnet"

property. Connecting packaging, TV and traditional media to mobile is a good place to start.

Take it one step further with interactive tables (surface computers[115]) in retail for example – what story could we tell as a consumer places their mobile on the table and it connects in real time? What should happen next? The creative format is made up of multiple elements like the surface-computer screen, the connected device, the retail environment and a few other sensors such as the mobile's camera or sound from the speaker. There is a lot to play with. What would an advertisement look like across these devices? What would a brand experience be in this format? If your brand is a service, could it have a new digital personality once it is connected?

2. Hyper-connected applications

Mobile and web applications and the personal and public profile information within them have also become hyper-connected. Think of things like social profiles, real-time media habits and purchase preferences: for example, Facebook, Zeebox and Red Laser profiles connecting with Amazon, iTunes and eBay. Coupled with connected devices, these connected profiles are having a significant impact on the way we do everyday things like shopping, travelling and consuming media/entertainment.

If the way people shop has changed, then also the way that people consume media has changed. Connected television viewing, dual screening with mobile and m-commerce is one example. The digital socialization of TV is already in full swing.[116]

Imagine for a moment that we are watching a Bond film on an internet TV. The computer controlling our TV is connected to our various wireless devices and online it is connected to our various personal and commercial profiles. These profiles act as our spam filters. They do not allow irrelevant or unwanted messages to reach us, but they are open to new messages from brands which are relevant for that given place or time. Bond movies are

---

[115]A surface computer interacts with the user through the surface of an ordinary object, rather than through a monitor and keyboard. A table is the most widely used example

[116]Zeebox: http://cipr.co/VDOupG

famous for their product placement; which is great if you are in the market for an Aston Martin DB7, but most people are not and many have relatively niche hobbies and interests. Only when Bond uses a product or service that is hyper-relevant to our profile will the mobile buzz with an opportunity to have it delivered.

This kind of marketing is not "futurology" – it is literally just around the corner.

Implications for brand strategy

At first glance it looks like the hyper-connection of profile information creates a world where our mobiles buzz all the time and hassle us to buy too many things. This is not actually the case. When we log in to mobile apps via Facebook Connect we do not get inundated with "push notifications", quite the opposite – it makes log-in faster for the user. In retrospect we might see something a bit different than the early days of "spam" on mobile. The meshing of profile data, with connected devices and digital objects through trusted infrastructures (e.g. Google) is acting as a filter through which irrelevant material will be blocked. The user should be in control of their digital persona. This raises some challenges for brands, in that the audience will be in control of their "filter" and those brands will need to be even more relevant. In theory it will be much harder to reach the audience. But on the other hand the filter will allow full access for trusted brands with relevant messages.

In a culture of hyper-connectivity there will be no room for spam but lots of room, even preference for, relevant and contextual brand engagements. Can marketing thus become a service rather than an irritating interruption?[117]

3. The mobile hub

As hardware and software became increasingly hyper-connected, the mobile phone has evolved into a digital hub. We see more mobile "phones" connecting

---

[117]This could lead to negative consequences. An insight into how is provided in *Filter Bubble* by Eli Pariser. The argument is that technology that filters out what it sees as irrelevant material can mean individuals are sheltered from viewpoints that challenge their ideas or preferences

with all sorts of things as we move around. Things like train ticket barriers, bus stops, parking meters, EPoS systems, televisions, magazines, points of sale, packaging, outdoor billboards, household devices – fridges, stereos, heating and lighting systems – and cars. Mobile is acting as a wallet or train ticket, but also as a receptacle for (connected) media distribution. One example might be when we pick up a free movie or track on our mobile from a product or advertisement. People will get used to "picking things up" from locations with their mobile device.

Implications for brand strategy

We should think about a future where our communications properties (including packaging and in-store media) are like origins for media engagements. Think of them like stations where the brand can broadcast digital experiences. If a customer connects their device to a press ad – or if they dual screen with an advert on TV – what should we do next? What would the brand's connected personality do? If they then go in-store, should they be able to get out their digital hub (mobile phone) and pick up something really special in the aisle, because of their previous interaction?

4. Mobile-directed experience

The new mobile media audience has more power and control than traditional media audiences. We are seeing audiences that are naturally used to manually controlling their experiences. Recent examples of brand response to this would be the Renault 360 iPad experience, The Gadget Show 360 iPad dual screen[118] and a 360-degree brand experience created for NS, the Dutch rail company, in The Netherlands[119] which won an award this year at the Cannes Lions international festival of creativity.

The audience of today is increasingly able to use the mobile device (as a digital hub) to direct the flow of media. With the arrival of 4G, they are now able to send media to other devices almost instantly. The mobile has already

---

[118]See http://cipr.co/11KUMeg and search for Gadget Show 360
[119]Search "NS Royal Waiting Rooms"

become the ultimate remote control. For example, the top of the range Mercedes Benz comes with a mobile app to control its ignition, windows and all sorts of other functions.

The A-class, Mercedes' entry-level model, has Apple's Siri software integrated into its on-board controls for voice control via iPhone. The phone connects with the car (hardware) and your Apple profile connects with Siri (software) to direct the on-board controls. In some cars it is already possible to pick up a video on your mobile and play it on the dashboard. In a different scenario we might be able to pick up a mobile media recipe for making sushi from the fish counter at the supermarket. Then take it home and transfer it from our mobile to the screen in the kitchen, or play it on our iPad with a swish of the hand.

Implications for brand strategy

The emphasis has shifted from "push" to "pull" media and communications. Brands will reap more rewards by organizing their assets into a usable suite of digital units (apps, connected media programmes, connected services, etc) and then inviting the audience to engage with them through traditional media and mobile. Setting up a "connected stall" if you will – and then inviting engagement. When they do engage, give them something entertaining or useful as a result and allow them to take it away and use it elsewhere.

5. A new creative landscape

Advertising is no longer about the powerful preaching to the grateful. We still remember the great ads from the 80s. The best new TV ads would break in the middle of Christmas blockbuster movies. If they were entertaining we would be grateful for them. A remarkable one was the Heineken three-part ad, the first one spanned the entire commercial break and had other ads interspersed in between each part: the first part showed an Aussie rancher hunting in the outback, throwing about 20 boomerangs but nothing coming back. Next you saw another ad from the schedule, for a car or insurance or something else. Then the second part came on. You realized that they were linked but unbranded – the film cut to the same guy throwing lots of boomerangs, perhaps another 20, but nothing coming back. After another unrelated (but real) advert you see him again. This time he takes out a Heineken and has a long drink. This is when you learn that the last two unbranded ads were for Heineken. Finally we see the payoff. All the boomerangs come back at once, and the line says "Heineken refreshes the parts that other beers cannot reach". The kangaroo hops past unaffected.

The first time we saw ads like this we were entertained. We were grateful for the story, the new format and the craft/execution. Today the audience is not so grateful and the brand not so powerful. The roles are reversing in this respect. We can already see the power tipping towards the audience on Twitter for example.

So advertising (creative work) has changed.

Marketers are still in the business of human understanding – we use human understanding to create business advantage but mobile marketing means understanding the way people adopt connected media technologies. Today we are in the mode of making insight-driven brand experiences. Platform ideas that grow beyond a single media channel. Advertising is changing again. Creative work will evolve into giving ideas to the audience: ideas of real value, as advertisements. We will be creating connected media campaigns that contain ideas that the audience can use right away. Campaigns that invite engagement from the audience and enable brands to give valuable ideas to customers, through connected media and devices.

For example: take the supermarket again. This time not at the fish counter, but walking down the condiments aisle. We are starting to see connected devices in the home like the internet fridge, which knows what is in it and how long it has been there. Also there are apps (like the Tesco app) from which we can scan our food as we use it and have it delivered with our next order. Let's say we are on our way to the supermarket, or walking past a shelf wobbler for Hellmann's Mayonnaise in the condiments aisle – we choose to receive a connected media advert from the Hellmann's package. Because the fridge and our phone are connected, the advert tells us that we have some chicken and pasta in the fridge and both are going out of date tomorrow. It offers a great new recipe based on chicken and pasta, if we grab that jar of Hellmann's. The brand gives us an idea for using up the food before it goes out of date. In this scenario, connected media devices are enabling brands to give ideas of value, as adverts.

Overall implications for brand strategy

A connected media (mobile marketing) landscape enables brand communications to become a service. With all the power going to the consumer and the mobile mode being "pull communications" then brands could need to plan how to be creative and tell stories across devices and locations.

In the early stages, most people are dual screening on their mobile devices while watching TV, or scanning barcodes for information in store – what could your brand do to make the most of that? One response would be to take a look at your various mobile internet sites and how they present themselves via different types of search on mobile.

The bottom line is this: whether they are experiencing your brand through traditional media, through the packaging or the product itself, they have a connected media device in their hand. There are many more connected things out there than you think – and a lot of these things are already connected to each other. Now is the time to plan a digital personality for your brand and start to work out how it might be able to help people (or even the planet) when the world's connected media infrastructure is fully established.

Biography

Scott (@scottseaborn) has worked in the creative industries for 15 years and with mobile technologies for the past 12. He began his career in broadcast media, then worked through digital before concentrating purely on mobile. He has owned a small agency and was Creative Director at a digital media network before founding Ogilvy Group's mobile division and then moving to his current role of Executive Creative Director at XS2. In the past 10 years Scott has won nearly 40 awards including some prestigious Cannes Lions, D&AD and London Internationals. He lives in Surrey and now and then he goes out to hug the trees.

Chapter 14

Dan Tyte

From Flickr's photo sharing to Facebook's social snaps, Instagram's instant on-the-go cool to the beautiful boards of Pinterest, this chapter explores the channels and the content which turned the web from words to wow.

A bird's eye view

If the old adage "a picture's worth a thousand words" is to be believed, today's web has got enough for a team of travelling encyclopedia salesmen. If web 1.0 was characterized by copy, images are now the king of online content with millions being tagged, tweeted and tumbled each and every second.

The visual web has been the hottest online trend of 2012 and the march of the megapixel is inherently linked to the rise of mobile web. 1.2 billion smartphones and tablets are predicted by Gartner to be sold worldwide in 2013 and 20% of web visits are now on the go.[120] The latest mobiles from big players Apple and Samsung, the iPhone 5 and Galaxy S III, come equipped with an 8 megapixel camera. Almost overnight, the streets and sidewalks have become populated with people with the ability in their pockets to photo-document their lives, loves, friends, families, communities and campaigns.

Let's take a look at three of the biggest image-led networks, Flickr, Face-book and Instagram, to explore how the visual web has developed over a

---

[120]In the US, according to advertising network Chitika in May 2012: http://cipr.co/Z9XKbs

relatively short space of time. Image host Flickr was (emphasis on the "was") the web's online photo album of choice, with bloggers big fans of its functionality. A child of unintended consequences, the site emerged from services created for a multiplayer online game. When Yahoo signed a cheque for the start-up in 2005, the fledgling Facebook only allowed users to upload an image for their profile picture. A cursory scroll of my feed in December 2012, filled as it is with cats dressed up as reindeer and Coca-Cola Christmas trucks, illustrates quite how much that has changed.

Where Flickr got left behind was in its social sharing elements.

Notwithstanding some aggravation to early adopters caused by the new owners – anyone arm-wrestled into a Yahoo account to sign in to the service back in 2007 will testify to this.

Sure, Flickr had groups and comment options, but when Facebook put the picture at the front and centre of its community, integrated with its other functionality, everything from marketing a gig to being nudged to wish your old school friends a happy birthday, there was only going to be one winner as the go-to gallery for those summer holiday snaps. Despite some new filter features, Flickr is now in danger of becoming the online equivalent of a dusty box of sepia-tinged snaps in the attic.

While Facebook was photo-friendly and share-centric, its slow-moving mobile app wasn't delivering the user experience today's web wanderer demanded.[121] Champs don't stay champs through complacency (just ask Mike Tyson about Buster Douglas). The network's emphasis on mobile since its February 2012 IPO has been a necessary step. In September 2012, the company announced that a new mobile app would be released every four to eight weeks in order to improve performance, develop new features and keep fresh-air Facebookers in the family. Latest figures[122] on Facebook's mobile use, up from 425 million users in February to 600 million monthly active users with 10% of these only accessing via their handheld devices, show the strategy is working.

Then, like Roman Abramovich[123] on a January transfer window spending spree, Zuckerberg and co bought Instagram for a cool $1 billion. Launched

---

[121]"Facebook users in iPhone app revolt", *Financial Times*, 22 July 2011: http://cipr.co/VUan4b
[122]Techcrunch, October 2012: http://cipr.co/YcHAJs
[123]Billionaire Russian oligarch and Chelsea FC owner for you non-football fans/Americans

in 2010 and developed with mobile in mind, Instagram has shareability at its very core. Why wouldn't you want to pass on pictures that look like a sun-kissed Santa Monica scene even if they were taken in a wet and windy Wales?

With over one hundred million registered users[124] uploading over one billion photographs, numbers post-Facebook integration were on a steep upward curve (users were at 27 million before the buyout). But before the ink was dry on the marriage certificate, Instagram caught flak from fans for giving in to its new partner's demands. A proposed change in the Terms of Service, which was interpreted as meaning images and information could be sold to advertisers, went down like a drunken sailor.

The data behind the storm seems to show that despite a big fall in daily average users (from 15.6 million in December '12 to 9 million in January '13[125]), monthly average users are still steadily increasing (up from 41.5 million to 46.1 million over the same period). Power users got peeved, but Instagram is still being used by more people each month.

The digital archivists of the future could well be scratching their heads at how their forefathers' photos seem to skip from the noughties back to the 1970s. Those Walden and Lo-Fi filters will have a lot to answer for.

Contrast Instagram's on-the-go omnipotence against the fact that Flickr's not even in the top 50 iPhone photo apps and you can see where the networks of now are syncing perfectly with today's web-browsing trends while the old guard get left behind.

Networks and top tips

But it's not all about Flickr and Facegram. Here's a rundown of some of the most crucial of the visual web:

Tumblr: A rich content, youth-driven[126] micro-blogging site, Tumblr's clean interface and mobile integration ensure it lives up to its strapline of

---

[124]Mark Zuckerberg, TechCrunch Disrupt Conference, San Francisco, September 2012: http://cipr.co/VSfGXd

[125]AppStats, January 2013: http://cipr.co/VSfK9p

[126]"Over half of users are under the age of 25", comScore, Jan 2012: http://cipr.co/Wlnw8m

being "the easiest way to blog". Its quick set-up process and simple upload system make it the perfect choice for those who want to share imagery through a blog without delay.

Do: Follow bloggers belonging to your target audience and post short, snappy and visually-led content for the best response from the younger demographic that make up the community. *Rolling Stone* magazine *does* have a direction home (in contradiction to the Bob Dylan song) and uses its Tumblr feed to drip feed content and tease people back to its website. Could this work for you?

Don't: Expect in-depth exchanges on your content. Snap, upload, share and repeat.

Pinterest: Taking the marketing moodboard online, Pinterest became the fastest growing community around in 2012.[127] An idea-collecting platform where users can "pin" pictures from across the web to their boards, content is dominated by home decor, fashion, food and crafts. Appealing to the lazy sides of social curators, the way Pinterest allows users to consume and order images in a simple and structured grid is having a big impact on the design of shopping sites across the web. Spin-offs include Trippy, a travel-focused network perfect for planning sojourns to sundrenched destinations on dreary days.

Do: If you're a retailer, integrate pinning buttons on your site and watch sales soar. Jewellery and accessories site Bottica.com reported that Pinterest drives more new visitors than Facebook (86% of visits versus 56%), with Pinners now accounting for 10% of sales (compared to 7% from Facebook), and spending twice as much ($180 versus $85).

Don't: Use for a campaign targeting men in the US. Over 80% of users Stateside are female and typically aged 35–44,[128] with Michelle Obama and Ann Romney hitting the boards in the battle to become First Lady. In the

---

[127]For January 2012 comScore reported the site had 11.7 million unique US visitors, making it the fastest site ever to break through the 10 million unique visitor mark: http://cipr.co/12Lf7jP
[128]Econsultancy, Feb 2012 : http://cipr.co/15bM6NX

UK, users are skewed more towards the male. Maybe we have Laurence Llewelyn-Bowen to thank.

Twitter: While not a visual network per se, around 1/12th of links shared on tweets are images, accounting for over 41.5 million pictures a day.[129] After years of reliance on third-party hosts like Twitpic and yfrog, Twitter's native photo app has evolved to take the fight to current photo trendsetters. The December 2012 release of tools included a "magic wand" to improve images, crop tools and Instagram-like filters. It remains to be seen whether Instagram users will exit their X-Pro II for this copycat functionality.

Do: Sticking with the Obamas, the man of the house's 2012 victory tweet became the most retweeted of all time. But what can we learn from it? The image, of the couple sharing an embrace, displayed honesty, emotion and crucially gave followers a behind-the-scenes look at the campaign. Could you show a peek of your MD's scribbled, crossed out and rewritten notes ahead of a big speech? Or your chef sweating (not literally) over that evening's special dish?

Don't: Choose a banner picture of a white-sand beach. Your bio, vital for other users to verify if you're worth connecting with, won't read well against a light backdrop.

Okay, we'll look at Instagram too (I couldn't resist):

Instagram: Flip reversing the path trodden by others, the ultimate mobile network hit desktops in November 2012. Looking a bit like parent Facebook's hand-me-down profile pants, it's an albeit useful addition for brands to anchor their snaps to the static. Joining the Facebook family seems to have been a good move so far, with Instagram's biggest day to date coming on Thanksgiving 2012 when over 10 million Toaster-effect turkeys were shared. But on-the-go is where Instagram's functionality and community comes into its own.

---

[129]Twitter processes 500 million tweets a day according to CEO Dick Costolo in October 2012: http://cipr.co/VSfS8Q

Do: Use hashtags to track your images and expose them (no pun intended) to a wider audience. Search to see if you can piggyback on existing ones that relate to your content. Perennially popular tags include #photoofthe-day, #instagood and, erm, #bieber.

Don't: Use the filter to try and imbue your subject with instant street cred. If your CEO doesn't look cool in real life, don't Nashville him up. It's the social media equivalent of your dad dancing to rap music.

The new press release?

In the aftermath of the 1906 Atlantic City train wreck, Ivy Lee issued what's widely considered to be the first ever press release. The impact his tool had on information distribution and influence has been palpable to this day.

It'll be clear to everyone reading this book that in this social age, communicating through the conduit of the traditional media can be bypassed by direct interaction with online communities. As such, it's increasingly "data visualized", or infographics, that we're sharing on the networks mentioned earlier in this chapter. But could the infographic be the new press release? Well, yes it could.

When today's average attention span is shorter than that of an amnesiac goldfish with a hangover, any way that communications can stand out from the noise and be more easily understood is going to give you a puncher's chance of message penetration. Whether on Twitter or in a journalist's inbox, a visually striking infographic which combines data or text with imagery certainly makes you stand out from the crowd.

Add to that the speed with which the information contained can be scanned and understood (65% of the population are said to be visual learners[130]) and you'll begin to understand why "data visualized" could really signal if not the death of the press release, then a snap at the ankles of old Ivy's invention.

Everything from complex health data to new studies on the impact of food waste disposal systems has been given the infographic treatment, turning dense (and, let's face it, potentially dull) information into easily understandable information. As well as making the complex comprehensible quickly, an

---

[130]According to the Visual Teaching Alliance: http://cipr.co/Y8nHl7

infographic pulls out facts and figures and feeds them ready for reporters to hang their story on. Beautiful isn't it?

A campaign my agency worked on proved the long-form feature could benefit from the infographic treatment too. Upon the promotion of their local football team to the Premier League, City & County of Swansea Council realized they had a once-in-a-lifetime shot at marketing the area. With Swansea City being given little hope by the media of maintaining their top flight status beyond a solitary season, the world spotlight (the Premier League is broadcast in 212 territories with a television audience of 4.7 billion) would be on the region for potentially just ten months.

We worked with the council's tourism arm, Visit Swansea Bay, Mumbles & Gower, on a campaign to showcase the area to football fans and the wider public. Alongside the journalist junkets you'd expect of a destination campaign, we produced a series of infographics which used football as a foot-in-the-door to highlight the region's offer in a fun, informative and shareable way. Kicking off with one where users could measure out landmarks in (beanpole England striker) Peter Crouches, we followed up with a WAGs guide to the area for Mrs Wayne Rooney, weekend packing advice for Aston Villa fans (riffing off the Birmingham team's motto of "Prepared") and #Swanselona, where an existing on-the-pitch conversation comparing Swansea and Barcelona was taken to weigh up their respective tourist trappings.

People love to content curate through a click, and a shareable infographic can really deliver traffic back to your website. Within an hour of seeding the Crouch-o-Metre on social media, the Visit Swansea Bay website crashed due to the volume of traffic. Visitors to the site rose by 44% on the same period in the previous year and four of the six top regions for Facebook fans reflected Premier League cities, representing ten teams. Our innovative tactics made front pages, street billboards and praise in Premier League's 2011/12 season review.

Before you commit your story to an infographic, ask yourself these questions:

- Do you have a story or statistics that could move a conversation on?
- Do you have an existing online community with whom to share it?
- Is your target medium open to carrying infographics?
- Do you have the design capability to turn your digits and words into wow?

Biography

Dan Tyte (@dantyte) worked in PR pre-social networks and has run campaigns for professional sports teams, pop musicians and alcoholic drinks using on and offline tools. A director at Working Word and committee member of CIPR Cymru Wales, Dan's debut novel, *Half Plus Seven*, set in a PR and digital agency, will be published in spring 2014 by Parthian Books.

Chapter 15

Matt Appleby

Carrying a powerful GPS-enabled computer in our pockets every day has created new ways for us to interact with the web and social networks. We are continually blurring the lines between the online and offline worlds in a way which has massive potential impact for professional communicators.

Checking-in and geotagging photos has become as natural as updating our status. We are increasingly creating new layers of content with our smartphones and tablets tied to real-world places for others to find, share and review.

As smartphone use increases, the opportunities for location-based services will expand, and we have already seen widespread adoption of the technology over the last three/four years.

Between 2011 and 2012 smartphone take-up rose from 27% to 39% of UK adults.[131] In the UK, a greater proportion of website traffic is generated from smartphones, tablets and other connected devices than in any comparable European country. The UK is a nation of smartphone addicts.[132]

From a marketing perspective, it's an attractive audience, increasingly difficult to reach through other channels. Smartphone use is unsurprisingly

---

[131]Usage stats taken from *The Communications Market*, Ofcom, July 2012 unless stated otherwise

[132]Just over four in ten smartphone users indicated high levels for addiction – 7 or higher on a scale of 1–10 where 10 is "I'm completely addicted to my mobile phone"

higher in younger groups: 66% of 16–24-year-olds and 60% of those aged 25–34 have one, as do 46% in the ABC1 socio-economic group.

Retail and leisure have arguably seen the greatest impact – more than half of smartphone users say they've used their handset in some way when out shopping. This includes taking a photo of a product (31%), making price comparisons (25%) and reading online reviews (19%). In 2012 smartphones influenced more than £15 billion (6%) of in-store sales – 15 times the value of direct purchases made through mobiles.[133]

Bernoff and Schadler (2010) make the implications for business clear: "Customers have more information power than ever before. Mobile browsing and mobile applications have made that power ubiquitous. You have a choice to make. You can line yourself up with them, empowering them with mobile offers, mobile information, and mobile customer services. Or you can let them find that stuff on their own" (*empowered*, Harvard Business School Press, 2010, p. 70).

Content will always be king, but context is rapidly becoming as influential – reaching people when they are in the place where you want them to take a desired action, whether that's choosing a restaurant, playing a game or buying a new gadget.

Where will you check in?

Location-based networks started to make headlines in 2009. In a short space of time they have had to evolve – the novelty of just checking in faded quickly as more established networks added geo-location features and new apps appeared.

While competitive checking in was fun for a while, being able to add location information to familiar social media activities – updating status, sharing pictures, reading reviews – was more natural than adding another new network which needed to be checked and managed. What it brought was a new, more immersive experience to many familiar tools.

Discovery is a key theme – whether that's finding a new restaurant that your friends are recommending, meeting new like-minded people, checking hotel reviews or sharing pictures. Value is the other – why should people

---

[133]The dawn of mobile influence, Deloitte: http://cipr.co/XuYval

check in? Brands and venues quickly realized that if they expected users to promote their service (by publishing their location through their social media networks) then they would expect something in return.

The picture today is broadly a threefold mix: surviving standalone location-based social networks; mainstream networks with enhanced mobile/local features; new location-based technologies, e.g. augmented reality.

Any roundup of current services will inevitably date quickly as they continuously evolve – but it is worth reviewing the location features of a selection of those that have the critical mass to be mainstream in most social media users' experience.

Foursquare

Since it first arrived on the scene in 2009 and was the talk of that year's SXSW Festival, Foursquare has outlasted several of its competitors. It says on its blog it is "a free app that helps you and your friends make the most of where you are. Share and save your experiences at the places you visit and get personalized recommendations for where to go."

It differentiated itself by offering Mayorships earned by being the most frequent visitor to a venue, competitive check-in rankings between friends and a wide range of badges to be earned. Its platform for businesses enables venues to offer different promotions to reward loyalty, encourage repeat visits or incentivize checking in with friends and includes valuable check-in data and the ability to post updates to loyal customers.

Foursquare has evolved over time. It has always positioned itself as a tool to make the most of your local area – find new things and share experiences with friends. The latest update has made this even more prominent, with enhanced venue information, images and user tips. The game element has become less central to the app over time.

There are over 25 million worldwide users and over 1 million venues using the merchant platform.[134] With over 25,000 developers using the Foursquare platform[135] it is also powering location services for a range of other apps like Instagram, Foodspotting and Untappd.

---

[134]As of September 2012: http://cipr.co/XjvkHd
[135]As of June 2012: http://cipr.co/XjvkHd

Facebook

Facebook is the most popular social networking site in the UK, so it brings massive numbers of users to whatever it does in the location space.

It launched Places to great fanfare in 2010 and it was assumed that it would easily dominate smaller rivals such as Foursquare and Gowalla (which it did later buy and shut down). Location is obviously an important element in the move to letting users document their lives through Timeline and Places as a standalone feature lasted around a year before being integrated into the main status update system.

Users can check in to venues and this feature offers valuable insight data to page managers who can see gender, age and home town of people visiting.

Facebook promotes the value of adding location to a status update to help remember where photos were taken, let friends know where you are so you can meet up or share where you're going so you can get tips. It makes more sense to users as a logical additional aspect of an update than as a standalone feature.

Google

Google has integrated location-based features across its services and apps. Its dominance in search, mapping, as a mobile operating system and browser puts it in a leading position in this space for users and businesses.

The latest version of the Google+ app includes the ability to check in with geotagged images, localized events and mapping. Its Local app uses location to serve up nearby local search results (including maps, business listings and reviews) and includes a useful category browsing facility. The same user reviews now also feature in the popular Google Maps app, reaching an even bigger potential audience on the move.

Local listings are invaluable for businesses, they're free to complete (add images, services, share updates), come with useful analytics and ensure you appear in web, map, local and G+ searches. In the US businesses can also create offers tied to their location, a useful incentive to turn web traffic into footfall if it comes to the UK.

Google Maps has long been a useful tool for displaying data creatively and is a staple of news reporting and blogging, as it is easy to create and share custom maps.

What Google does next within the location space will bring content and context more seamlessly together, "keeping people in the moment"[136] by replacing the barrier of a handheld device with connected augmented reality glasses. Its Project Glass video[137] has racked up 18.6 million views on YouTube already (December 2012) and with Microsoft and Apple reportedly working on similar technology we need to get used to the idea of even better-connected people accessing location-specific content all day, every day.

Twitter

Twitter added a location feature in 2010 amid a certain amount of controversy over privacy. It includes the ability in its search tool to filter by location and rolled out localized trends information to a range of UK cities in December 2012.

While Twitter itself has not added particularly rich location-based features, other location-based apps can be used to map or view tweets nearby through an augmented reality lens.

Yelp

Yelp is a directory and review service which launched in 2004 with a mission to help people find local businesses. Listings are free for businesses and Yelp emphasizes the impartiality of its reviews and the lengths it goes to in ensuring suspicious reviews are suppressed. The service is all about local discovery, so the mobile version puts reviews in your pocket while you're potentially standing in the street making the decision about which business to choose.

Its mobile app has an augmented reality (AR) viewer called Monocle, which adds a layer of Yelp reviews to what the camera sees, enabling you to scan a whole street and see instant star ratings. While it may have a reputation for being all about leisure venues, only 20% of the businesses reviewed are restaurants[138] – no local business should be ignoring its potential to influence customers.

---

[136]Project Glass is the Future of Google, TechCrunch: http://cipr.co/WQJnCR.

[137]Project Glass: One day . . ., YouTube: http://cipr.co/VUYahr

[138]Yelp factsheet: http://cipr.co/17p3YFy.

Augmented reality apps

The fusing of a real-world view, usually through a phone camera, with web or social media content has opened up new possibilities for innovation and delivering relevant content when it has the greatest potential utility and impact.

Wikitude was a pioneer of AR browsing (layering web content over a smartphone camera view) when it launched in 2008 and now, according to its website, boasts 20,000 developers using the platform. The Wikitude app adds content layers over a map or through a smartphone camera. Users can find new places to visit, see reviews, view photographs or find social media activity like nearby tweets. It is a relatively simple process to publish your own "Worlds" to Wikitude which can be found by anyone using the app.

The next area where AR has made major inroads is in augmenting traditional publishing.[139] *The Sunday Times Magazine* of 24 November 2012 claimed to be "The First Augmented Reality Supplement" and increasingly catalogues (e.g. Ikea), customer magazines (e.g. M&S), advertising (e.g. O2) and even packaging (e.g. Lego) or menus (e.g. Wagamama) are using the technology to enrich the printed experience.

The final example is in generating news through stunts – the technology is still new enough that good examples of its use remain newsworthy. This is the area which many people may be most familiar with, as high-profile stunts have been used to generate buzz around quirky AR innovations.

Lynx grabbed headlines and viral success for its Fallen Angels stunt in March 2011. Bringing its TV advertising to life, it set up an AR system through the big screen at Victoria Station. As commuters passed through a fixed point which a camera relayed to the screen, they saw the Lynx Angels falling down around them.

At the end of 2012 One Direction launched a new exclusive box set which came with a virtual AR picture book app. It was just one example of increasing

---

[139]Many of these examples use the Aurasma or Blippar platforms, both of which make it easy for users to make their own AR markers and link to content and have showcases of recent campaigns on their websites

use of AR in the music business reported by *The Guardian*[140] at the time. Aurasma reported that 24% of the people who interacted with its Rolling Stones AR app clicked through to the pre-order site in the same story.

Either as an experience, or as an added value offer with a premium product, the fact that it was innovative, high-impact use of the technology has driven the reporting. The novelty factor clearly has a shelf life, so it is important to keep track of what's on the horizon to be able to stay ahead creatively.

Putting PR on the map

Social media has seen a massive shift of power from corporation to consumer. Location-based networks have shifted that power even further.

Professional PR practitioners need to be alert to even better informed customers, more powerful online reviews, new ways to engage directly with consumers and more relevant location-specific social word of mouth. What does that mean in practice?

1. Adapt content to context – what is the functionality that a customer will want on the go? Keep it quick and simple to use.
2. Strategically, what location features would add value? It's more obvious for venues and consumer businesses but in a B2B context[141] could they, for example, be offering localized insight/expertise, technical support, seminars/events or a reason to check in to your office?
3. Are businesses monitoring what's being said? Reviews and customer service are more powerful if they are tied to the location where customers are making a buying decision. Listen, adapt and respond quickly.
4. Respect privacy. It's an even more sensitive subject with location-based services and even the big networks have misfired here. Give people a reason or incentive to opt in.

---

[140]"One Direction? There's an augmented reality picture book app for them . . .". *The Guardian*: http://cipr.co/14Sb5FF

[141]"Location may not be hugely applicable for B2B companies, but when it comes to trade shows, it is another tool in your marketing superhero utility belt": K. Bodnar and J.L. Cohen, *The B2B Social Media Book*, p. 173, John Wiley & Sons, 2012, ISBN: 1118167767

5. Remember that you are asking people to help you promote your business through their networks if they check in. Be up front – tell them what their check-in means to you and offer something valuable in return.

6. Be clear on what you want to get out of it – increased sales, improved customer loyalty, higher frequency of visit, promotion of a specific offer?

7. Decide what you'll do with the data you collect and the insights about your customers.

8. How will you promote your localized online presence? It needs to be promoted through all your other social networks, website, PR, POS, advertising, e-newsletter and so on.

9. To be effective, augmented reality needs to add something valuable. The novelty of animated ads has already worn off – content has to be as novel and innovative as context.

10. Make the most of Google Local listings – it's free and very (increasingly) powerful.

Empowering people with information right at the point of decision – adding context to content – adds a new dimension of influence. As technology, and particularly mobile devices, evolves this will only become even more widespread, pervasive and powerful.

Biography

Matt Appleby (@mattappleby) is MD of Golley Slater PR Cardiff and leads its UK social media arm GolleyEngage. He has more than 15 years' experience in corporate and consumer PR consultancy for many of the best-known brands and organizations in Wales. He is heavily involved in the social media scene in Wales, writing a food blog, editing a hyperlocal community news site in Cardiff and supporting the Social Media Surgery network. Matt is a CIPR Chartered PR Practitioner, a Fellow of the CIPR and former chair of the award-winning CIPR Cymru Wales group.

Chapter 16

CONNECTED EMPLOYEES

Kevin Ruck

A review of how employees are using social media inside organizations, how this enables greater employee engagement, connected and unconnected employees and the rise of "bring your own device" to work – the chapter draws on crowdsourcing at CIPR Inside's annual conference that took place in November 2012. Delegates debated how to use social media to generate greater employee engagement and how to connect with unconnected employees. Discussions were summarized and recorded on a crowdsourcing system using iPads configured specifically for the event.

What is employee engagement?

Only around one third of UK workers say that they are engaged, leaving the UK ranked ninth for engagement amongst the world's 12 largest economies.[142] That is why employee engagement is such a hot topic and why the UK government is supporting a high-profile Engage for Success movement.

Before exploring how internal social media can generate higher levels of engagement it is important to understand what enables engagement. This is not as straightforward as it might seem. Employee engagement is a strongly contested concept. However, the Engaging for Success Report,[143] published in 2009, identifies four enablers:

---

[142]Engage for Success: The Evidence, Employee Engagement Task Force "Nailing the evidence" workgroup: http://cipr.co/YDtG3U

[143]Engaging for Success; enhancing performance through employee engagement: http://cipr.co/WQLztZ

- Visible, empowering leadership providing a *strong strategic narrative* about the organization, where it's come from and where it's going.
- *Engaging managers* who focus their people and give them scope, treat their people as individuals and coach and stretch their people.
- There is *employee voice* throughout the organizations, for reinforcing and challenging views, between functions and externally; employees are seen as central to the solution.
- There is organizational integrity – the values on the wall are reflected in day-to-day behaviours. There is no "say-do" gap.

Of these four enablers, a strong strategic narrative and employee voice are core internal communication activities. They also reinforce academic research conducted in 2006[144] that identified three drivers of engagement:

- Feeling well informed about what is happening in the organization.
- Having opportunities to feed your views upwards.
- Thinking that your manager is committed to your organization.

However, when it comes to keeping employees informed, a question that is not often asked is what do employees want to know? It seems that employees are, unsurprisingly, very interested in being kept informed about work-related matters, such as pay, benefits, recognition, reward and understanding how the job fits into the wider organization. Employees are also very interested in information about the organization's vision, values, plans, priorities, successes and failures. Interestingly, correlations between organizational content and the feeling that the organization is a good one to work for are higher than correlations with work-related content.[145] So, an employee's identification with the organization is very important and a useful distinction can be made between *work* engagement and *organizational* engagement, where work engagement is a hygiene factor and organizational engagement is a more emotional and higher order factor.

---

[144]CIPD Report: Working Life: Employee Attitudes and Engagement 2006
[145]Author's unpublished PhD research

Informed employee voice

From an internal communication perspective, it is clear that focusing on a combination of keeping employees informed about important organizational level matters and combining this with employee voice will make a significant contribution to higher levels of employee engagement.

The second enabler, employee voice, can be categorized as individual, formal group or organization.

Individual/informal group	Formal group	Organization
Exchange of views on specific issues	Collective bargaining	Opportunity to have a say as part of the culture
Problem solving	Joint consultation	
Management decision making	Team briefings	Partnership approach for long-term sustainability of the organization
	Problem solving	
	Management decision making	

Categorizing employee voice

For internal communication practitioners, the aim is to establish employee voice as an organization-wide process. However, the basis on which views and opinions are expressed has to be a transparent, authentic and timely approach to information sharing, otherwise any views or comments expressed may not be well enough informed.

Employee voice is not an annual survey or a "one-off" project. It is an ongoing process. It also has to be treated seriously; what is said has to be carefully considered and responses provided. This can be a challenge for many organizations. From research conducted in 2011 with internal communication practitioners,[146] it is clear that time devoted to employee voice is currently minimal at around 9%. Furthermore, only 24% of practitioners reported that they believe the board think communication is really important (see Figure 16.1).

---

[146]Communicating for Engagement: PR Academy, Kevin Ruck and Sean Trainor

Percentage of practitioners spending more than 25% of time on:

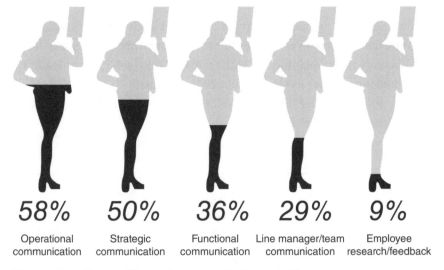

58%	50%	36%	29%	9%
Operational communication	Strategic communication	Functional communication	Line manager/team communication	Employee research/feedback

Figure 16.1: Focus of internal communication activities

Social media and employee engagement

Delegates at the CIPR Inside conference suggested a number of ways that using internal social media contributes to employee engagement. These can be summarized as:

- Real-time information
- Authentic
- Transparent dialogue
- It is not moderated
- You can involve people earlier in strategy
- Wider input on water cooler conversations
- It enables you to cut through layers of bureaucracy
- Generates more interest.

However, they also reported significant issues around leadership understanding and commitment to using internal social media. As one delegate noted, "It is only meaningful if there is a commitment to read, reflect and respond."

This highlights the challenges for adopting social media inside organizations. Senior managers may not want to blog and they do not always see the value of employee conversations and dialogue. On the other hand, employees may be more circumspect about expressing views about work in full view of colleagues and managers than they are expressing views about their personal lives on Facebook or Twitter.

Research[147] suggests that the top five barriers for organizations to embrace internal social media are:

1. Knowledge and understanding – about how to mobilize communities.
2. Leadership – a lack of skills and awareness.
3. Loss of control – dealing with increased transparency.
4. Fear – of failure, change, abuse, reputational damage, merging work and personal lives, security violations, IP leakage and breaking down of functional barriers.
5. Resources – unwillingness (or inability) to commit sufficient and sustained resources.

The culture of the organization is therefore a critical consideration. A way to map internal social media and culture is to apply Li and Bernoff's[148] social technographic profiles against an open or closed organizational culture (see Figure 16.2).[149] Understanding the likely technographics and the known culture for specific departments within an organization informs where to start with internal social media, or where to go next. For example, if a department can be described as "closet communicators" the focus should be on working with senior managers to identify the benefits of extending what is being achieved through using internal social media. In a more "open" organization, the challenge may be the availability of the best tools and therefore working with IT might be the more productive approach.

---

[147]The Social Media Garden: A Digital Era Research Study into Social Media at Work: http://cipr.co/UXVPTS

[148]C. Li and J. Bernoff, *Groundswell, Winning in a World Transformed by Social Technologies*, Forrester Research, Inc., 2011, ISBN 1422161986

[149]T. Playle, "Internal Social Media: enterprise 2.0, 3.0 and beyond" in K. Ruck ed, *Exploring Internal Communication*, Pearson, 2012, ASIN 1849595968

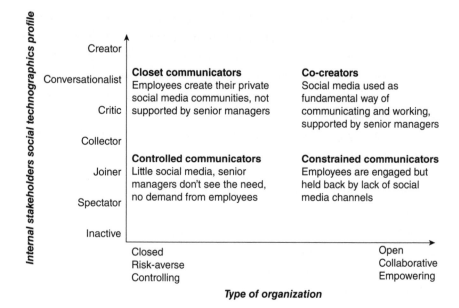

Figure 16.2: Mapping social technographics to organizational culture

Delegates at the CIPR Inside conference offered suggestions about how to introduce internal social media:

- Use it during times of change to capture video feedback and get leaders to respond.
- Start small . . . choose the audience carefully, give it time to grow.
- Create collaborative groups.
- Baby steps . . . help them to write and teach them how and then get them to blog on their own.
- Don't ask for permission, just do and be a little bit "maverick".
- People tend to listen to peers more than credible leaders.
- Blur the lines from internal and external and be social in an open forum.
- Stop communicating some information via other channels to create a need.

At a leadership level, delegates identified a number of reasons for engaging leaders in the use of internal social media, with trust emerging as a strong theme:

- Exposing issues is a good thing, it develops trust.
- Trust comes as the executive becomes accessible.
- These conversations are happening anyway, social media enables them to get involved and develop a closer, more trusting relationship with their staff both online and face-to-face.
- Social media enables leaders to be seen as "people" – puts a personality/face to leaders.
- Raw and real content resonates more with employees than polished content.
- Leaders are already social, they just don't know it!

Connecting with unconnected employees

For many internal communication practitioners, connecting with employees who may not have easy access to the intranet or email has presented difficulties for many years.

Conference delegates highlighted the need to integrate internal social media with more traditional channels, such as print media, face-to-face roadshows, visits and meetings to ensure that "unconnected" employees are informed and have a say in what is happening. This is a challenge that the Go-Ahead Group, a leading train and bus operator, takes very seriously (see mini case study). As one delegate put it: "Face to face is still valuable. You need to create a bridge between online and offline conversations with 'unconnected' teams." Other delegates are starting to use touchscreens or iPads more in communal areas.

A suggestion was:

> "Ask non-deskers to offer their stories. A campaign purely for them to relay their insights to other parts of the company. Capture these via road shows/canteen/mobile app. Explain benefits to encourage involvement – better understanding of their issues and successes."

The obvious solution to connecting with "unconnected" employees is to provide them with smartphones or tablets. Some ambulance trusts are, for example, providing the iPad mini to paramedics and first response units so

Go-Ahead mini case study

Go-Ahead is one of the UK's leading providers of passenger transport, delivering bus and rail services to predominantly urban markets. It employs around 23,000 people across the country and over one billion passenger journeys are taken on its bus and rail services each year.

Train operator, Southeastern, is part of the group and has a range of corporate channels:

- Weekly newsletter.
- *Voyage* employee magazine.
- "Workmate" social intranet.
- "The Open Line" employee phone-in.
- Senior Management Forum.
- Quarterly Management Forum.
- Noticeboards at high-density locations.

Southeastern integrates written briefings with face-to-face briefings and posters. However, it is now making greater use of videos and audio (streaming and download) in a range of formats so that they are more accessible.

The social intranet and open phone-in have led to improved dialogue and during the Olympics the operator enjoyed its best ever period of train performance and increased customer satisfaction.

that they can keep in touch whilst they are in a lay-by waiting for a 999 deployment.

Another alternative approach is to enable employees to access information on their own personal devices. This is known as "Bring Your Own Device" to work (BYOD).

Two trends are driving the rapid emergence of BYOD:

1. The increase in smartphone and tablet ownership.
2. Cloud computing.

There are clear hardware cost savings for organizations. For employees, the benefits are familiarity with technology that they have personally chosen and remote access to email and the intranet. Many security concerns can be addressed through the use of cloud computing and "secure containers" that also reduce downloading time. According to research conducted by BT,[150] almost four in five (77%) employers now permit the use of personal devices at work and almost half (47%) of employees already use their own devices for work purposes.

The benefits cited for BYOD have so far largely ignored the potential increase in employee engagement through the improved ability to connect with "unconnected" employees. Until recently, the main way to communicate with field-based employees was through a print newspaper or posters in depots. As one conference delegate observed, "many 'unconnected' employees have mobile devices and talk about work on social networks", so this provides a great opportunity for organizations to have more meaningful conversations with front-line employees. It also potentially unlocks innovation, more easily enabling employees who serve customers directly to be able to feed back valuable market knowledge and suggestions for improved service. The potential for BYOD is not restricted to the private sector. Many public sector bodies are also embracing it, for example, one in five local authorities in England are reported to be looking at the idea of allowing their staff to use their own mobile phones, laptops and other devices at work.[151]

Conference delegates generally saw the positive benefits of BYOD. These focused on "freedom from IT", "no technical training requirements" and "allows individuals to use the most modern technology". Some issues were raised, such as "financial support or subsidies should be provided/agreed when people are using their own devices for work". Another point made was "we need to ask people if they want to use their devices. Has to be opt in."

The adoption of social media within organizations has lagged behind the way it has transformed external communication. However, things are now changing fast. Internal platforms, such as yammer and chatter, are now well

---

[150]BT Press Release, 27 September 2012, Businesses failing to communicate "Bring Your Own Device" best practice to employees
[151]BBC News, Will councils benefit from allowing staff to use their own laptops at work?: http://cipr.co/11LhgvK

established. And, although a closed internal culture may still be an obstacle, the onset of BYOD looks set to become an unstoppable force. This offers organizations new ways to keep employees informed and to give them a say in what goes on that could unlock the door to greater employee engagement and performance.

Biography

Kevin Ruck (@AcademyKev) is a co-founder of PR Academy, the largest CIPR accredited teaching centre. He developed the CIPR's internal communication certificate and diploma qualifications and edits the textbook *Exploring Internal Communication*. He is a PhD student at the University of Central Lancashire, researching how to rethink internal communication measurement and was chair of CIPR Inside for 2012.

Acknowledgment: Kevin thanks all the delegates at the CIPR Inside conference who contributed to the crowdsourcing session.

Part V

Professional Practice

Chapter 17

Hanna Basha

Here we review the law governing social media including defamation, privacy, confidence data protection and copyright. It's a massive topic and it's not possible to set out all the legal issues, so this chapter briefly discusses the main risks for those involved in public relations and tries to offer practical tips to prevent legal action.

Social networking platforms are often referred to by lawyers as "cowboy country", because they seem to operate outside of normal social laws and rules. People have the ability to communicate instantly and informally and this gives many a sense that they are chatting to friends, when in fact they are publishing their thoughts to the world, often with a greater impact and circulation than traditional forms of media.

Unlike newspapers and broadcasters, who have internal legal departments, the public publishing via social media do not. There is therefore no one assessing or mitigating the risks or threats of litigation before publication.

The problem is that there are risks and threats of litigation as the same laws and rules do operate online. Publication of information on social media sites brings with it the threat of legal action from people and companies who wish to enforce their legal rights, be it a right to reputation, confidence or intellectual property. Of course the issue with social media is often enforcement, as it can be difficult to find the person who has published and bring a meaningful claim against them, especially when they could be hiding behind anonymity or publishing from outside of England and Wales.

Defamation

A defamatory statement is one which lowers someone's reputation in the eyes of reasonable people. There are various defences, which I come onto below, but if you are saying something derogatory, critical or offensive about a person, company or brand, be aware that they could have a claim against you. All a potential claimant has to prove is that the allegations are defamatory and that they have been published.

In relation to publication, the interesting thing about the internet is that often it is possible to give precise numbers of people who have read the allegations, or even identify them. Whilst publication to even one person can result in a claim, the Court will consider carefully whether any damage has been done if only a few people have read the allegations. If there is no damage, or minimal damage to reputation, then a claimant risks the claim being dismissed even though it would have been actionable had the damage been more substantial.

Liability online

There are many rumours, untruths and half-truths circulating about the liability of individuals who publish statements online. In fact liability for statements online is exactly the same as liability for publication in a newspaper.

There are common mistakes and misapprehensions, so it is worth being aware that:

- Repeating what someone else has said or forwarding a defamatory statement makes you liable for the content of that statement. It is not a defence to say that you were only repeating what someone else said, or that you believed them.
- Posting a link to a defamatory statement, without repeating the statement or any of its contents, makes you liable for the content of that statement. Again, it is not a defence to say that you did not realize that the allegations were untrue or that you did not intend to defame anyone.
- If you contribute to a defamatory press release or statement, because you have either prepared the first draft or issued the statement or because your words have been quoted in it, then you can be liable in defamation.

- Speculating or adding "allegedly" before a defamatory statement does not get you off the hook. It may change the meaning of the allegation, for example speculating that someone is a crook is better than asserting that they are a crook, but it is not much better.
- Just because someone has made the allegations before and not been sued, does not mean that you will not be.
- Just because you do not name someone, they could still have a claim against you. This can be either because you describe them sufficiently clearly (such as the chief executive of a company) or because someone else names them.
- Even if a post or statement is anonymous, there are circumstances in which you can be located or a Court can order disclosure of your details.

Receiving a complaint

If you receive a complaint over something you have published, it is important to assess the merits of the claim quickly as conduct post-publication can increase or decrease damages. Just because the allegation is published on a social media website does not mean that damages are low; damages can still be tens or hundreds of thousands of pounds.

Also, often all a potential claimant wants is an apology and for the allegations to be taken down and if this can be done quickly, then it may be possible to settle without paying a vast sum of money in damages or costs. Therefore if you do receive a complaint it is important to assess possible defences as soon as possible.

There are a number of defences to a defamation claim and below are listed only those which are most likely to be available.

Justification

The most straightforward defence is that you have published a factual allegation, the meaning of which is true (known as justification). This does not mean that each and every word has to be accurate, but only that the thrust of the allegation is true. The burden is on you to prove truth, rather than the person complaining to prove falsity.

The Court will interpret what has been said in context. It gives some latitude for the informality of social forums. This is not because they have any special status, but because, by their nature, they are informal. Depending on the forum, people reading a potentially defamatory message may be less likely to take it seriously. Also, it is worth bearing in mind that the thread of the forum must be considered as a whole, so a rebuttal or clarification later may make the initial post no longer actionable.

Honest comment

The second main defence is that you have expressed an honestly held opinion based on facts that are true (known as fair or honest comment or opinion). The law in this area is in flux at the moment and currently the opinion must be on a matter of public interest, but that may shortly change. It is often tricky to determine whether the words are a factual allegation or an expression of opinion and therefore whether the defence of justification or honest comment may apply.

Privilege

The third main defence is privilege. A statement may be protected from a claim in defamation on grounds of public policy or if the publisher has behaved responsibly and is reporting a matter of public interest. There are a number of different situations where words can be published under privilege but it is worth noting for these purposes that your defence to a complaint in defamation may not fail just because the allegation is false and defamatory.

Think before you publish. It is worth considering the following before publishing:

- Is what you are saying true and do you have evidence to back it up? If you can only prove that there are grounds to suspect someone is a crook, do not allege that in fact they are a crook. Or, safer still, set out the facts and let the reader draw the conclusion.
- If you are expressing an opinion, is it one you hold and one an honest person could hold (however radical)? It is worth setting out the basis for the opinion and not simply forwarding someone else's view, especially in circumstances where their view is questionable.

- What is the context of the statement? If you are posting in a forum, do the other posts change the meaning of what you are trying to say?

Privacy, confidence and data protection

The very point of social networking platforms is for individuals to communicate and share information. The downside is that information is often shared without proper thought for whether it should be and in particular without concern for the privacy of others. Everyone has a right to keep certain matters private and confidential and companies also have the right to protect their commercially sensitive information.

Before posting or forwarding information, it is important to focus on the content of the information as you are potentially publishing it to the whole world. You should be trying to assess whether anyone will complain if you share information and if so, whether they have a legitimate complaint.

Assessing whether a complaint may be legitimate is difficult because the precise ambit of protection for private and confidential information depends on a complex matrix. This matrix hinges on factors such as how sensitive the information is: information about private relationships, medical details and corporate secrets has more protection. Another factor is whether anyone has taken steps to keep the information out of the public eye: has it been kept under lock and key? Lastly it is important to consider whether there is any public interest in its publication (such as exposing a crime) or whether you have a right to tell the story despite someone's competing rights to keep it private.

Considerations and tips

It is worth considering the following before publishing:

- Does the information seem to be private or confidential? If it feels as if you are intruding or exposing secret information then you may well be. There is a particular sensitivity with photographs which can capture more than words can express.

- Was the information given to you in circumstances which gave you an obligation to keep it secret? This could include receiving information from a client, a consultant or during employment.
- Just because information is untrue does not mean that it is not private.
- Even if information has been published already, you can still be liable for breaching someone's privacy or confidence by re-publishing.
- Is the information about litigation or a crime? If so the Court could have put restrictions in place to prevent reporting certain matters and if you do publish then not only could you be liable for an invasion of privacy but also for contempt of Court.

Copyright

A work attracts copyright protection if it is an original work which was made with a degree of labour, skill or judgement. Copyright protection may well attach to press releases, slogans and catchphrases. It is especially important when communicating online to make sure that you protect your own work as it is easy to infringe copyright works on the internet simply because it is easy to copy material and republish it. It is equally important to make sure that you do not infringe the work of others and this means copying a "substantial" part of the material. The whole work does not need to be copied and only copying a few key important lines could be enough for an infringement.

As always, there are defences, the main one being if there is "fair use" of the copyright work, for instance for criticism or reporting current events. The other major one is that the work is no longer protected by copyright because the time for protection has expired. Although this period changes in different situations, the general rule in England and Wales is that protection lasts for 70 years after the author's death.

Protecting your work

It is easy to be the victim of copyright infringement as it is difficult to tell whether a work has copyright protection. Under the laws in England and Wales, there is no need to register the work. However, if you are publishing online, it is worth marking the material with the copyright symbol © followed by your name and the date of creation. If you are being ultra-careful, you should also include your details and ask that people contact you if they wish to license the work.

If your copyright has been infringed it is important to take steps quickly. It may be difficult to enforce your rights, not least because the infringer could be based overseas or because it is difficult to find them. However, if you cannot find the person who infringed your copyright it is worth contacting the internet service provider or the host of the site. Many social networking sites, realizing how problematic it can be to enforce copyright, have strict policies on taking down material which is subject to a legitimate complaint. Therefore, check the terms and policies of the site which is publishing your material.

Avoiding infringement

Protecting your own work is only one side of the coin. The other is not infringing the work of others. To be safe, only use work where you have permission of the copyright owner or the work has fallen outside of the period of copyright protection. If neither of these apply then only use the work if what you are doing amounts to "fair use" and only if you are using the work for comment, review, criticism or reporting current events.

There are some key tips to remember:

- There may be no symbol at all to indicate that the work is protected by copyright. However, if the material has an author's name on it, or looks as if effort went into creating it, then be careful.
- Just because the work has been put on another website or published elsewhere, does not mean that it can be published again without payment.
- Even if you are making no money from using the copyright work, or you are not intending to use the work for commercial gain, this does not give you a defence.
- Giving the author a credit does not give you a defence.

Trademarks and passing off

Another issue to be aware of is the use of trademarks owned by a company or celebrity endorsements. Celebrities are very aware of the commercial value of their images and the value to a brand or company of drawing an association with them. As such it is important to be careful using images, voices, names or anything which might appear to show that a brand or company has celebrity endorsement when it does not.

This can be a thorny issue online as celebrities may be happy to share information as to what products they use, but this does not necessarily give you a right to say that the product has celebrity endorsement.

There are more laws than can be covered in this chapter. The main issues which are faced by public relations advisors and communications agencies are dealt with above. However, they are by no means the totality. Whilst it would be unlikely for public relations advisors to be engaging in bad behaviour online, there are laws governing harassment, malicious communications, and incitement to racial hatred which have serious penalties.

Biography

Hanna Basha (@hannabasha) is a solicitor specializing in defamation, privacy and sports law, as well as more general media litigation and acts for a wide range of clients including celebrities, high-profile individuals, businessmen, sportsmen, football clubs, private equity companies, film companies and other corporations. As well as representing clients in Court, she provides legal and practical reputation and crisis management advice when clients are faced with more extensive press scrutiny, working closely with their external and in-house public relations advisors. Hanna has had considerable success preventing publication of information about her clients, either by negotiation or by applying to Court for an injunction, often on an emergency basis.

Chapter 18

Chris Norton

In the era of 24-hour news, social media and mobile devices, news spreads quicker than ever before. Organizations don't have as much control over their marketing messages and, as a result, news of a crisis can travel in seconds. This chapter explores the increasing risk of an online crisis and offers advice, guidance and examples on how to identify and respond to an online crisis efficiently.

With the increasing popularity of forums, social media and 24-hour online news, our fans and followers out there are now liking, commenting and sharing our content around the clock. This is great when things are positive, but in times of crisis it can cause a problem. The growth of citizen journalism can make it feel as though everybody has a voice and they are just waiting to criticize.

The most worrying aspect is that a controversial story can be trending before you have even sat down at your desk. News spreads instantly and often isn't properly checked and doesn't abide by the rules that traditional media do.

A crisis can rapidly result in damage to stakeholders, losses or, even worse, the end of the organization. Handling the communication around a crisis effectively is critical and PR practitioners should form an integral part of any crisis management team and, more importantly, should understand the ethics and rules of digital media.

A crisis can be damaging to the value of the organization. A report by the Oxford Executive found that firms affected by catastrophes fell into two distinct groups; recoverers and non-recoverers, with the initial shareholder loss at approximately 5% for recoverers and around 11% for non-recoverers.[152]

Defining a crisis

A crisis is defined by Wikipedia[153] as:

> "Any event that is, or expected to lead to, an unstable and dangerous situation affecting an individual, group, community or whole society. Crises are deemed to be negative changes in the security, economic, political, societal or environmental affairs, especially when they occur abruptly, with little or no warning."

Crisis management has been developed to help protect an organization from threats and to reduce the impact inflicted by those threats. It can be separated into three stages:

1. Pre-crisis
2. Crisis response
3. Post-crisis evaluation.

An online crisis[154] typically creates a spike in comments, shares and engagement and the conversations are characteristically negative. The modern practitioner needs to learn how to monitor a brand's reputation, track what is being said and respond immediately.

---

[152]The Impact of Catastrophes on Shareholder Value – asse.com: http://cipr.co/WOVDaa.
[153]Wikipedia definition of crisis: http://cipr.co/WQRHT6
[154]3 Ways to tell a social media problem from a crisis – Convince and convert: http://cipr.co/WuzLB9

1. Create a plan and run test exercises.
2. Use tools like SMS, Yammer, blogs and private groups to liaise with the crisis team.
3. Build a dark site in preparation.
4. Create a response strategy for negative comments.
5. Use social monitoring tools – track the sources of comments and check who is influencing whom.
6. Acknowledge any issues and be prepared for negative responses no matter what.
7. Assume people are intelligent.
8. Use pay per click (PPC) advertisements to combat negative websites.
9. Use repetition to ensure people remember positives.
10. Have a friendly network of online influencers, to help you disseminate messages.
11. Don't engage everybody – target the influencers and keep a record of who you engaged with.
12. Using video content is more authentic than written statements.
13. Don't get involved in arguments.

A summary of the issues to consider when preparing for and managing a crisis

Crisis planning

The pre-crisis phase is focused on preparation and prevention. The best way to prepare for a crisis is to avoid one altogether and PR professionals are doing this on a daily basis, you just don't hear about it because they are doing their jobs successfully.

Effective preparation means creating a crisis management plan, selecting the response team and conducting a number of exercises to test the team's adaptability.

Brand monitoring

One of the most valuable elements of social media is that you can listen to what people are saying about your brand both retrospectively and in real time. There are a plethora of monitoring tools that enable you to listen to the thousands of conversations occurring on blogs, forums, news sites and Twitter. You may have had calls from organizations like Brandwatch, Radian6 and

Sysomos and the truth is they are all very similar, but they are useful for tracking sentiment and the sources of online influence.

This type of qualitative analysis used to be expensive but with digital tools pricing becomes competitive. Listening, analyzing and understanding the overall tone and feel for the crisis could be invaluable when crafting your response.

The response to a negative comment on the Bodyform Facebook Page by its PR team was brilliant;[155] they listened to the response from the crowd and gave a tongue-in-cheek reply which had a phenomenal viral effect and will now shape its marketing campaign for the next few years.

Crisis management plan

A crisis management plan should act as a reference document and contain all of the necessary contact details, the process to follow and any templates required. The plan saves time by pre-assigning tasks and collating important information. All members of the crisis team should understand their roles and be given autonomy.

Crisis management team

Time is saved by creating a team because they already know who will do the basic tasks required in a crisis. Each crisis is different which means the team will have to make important decisions.

Pre-draft updates

The team can pre-draft templates for messages, tweets or blog posts with blank sections for when everything is confirmed. Legal teams can pre-approve the use of the messages which lets the communications team send them quickly on whichever platform they wish.

---

[155]Ibid

Using a holding statement should never be underestimated – as often saying "We are going to release a statement at 4pm" can stop the floods of tweets, messages and calls flying in.

Communication channels

Although video replies have become the standard in online crisis management, if a discussion starts on Twitter, try to keep it there and don't move it to another social channel – you could be spreading the issue rather than containing it. Twitter has an immediacy that can be used to your advantage if statements need to be shared immediately.

Online newsrooms or corporate blogs

If you have an online newsroom or blog, it must have some form of social shareability and should help to bring all of your networks together, making it easier for your readers to find you.

If the crisis is minor, sometimes the best place to deal with it can be within your newsroom, as here you can control the statements, tone and offer materials. However, you should be cautious – if the crisis is likely to be protracted you don't want it to take over your newsroom. You may want to portray an external image of it's "Business as Usual".

Create a terms of use policy

Make sure you have something that outlines how people can and can't behave across your channels. This should sit in your "About Us" section and be clearly labelled. If you have a policy, you can direct people to it and warn them before taking things further.

Scoop up those negative domain and user names

Make sure you have considered all of the domain names that could be created to attack your company and buy as many of the negative versions as you can such as www.ihatestarbucks.com. You may have to incur domain name referral fees annually but it could stop you from having a high authority site with an easy to remember name sharing destructive stories about your company.

Try to guess the usernames that could be used against you. Use a free tool such as Namechk[156] to check which names are available. Make sure your team has registered as many of these as possible. If you control them, they can't be used against your campaign.

Dark sites

A "dark site"[157] is an online hub which remains unpublished or "dark" until a crisis breaks. Organizations create them so there is a ready-made online resource to respond and direct the conversation. It usually contains a few pages such as a message from the CEO, emergency contact details and statements on what is being done to resolve the crisis. The team can utilize the social media channels to drive the conversations towards this site.

Key parts of the site are usually blank until details are confirmed. The site must have enough bandwidth ready to handle a colossal amount of hits in an extremely tight timeframe.

Mobilize your team

Skype can be considered when organizing your response team if it is spread out geographically. It's one of the safest channels for peer-to-peer communication and the sharing of sensitive information.

Targeted advertising

Advertising can be a useful weapon in reputation management if it is used intelligently to control the search results delivered by Google or Bing. Using advertising can be a bold statement and you must be sure your messages are correct and fit with the rest of your strategy.

In June 2010,[158] following the Deepwater Horizon Catastrophe,[159] BP used huge amounts of PPC advertising to try and control which search results were

---

[156]Namechk: http://cipr.co/Z1rgAg

[157]Online Crisis Communications: Beware of the dark site, young Skywalker, Cision blog: http://cipr.co/WOV5Rm

[158]Wikipedia: http://cipr.co/WuA8vA

[159]The Peak Oil Crisis: Deepwater Horizon – FCNP: http://cipr.co/14EdXoO

delivered for searches such as "Oil Spill".[160] Although it was a clever tactic, the execution was rather clumsy – the BP dark site felt like it had been written by robots rather than human beings. It initially focused on the amount of money that was being invested in the area and the public felt it lacked the more personal, sympathetic touch that was required.

Internal communications

Employees will need to know what happened, what they should do and how the crisis will affect them. Don't underestimate the power of them at times of crisis, as people will ask them for their opinion. Keep them in the loop on the intranet or using internal messaging systems such as Yammer.

Crisis response

The initial response must always be quick, accurate and consistent; when a crisis occurs, people want to know what happened. The online and broadcast media will attempt to fill the information vacuum as our news channels are 24-7 and they require their angle.

A statement released early may not have much "new" content but you have positioned yourself as a vital source and this should indicate that you are now in control.

The crisis team needs to share information so that spokespeople can deliver consistent messages. They should be briefed on the key points you want to get across and any other instructions.

Genuine expressions of concern help to lessen reputational damage and could reduce financial losses. If a company has a history of similar problems, or an existing bad reputation, the threat will be increased.

Don't be afraid of the #hashtag

If a crisis does go viral, a campaign #hashtag can create a genuine opportunity. After all, if all of the conversations are using it you can use it too, even

---

[160]BP buys oil spill PPC ads: Nice idea, poor execution. Econsultancy blog: http://cipr.co/VVfRgQ

if it is a negative one. If you use the #hashtag to reply, you can start to steer the conversation to direct people to your dark site or hub.

Use your online advocates

Encourage your online advocates to share constructive stories about you on their channels during the crisis. Try and ask them for their own opinion because, if you can get them talking actively about your organization, it will help to spread some positive vibes across the social web.

Crisis case study: Asda and the chicken licker

The Asda Chicken Licking video[161] was created by a disgruntled former employee and included a series of nasty short clips at the Fulwood branch of Asda supermarket in Preston. The clips were posted on YouTube and quickly went viral as they showed him hurling raw eggs at the wall of a stockroom.

In other scenes, Ayub, who was dressed in an Asda uniform, entered the staff room and slit holes in other employees' clothing and was later seen urinating in a bin. The scene that disgusted most was of him peeling back the film around a fresh chicken and licking it before placing it back. The clips made national news, with coverage all across the country.

The response from Asda's PR team was swift and clever as it included an interview with the store manager, a security guard and several other workers talking about their personal disgust that a former employee could even do something like that. The reason this response was especially well thought out was because it used an informal video to get a simple but important message across. Asda's staff were seen to care and were clearly shocked. The video response was covered in various places and received positive responses from almost everyone. The fact that it didn't feel forced or scripted clearly helped its credibility.

---

[161]BP buys oil spill PPC ads: Nice idea, poor execution. Econsultancy blog. http://cipr.co/VVfRgQ

Moderate commenting on your channels

If your blog or social channels are being overrun with negativity, you may consider changing your pages to allow approved comments only – turning off the ability for everyone to comment gives you a small element of control. After all, these are your spaces, so control them.

Post-crisis phase

The final phase is post-crisis, when a company returns to "business as usual" and the digital channels are used for more proactive communications campaigns.

Once it feels right, you can slowly and carefully return to your normal content programme, but be sensitive to the issue. If all goes well, open your pages back up for people to comment on and resume service as normal, monitoring and moderating carefully as you proceed.

You should ensure that all of the promises for information are fulfilled to maintain the trust with your contacts. You will need to release any important updates on the recovery and any investigations taking place.

This is a time for reflection and the team must go through what worked and what needed to be improved.

Appoint an evaluation team to assess the handling of the crisis and recommend changes in procedure. The evaluation team should be different from the original crisis team members. They should be asking themselves these questions:

- Did the plan work?
- What were the conversation triggers?
- Where did it fall down?
- What should be added?
- What was unnecessary?
- Which #hashtags did people use?
- Who should be in the next team?

While most crises start as a negative threat, effective crisis management can actually help contain the damage and, in some cases, provide a unique opportunity to even strengthen the brand. The best way to avoid and survive an online crisis is to prepare effectively.

Biography

Chris Norton (@chris_norton) is the founder of Dinosaur PR and an award-winning PR practitioner with more than 15 years' experience, having worked both in-house and in a number of international consultancies. He is a regular speaker and lecturer on online communications and his Dead Dinosaur blog on the evolution of communication is listed by Brand Republic as one of the most influential marketing sites on the planet. Chris sits on the CIPR Committee as its social media coordinator and has delivered online PR campaigns for clients such as: Ronseal, Sony Ericsson, Audio Technica, Ultralase, George Foreman, Russell Hobbs and Hallmark Cards.

Chapter 19

WIKIPEDIA AND REPUTATION MANAGEMENT

WIKIPEDIA AND REPUTATION MANAGEMENT

Stephen Waddington

Wikipedia is an online community of more than 100,000 active contributors. It is the first place that millions of people seek out when researching a topic. Here we tackle the often fractious relationship between the public relations industry and Wikipedia, with the goal of providing clear guidance to practitioners.

Wikipedia is the sixth most popular website in the world according to web information firm Alexa; beaten only by Facebook, Google, YouTube, Yahoo and Baidu.com. It is a crowdsourced online encyclopaedia of more than 20 million topics in 285 different languages and is frequently the starting point for online research.

Building a crowdsourced encyclopaedia

Wikipedia was launched in January 2001 by internet entrepreneur Jimmy Wales using a social media technology called a wiki. This is a web platform that allows content to be added, modified, or deleted via a web browser.

Initially Wikipedia was created as a site for amateur contributors to complement an online encyclopaedia created by subject-matter experts called Nupedia. Wikipedia had none of the formality of its counterpart. It could be modified live whereas Nupedia had a seven-step approval process to control the content of articles contributed to the site. Wikipedia quickly overtook the site that inspired its creation and Nupedia was shut down in 2003.

Wikipedia remains an open community funded by the Wikimedia Foundation, a US charitable organization, whose goal is to bring free educational content to the world. Wikipedia founder Jimmy Wales is a trustee of Wikimedia and an ardent advocate of Wikipedia's community status. Wikipedia has established a strong brand and has become a destination site on the web. It also ranks highly for search. These two features combined mean that Wikipedia has a significant reputational impact for any individual or organization that is discussed in its articles.

A study in February 2012 by search tool provider Intelligent Positioning[162] found that Wikipedia ranked on the first page of Google for 1,000 search terms selected by a random noun generator. This provided ammunition to critics of the two organizations to claim that Wikipedia is receiving undue prominence from Google. The reality is that Wikipedia has earned its search ranking dominance because it is incredibly well optimized for keywords and has built a large number of inbound links.

Reputation management

Critics claim that Wikipedia has become too powerful and that it operates without the recognized processes or oversight common for more traditional media. This is the issue that puts Wikipedia in conflict with the public relations industry. Errors in traditional media can be dealt with swiftly through well-established processes. Correcting content in a Wikipedia article requires engagement with the community and, crucially, adherence to its rules.

The reputation of an organization can be attacked in a matter of hours through changes to its Wikipedia page. Monitoring Wikipedia pages for modifications has become a key part of managing the reputation of an organization. In reality, rogue attacks on Wikipedia pages are few and far between, but when they occur an organization has no option, for now, but to seek redress via the community's own workflow.

So-called Wikipedia vandalism tends to be associated with high-profile individuals and organizations. But damage can also be done by micro-edits.

---

[162]Wikipedia: Page one of Google UK for 99% of searches: http://cipr.co/Y7epq7

Repeated changes in a short period of time can go unnoticed but have the effect of dramatically changing the content of an article. You don't have to look hard to find cases of pages that have been wilfully edited with factually incorrect content that is shared via social and traditional media before its authenticity is verified.

The so-called Seigenthaler incident in May 2005 saw a hoax article posted on Wikipedia falsely accusing US journalist John Seigenthaler as a suspect in the assassinations of US President John F. Kennedy and Attorney General Robert F. Kennedy. The entry went uncorrected for four months. The incident led to unregistered users being banned from creating new articles.

Crisis situations inevitably make headlines and make good content for discussion on the social web, but there is a more fundamental issue. Wikipedia is an important reference source yet many of its articles contain outdated or incorrect information such as spelling mistakes in the names of company executives and incorrect financial information.

A US survey of more than 1,200 individual members of CIPR, IABC, NIRI, PRSA and WOMMA, published by Marcia W. DiStaso, a communications assistant professor at Pennsylvania State University published in the PRSA's *PR Journal* for Spring 2012, found that 60% of Wikipedia articles contained factual errors.[163] Under Wikipedia's current rules these errors cannot be corrected by anyone that has a direct interest in the subject and who would arguably be best placed to make a correction. The study was criticized by the Wikipedia community for being self-selecting and narrow in its definition of what constitutes an error.

Relationship with public relations practitioners

The relationship between the public relations industry and Wikipedia is an uneasy one although there have been numerous efforts in recent times to bring the two constituencies closer together.

Herein lies the issue. Wikipedia did not set out to create a business directory.

---

[163]Measuring Public Relations Wikipedia Engagement: How Bright is the Rule?: http://cipr.co/YDHito

"The issue I have with PR editing is that it just takes up too much *time*. Wikipedians didn't turn up to help manage a business directory written by PR and advertising folk, they were attracted to Wikipedia for some far less worldly subject: philosophy, in my case, or military history or whatever it might be," said Tom Morris, a Wikipedia editor with more than 10 years' experience.

While an individual may contribute or edit articles on Wikipedia, they may not do so where you have a conflict of interest. That means that if you have a vested interest in an organization, individual, client or product you may not edit content.

The Wikipedia community claims that editors with a conflict of interest make bad Wikipedians.

"What I have found – and the evidence for this is pretty comprehensive – is that people who are acting as paid advocates do not make good editors. They insert puffery and spin. That's what they do because that is what paid advocates do," said Wikipedia founder Jimmy Wales.

A group of public relations practitioners has created a group called the Corporate Representatives for Ethical Wikipedia Engagement (CREWE)[164] to lobby Wales and the wider Wikipedia community to review the community's processes and policies in favour of improved corporate engagement. This remains a work in progress, although thanks to the efforts of CREWE and organizations such as the CIPR in the UK, and the PRSA in the US, the relationship and understanding between Wikipedia and the public relations industry is much improved.

Working with Wikipedia

To engage with the Wikipedia community, contribute articles and edit pages successfully you must have a good overview of the site and an understanding of its ethos. The community is ruthlessly transparent and you can review its governance on the Wikipedia site. Its core principles consist of five key pillars.

---

[164]Corporate Representatives for Ethical Wikipedia Engagement: http://cipr.co/YDH5ZK

1. Wikipedia is an encyclopaedia.
2. Wikipedia is written from a neutral point of view.
3. Wikipedia is free content that anyone can edit, use, modify, and distribute.
4. Editors should interact with each other in a respectful and civil manner.
5. Wikipedia does not have firm rules.

The Five Pillars of Wikipedia[165]

In addition to these key pillars Wikipedia has three core content policies covering neutrality, verification and attribution which public relations practitioners should understand.

Neutral point of view – All Wikipedia articles and other encyclopaedic content must be written from a neutral point of view, representing significant views fairly, proportionately and without bias.

Verifiability – Material challenged or likely to be challenged, and all quotations, must be attributed to a reliable, published source. In Wikipedia, verifiability means that people reading and editing the encyclopaedia can check that information comes from a reliable source.

No original research – Wikipedia does not publish original thought, all material in Wikipedia must be attributable to a reliable, published source. Articles may not contain any new analysis or synthesis of published material that serves to advance a position not clearly advanced by the sources.

Wikipedia core content policies[166]

---

[165]Wikipedia: Five Pillars of Wikipedia:
[166]Wikipedia: Core Content Policies: http://cipr.co/14Sp9is

How to help improve Wikipedia articles

This next section has been adapted from the CIPR's best practice guidance for public relations professionals.[167] This is a document produced by the CIPR's Social Media Panel that provides clear and detailed advice on how public relations practitioners should engage with the Wikipedia community. The document was written openly and collaboratively on an open wiki with input from both public relations practitioners and Wikipedians.[168] It remains a live document online.

All editing should be conducted in an open and honest manner. Public relations professionals should create an account with Wikipedia and create a user page associated with this which discloses their place of work and a list of their clients. Wikipedia policy doesn't allow user accounts to be shared, so each person should have their own account and user page.

Engaging with the community

Once you have registered with Wikipedia, head to the Talk section of the article where you are seeking changes to the article (the tab at the top of a Wikipedia entry labelled Talk).

"If something has been written about your client, tell them your client has a response, or a response that has been published elsewhere and should be on the site. Talk to the community with respect. State your job title, identity, interest and company. Escalate with kindness. This is effective almost always," says Wales.

Wales has a point. Marcia W. DiStaso's study into the relationship between the public relations industry and Wikipedia at Pennsylvania State University found that less than 35% of the respondents to the study had engaged with the Wikipedia community.

Engaging directly with the original editor or an editor of the page can prove effective. By going to the Toolbox section in the left-hand sidebar and looking

---

[167]CIPR Best Practice Guidance for Public Relations Practitioners: http://cipr.co/wiki-guide
[168]Draft Best Practice Guidance for PR: http://cipr.co/wiki-guidance

for their list of contributions, you will be able to check if they are still active on the site. If not then try other, more recent editors.

If you get no response from the Talk pages, proceed to a relevant notice-board. These pages are watched by groups of people with a particular interest: in effect, specialists. Noticeboard pages are very active and provide help quickly. If you are concerned about an entry for an individual, you can go to the Biography of Living Persons Noticeboard. If you want to make changes to a company page, or you think that someone editing the article is biased, it is a good idea to ask someone from the Conflict of Interest Noticeboard.

Inevitably there are sensitive situations where you may not want to dis-close your identity because it may inflame an already difficult issue. In such instances you should email info-en@wikimedia.org. This is managed by a small group of Wikipedians who will act as your advocate within the com-munity and offer advice. When you have a reply, keep the reference number so that any further correspondence can be tracked.

Dealing with disputes

If a subject is controversial, or there are repetitive edits better known as edit wars taking place, you can apply for the page to be protected. There are various stages, from full protection, where only a Wikipedia administrator can make an edit, to semi-protection, where only Wikipedia editors who have been registered on the site for more than four days and have made at least ten edits are allowed to make changes. To apply, ask an administrator or email info-en@wikimedia.org.

There is a dispute resolution system within Wikipedia, but the best advice, almost always, is to seek informal negotiation or mediation. The Administra-tors' Noticeboard can be effective in dealing with obnoxious conduct. Wikipedia's conflict resolution mechanisms are based on the simple tenet of good faith.

Administrators will almost never get involved in disagreements over the content of a page but they may ban one of the parties from the page or from the whole site for rude behaviour or sabotaging efforts to reach consensus. If an administrator does get involved then listen to any advice they have to give you, even if it is not what you want to hear or believe is correct.

The table below provides a quick reference summary of how to join and engage with the Wikipedia community.

---

1. Anyone can join the Wikipedia community and edit and contribute to content on the site. Register a personal rather than a corporate account and disclose your conflicts of interest on your user page.
2. If you are concerned about the accuracy of a Wikipedia article but have a conflict of interest you must address this via the community. Don't edit any page you have a conflict of interest on, except to remove vandalism.
3. Head to the Talk page for the Wikipedia article concerned and draft your response. This works in almost all situations. However, if you don't get a response then raise it on the relevant noticeboard.
4. Escalate with kindness and don't be an idiot. When faced with a situation where you have a choice to be an idiot or not be an idiot, choose not to be an idiot. Following this rule will mean you will very rarely get into difficult situations.
5. You can freely contribute articles related to your profession, hobbies and interests, where you do not have a conflict of interest. In fact, Wikipedia actively encourages this and it's a great way to get to know how Wikipedia works.

Working with Wikipedia

Wikipedia works

Wikipedia is a free-to-access online encyclopaedia first and foremost, but it is also a community. It is not a media property in the traditional sense of the definition and does not share the same structures, workflow or governance. But there are very clear processes for seeking redress and corrections.

When I asked my network recently for examples of significant reputational damage caused to an organization or individual by an article on Wikipedia in the last 12 to 24 months, examples were few and far between. Yes, there were plenty of examples of minor errors and content about past corporate activity that public relations practitioners would prefer to be erased, but by and large it appears that the Wikipedia community works.

Biography

Stephen Waddington (@wadds) is European digital and social media director for Ketchum. He has earned the reputation as a public relations modernizer, thought-leader and consumer engagement advocate working with organizations including The Associated Press, Cisco, *The Economist*, P&G, Philips, IBM and Tesco. He is a regular commentator on issues related to modern brand communications and reputation. His published work includes *Share This* (John Wiley & Sons, 2012) and he has written *Brand Anarchy* (Bloomsbury, 2012), a provocative book on brands, social media and public relations. You can connect with Stephen via his popular blog Two-Way Street.

Chapter 20

Becky McMichael

It has never been easier to find health information online. Be that via patient-oriented websites, NHS Online sources, user-generated forum content or a range of health, disease awareness and fitness applications available for mobile devices.

Healthcare professionals are increasingly using platforms such as doctors.net to communicate with each other and receive intelligence and share information about disease awareness and medicines in a more social and collaborative manner.

2012 saw the first mobile health app registered and regulated as a medical device in the UK, providing a strong indication that digital health tools are growing up. So what can healthcare organizations do to incorporate social platforms and digital tools into their campaign armoury and truly begin to benefit patient health outcomes?

The global healthcare landscape

Worldwide, governments aim to deliver effective, safe and affordable healthcare to their people with increasingly effective outcomes. And the budgets this sector attracts are not small change either from a political spend perspective or a PR perspective. In 2011[169] the World Health Organization (WHO)

---

[169]mHealth; McKinsey; 2012: http://cipr.co/WBz2MM

expected a global annual spend on healthcare to reach US$6 trillion and over the last 50 years, healthcare spend has outpaced GDP growth by about 2% a year. There are, says McKinsey, few signs that this trend will slow.

New approaches such as digital and mobile health, remote medicine delivery, remote diagnosis, patient-led monitoring and physician digital knowledge sharing are cited as key ways in which costs can be lowered and access increased between and across the developing and developed world. As these innovations become more commonplace and filter down from health-care practitioners to pharma companies and patients, technology becomes more than the delivery mechanism.

How patients approach digital health

According to the most recent research from Eurostat (see Figure 20.1), in the UK alone, 80% of us have access to broadband internet as of 1 January 2012 and over 36% search for health information online.

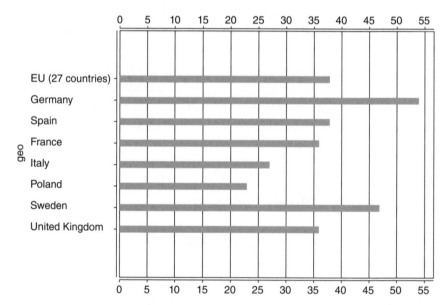

Figure 20.1:   Eurostat Information Statistics 2012[170]

---

[170]Individuals using the Internet for seeking health-related information; Eurostat; 2012: http://cipr.co/YchZPC

The annual survey by Experian Hitwise and Private Healthcare UK[171] outlines which sites are most visited and which issues UK citizens are most concerned about. The results show fat is more than a feminist issue with the British. Health seekers are more concerned with excess weight and how to lose it than any other health area.

In terms of where we go, the top five most visited healthcare websites in 2012 were:

1. NHS Choices
2. Boots
3. WeightWatchers
4. Patient UK
5. Netdoctor.co.uk.

Perhaps surprisingly, the trusted voice of the NHS online – NHS Direct – ranks 16th, putting it below commercial brand sites such as Holland & Barrett, BUPA and Specsavers.

Alongside an increase in high-speed broadband access in the UK and internet usage across all areas, the increase in smartphone penetration is a key driver in the digital health arena. In 2013, mobile phones will overtake PCs as the most common way to access the web[172] and analysts predict that the smartphone application market for mobile healthcare will reach US$1.3 billion in 2012 with 247 million users downloading an app worldwide (see Figure 20.2).

Healthcare professionals and the increased adoption of digital health

Healthcare professional (HCP) sources can be split into two key streams of "open" and "HCP only" social media. Both fulfil different roles and both are growing. Open channels tend to be used for research, information gathering and product searches whilst "HCP only" enables HCPs to connect with

---

[171]2012 Webwatch report; Private Healthcare UK; 2012: http://cipr.co/YFNJ1V
[172]Top 10 technology trends for 2013; Gartner; 2012: http://cipr.co/UDAX6E

1. People want health apps that will help them and the healthcare professionals who are working for them, manage practical aspects of healthcare or emergencies.

2. People are interested in health apps but usage is low post download.

3. People on Apple kit use health apps more than people on other devices.

4. Blackberry users find apps too hard to use on their devices.

5. At the moment health apps are the least popular apps, social media are the most popular.

6. 20% of respondents said they were very likely or fairly likely to use a health app before the end of the year.

7. Nearly a third of respondents said they'd view their medical records or get test results over an app.

Figure 20.2: mHealth: Consumer Attitudes Survey of 2,000 consumers (Ruder Finn/ YouGov June 2012)
Reproduced by permission of Ruder Finn UK Ltd

colleagues and share both perspectives and experiences. From a PR perspective, opportunities exist to engage HCPs in both streams of social media.

In Europe alone, the HCP-only community is fragmented. The large US-founded community WebMD recently entered Germany, where there were already half a dozen small networks. Similarly, a number of networks are also joining a partnership with doctors.net.uk in the UK. The site claims to have 40,000 daily users,[173] ranking it as Europe's biggest network. A recent survey[174] amongst European HCPs, showed those in the UK and Germany were most likely to use an online medical community.

As the time pressures on HCPs increase, they are less able to attend medical congresses and see pharmaceutical reps face-to-face – 52% of GPs did not see any pharmaceutical sales representatives in a typical week according to research from doctors.net.uk. As such, digital channels become an increasingly crucial way of sourcing independent product information. Nearly a quarter of them said they preferred to obtain their own product information via independent online resources. Only 3% of doctors think that online

---

[173]Doctors.net own web data; 2012

[174]Cegedim Strategic Data; 2012; Two-thirds of UK physicians aware of mobile applications for professional use: http://cipr.co/XRk0C4

pharma resources are credible and 42% never visit pharmaceutical websites, meaning the role of PR is increasingly important in ensuring that credible and validated information appears across a range of trusted sources.

Many HCPs' roles are inherently mobile – GPs on home visits, specialists moving around hospitals or clinics, midwives attending home births or paramedics on duty – and this increases the interest and relevance of mobile devices. Doctors, in particular, have embraced smartphones and tablets wholeheartedly and 26% of European doctors now have and use an iPad professionally, spending a quarter of their online time using the device.[175]

In terms of application usage, less than half[176] of HCPs were personally using mobile applications for professional purposes. Of those that did, a higher proportion were in secondary care and more likely to be physicians than nurses (see Figure 20.3).

Less than half of HCPs currently using mobile applications

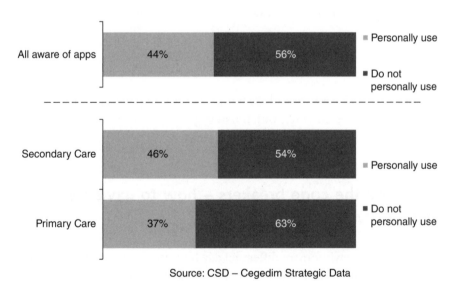

Source: CSD – Cegedim Strategic Data

Figure 20.3: What percentage of HCPs use mobile applications? – Cegedim Strategic Data 2012

---

[175]D. Tryer, Twenty six percent of European doctors own an iPad. 2012: http://cipr.co/Ycil8X
[176]Cegedim Strategic Data 2012; Two-thirds of UK physicians aware of mobile applications for professional use: http://cipr.co/XRkoC4

Physicians especially Rheumatologists & Urologists most aware of mobile applications

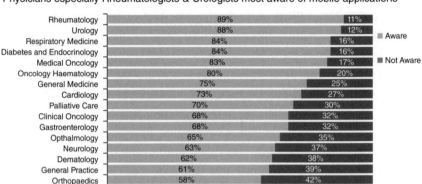

Source: CSD – Cegedim Strategic Data

Figure 20.4: Physicians most aware of mobile applications – Cegedim Strategic Data 2012

In terms of disease areas, there was greater use amongst clinical oncology, haematology and cardiology, with nursing, geriatrics and psychiatry rated the lowest users of mobile apps (see Figure 20.4).

Avoiding the code breakers – how to navigate regulatory responsibilities

The regulatory environment differs hugely from market to market and must be carefully considered at the outset of any global or pan-regional campaign. In terms of regulatory environment in the UK, the control of medical marketing is based on a long-established system of self-regulation supported by the Medicines and Healthcare Products Regulatory Agency (MHRA). The MHRA administers legal regulation on behalf of UK Health Ministers.

The Association of the British Pharmaceutical Industry (ABPI) Code of Practice for the Pharmaceutical Industry, administered by the PMCPA, is the self-regulatory system covering prescription medicines. The ABPI Code extends beyond UK law and provides guidance on marketing, digital and social media activity.

The ABPI Code does not cover the advertising or promotion of medicines that are available without prescription or "over the counter" (OTC). The Proprietary Association of Great Britain[177] (PAGB) regulates OTC medicines and food supplements. OTC products are far less restricted in terms of how they can be promoted than prescription only medicines (POMs).

In accordance with the ABPI Code,[178] the advertising and promotion of (POMs) to the public is prohibited. Therefore, any promotional material about POMs directed to a UK audience which is provided on the internet either in an owned site or on a social network must comply with all relevant requirements of the Code.

Therapeutic area/disease awareness websites can be sponsored by companies provided that all the material available at the site complies with the Code. However, according to the MHRA,[179] the primary purpose of a disease awareness campaign must be to increase awareness of a disease or diseases and to provide health educational information on that disease, *not* to promote the use of a particular pharmaceutical product or products. Websites for HCPs are possible as long as they have a clear firewall and require the viewer to confirm their HCP status.

A disease awareness campaign may make reference to the availability of treatment options but not specific medicines. And when there is only one treatment for a condition (i.e. no competitive drugs) disease awareness campaigns will naturally point to the only available drug on the market. In these circumstances, a campaign should only focus on general disease education with details of where to get appropriate advice and not on treatment options.

---

[177]Proprietary Association of Great Britain; Regulations and Guidance; 2012: http://cipr.co/VFLyc9

[178]Prescription Medicine Code of Practice Authority; The ABPI Code of Practice for the Pharmaceutical Industry; 2012: http://cipr.co/Ww6tCl

[179]Medicines and Healthcare products Regulatory Agency; The ABPI Code of Practice for the Pharmaceutical Industry; 2012: http://cipr.co/12vuJIo

Control and adversity

A large proportion of healthcare campaigns in the social media or digital areas are ultimately funded by pharmaceutical companies, either directly or through charity funding or grants. Either way, their involvement must be clearly declared and any assets created are liable for the same levels of scrutiny and responsibility as the pharma company's own website. As such, this often causes the more risk-averse pharma companies to back away from two-way dialogue and to run campaigns with closed walls and comments disabled. This not only affects the overall success of many campaigns but also throws questions over whether they are actually social at all.

The reason for this risk aversion is primarily due to a lack of control over the dialogue that happens on social media and a fear of being seen to be conducting promotional activity to the public.

Whilst disease awareness campaigns are permitted, pharma companies cannot ensure the conversation remains about disease. In extreme cases, campaigns that are deemed direct to consumer and promotional in nature can result in imprisonment for medical directors, so the stakes are high!

However, another large factor in using social tools for pharmaceutical marketing is adverse event (AE) reporting. An adverse event is where a consumer discusses ill effects that they had during the time that they were taking a medication. Under current regulations from the ABPI, any adverse event must be reported and acted upon immediately as soon as it is discovered.[180]

The ABPI[181] insists that monitoring should be frequent enough to ensure regulatory obligations can be met and daily monitoring of a campaign should be considered (it is important to note that the guideline does not specify round the clock monitoring).

If an adverse event is observed, there should be a robust procedure in place between the social media administrator, the pharmaceutical company's

---

[180]Association of the British Pharmaceutical Industry; 2012; Guidance notes on the management of adverse events and product complaints from pharmaceutical company sponsored websites: http://cipr.co/WBAQW2

[181]Association of the British Pharmaceutical Industry; Management of adverse events and product complaints from pharmaceutical company sponsored websites (section 7), 2011

pharmacovigilance team and the AE reporting expert in order to handle this, according to the usual regulations.

Getting creative with digital health communications

2012 saw health organizations embrace digital campaigns that used social media like never before.

1. Novartis Vaccines and Diagnostics supported a successful Meningitis Keep Watching campaign comprising a range of assets such as a short film, cinema advert, Facebook disease awareness page and social advertising campaign to reach thousands of mums with babies under one.
2. GE Healthcare used a digital data visualization built using Twitter data to illustrate the conversation happening worldwide about breast cancer.
3. St John Ambulance launched its Helpless campaign with an ad during ITV's *Downton Abbey* and an accompanying social media campaign to highlight that up to 140,000 people (as many as die from cancer) die each year in situations where First Aid could have helped save their lives. Additional assets included an app, a first aid guide and training courses, all housed on an area of the charity's website but publicized widely through social media channels.
4. A little public safety film made by a train safety organization in Melbourne, Australia turned all the rules on their head by receiving over 26 million views to its film in the first week on YouTube with no paid media support due to a clever mix of catchy song, cute animation and a subtle but powerful message. Giving hope to marketers everywhere!

What's next?

Last year, the forward-looking predictions covered by media and bloggers alike featured digital health prominently on the agenda. This is great news for communications experts as the future for digital health is both red hot and right now!

How do you kick things off?

Assuming you've got your risk analysis and AE reporting sorted, you understand your demographics and have a clear idea of what you want your campaign to achieve, the healthcare campaign world really is your creative oyster. There are many trends that can provide great creative fodder to your brainstorms. Here's some brain food to get you started:

- **Big Data** – looking at a disease awareness programme at a global level and allowing HCPs and media to work together to interpret the story from the data.
- **Mini data** – making the story of me. What does my digital health footprint reveal about me and how will it impact me in the future?
- **3D printing** – how can the new phenomenon in printer hardware impact healthcare professionals? How about printing models for plastic surgery or prosthetics? Or printing out a model of a tumour so the surgeon can hold it life size in his hands before he operates?
- **Quantified self applications** – look at the impact for consumers on mobile health – beyond exercise bragging rights and weight loss, how does this new trend to personal tracking impact everything from our health footprint to our insurance quotes? Can I finally get a complete personal health dashboard?
- **Gaming data** – how can gaming change negative health behaviour in the long term?
- **Creative events and storytelling** – using data and insights to inform your campaign, how can we start with finding the patient before we start to decide the tactics? Finally put a stop to starting with a website or an application . . . how can we put our data to work for us?
- **Visual campaigns** – how can platforms such as Pinterest, Vine or Instagram help with health conditions and redefine beauty for people with skin disease for example?
- **Original content** – How can pharmaceutical companies drive the development of original media and programming? An early example of this is Lilly's collaboration with Disney for a series of diabetes books.

Biography

Becky McMichael (@bmcmichael) is head of strategy and innovation at communications consultancy and digital studio, Ruder Finn UK. She has over 15 years of experience spanning many industries, including pharma, having worked on digital campaigns for organizations such as Abbott, Pfizer and Novartis. Becky has a real passion for technology and social tools, is a blogger and runs a community for working mums in marketing. She splits her time between London and Cornwall where she spends her free time walking at toddler speed to the beach.

Chapter 21

Rachel Miller

For today's corporate communication professional, it's now assumed that you have a solid understanding of social media. What if that's not the case? Here are case studies, research tools and resources to help you make appropriate decisions.

Are you being asked to advise your company on the correct social media strategy to fit with your culture? What if you've never even used Twitter, let alone know how Pinterest works, but are expected to know what's right for your business?

Internal communication is as important as external communication. Social media use is as crucial a conversation as explaining the profession of corporate communication or role of employee engagement. There will always be a requirement for organizations to engage with online communities, albeit the tools may change over time. You need to be able to demonstrate gravitas in this area, and fast.

Digital versus social

Even the term social media creates complications in some companies, which choose "digital", "social" or something entirely different. I think its use for corporate communication will become ingrained to the point where the focus is the communication, content and conversations rather than the name.

Management consultant Peter F. Drucker said the best way to predict the future is to create it. That's never been truer for corporate communication, particularly regarding social media. If you believe collaborative communication is right for your culture, choose the phrase that suits your workplace.

GAME, a large UK high street retailer of video games and consoles, uses tools for sharing best practice and tools for reducing inefficiencies. "Hardly catchy" says Paul Bennun, communications and engagement manager, "but they fit into a sense-making framework for our senior leaders."

The organization is currently exploring a media database for video/image sharing. If each of their 340 stores takes two photographs over a new product launch weekend, and only one in 50 creates a good video, it has 700 photos and seven videos to use internally or externally. GAME is equipping employees with information to prepare for this change.

Paul adds: "It's incredibly exciting and opens up a wealth of content we currently aren't using. It's about plugging the business into conversations, creating the arena for them and extracting value from the content, which in most cases is already there." In the words of Philippa Snare, Chief Marketing Officer at Microsoft UK: "Social is a mindset, not technology. Only do it if it comes naturally, or you could look like a dad on the dancefloor."

Role of 21st century corporate communicator

Corporate communication is a broad term. Underneath it can sit internal communication (with employees, stakeholders and interested parties such as shareholders), external communication (with customers and media), public and government affairs, corporate social responsibility, sponsorship, brand, events and more.

These disciplines often overlap and each one requires unique skill sets and dedication. An effective corporate communication function and team recognizes and celebrates this and aligns effort, content and timings to benefit the business and its customers.

The lines between internal and external communication continue to blur. You're only a forwarded email/status or misplaced employee magazine away from headlines.

Assuming that all information will stay purely internal is foolhardy. In heavily unionized workforces or in times of change such as mergers and acquisitions, the criticality of your communication's accuracy and mindfulness of audience cannot be underestimated.

Alex Smith, head of communications at the Target Ovarian Cancer charity, says: "We don't distinguish between internal and external communications as we have fantastic volunteer support from women with ovarian cancer, their families and friends, in fundraising and campaigning. I prefer to view our audiences as concentric circles with those most involved (staff and women with ovarian cancer) at the centre."

Ensure clear guidance is in place with regard to what can be shared via social media. Treat employees as an internal and external audience and create a framework of flexibility within boundaries, such as using a social media friendly mark. The Local Government Association (LGA) developed one in 2012 and I've secured permission for you to access the images and guidance.[182]

There are many arguments for and against having a policy. I recommend including employees in its creation to aid adoption, and you can find hundreds of examples online.[183]

Mayo Clinic Center for Social Media has a 12-word policy.[184] Could this be the basis for yours?

Don't lie. Don't pry. Don't cheat. Can't delete. Don't steal. Don't reveal.

Writing well is still important, but the focus is now on creating timely, shareable content for your organization to use, written in an appropriate style. In the words of Euan Semple's book, organizations don't tweet, people do.

Technologies are appearing within companies with the label "social media" but they aren't always sociable or indeed social. There is an undeniable feeling within the communications community that you have to be seen to "do social".

Brian Solis, digital analyst, sociologist and futurist says: "The challenge is the ability to link business objectives, social media strategies and the bottom line. Executives need to see how social fits in to the overall vision and goals

---

[182]Local Government Association Social Media Friendly Mark: http://cipr.co/YVJGCl
[183]Social Media Governance, Chris Boudreaux: http://cipr.co/WwbECj
[184]Mayo Clinic social media policy: http://cipr.co/Xq7IyG

of the organisation in order to lead a top down charge that changes how employees and customers connect and collaborate. There must be a purpose coupled with tangible results."[185]

There are a plethora of social media training courses available[186] to suit your time and budget, and you can't beat actually doing. I couldn't see a use for Pinterest until I tried it. Now I regularly pin on my own internal communication and social media boards[187] to collate shareable content. With the introduction of "secret boards", its suitability for corporate communication increases.

Etsy has more than 800,000 online shops and 15 million one-of-a-kind handmade items. Editor in chief Alison Feldmann says: "Our goal of using Pinterest is inspiration – not just sales. We showcase Etsy's values to drive loyalty and engagement, and we post things that resonate with our community. We maintain a careful balance of Etsy items and other content pinned to maintain authenticity with our audience."

Visual communication, such as infographics and visual roadmaps, are on the rise for corporate communication. They consider the receiver rather than the sender of the message and often generate positive feedback. They've been used by companies including Hallmark, Royal Bank of Scotland and GKN.[188]

Corporate reflections on social media

In October 2012 I conducted research into how internal communicators use social media, both personally and professionally (managing or writing on behalf of an organization). It revealed that 93% of communications professionals expect their professional use to increase. There is further information below and the full results are available as an infographic.[189]

Communications recruiters VMA Group led a Business Leaders in Communications Study[190] with 95 directors of communications in leading FTSE

---

[185]How Social Media Can Spur Organizational Transformation, Forbes: http://cipr.co/Xq7M1w
[186]Training courses via http://cipr.co/12vCZrB: http://cipr.co/YVKBmn
[187]Rachel Miller's Pinterest profile: http://cipr.co/14UtVfo
[188]Visual communication, Strategic Communication Management: http://cipr.co/12vD2ng
[189]Internal comms research, www.rachmiller.com: http://cipr.co/11OQoMS
[190]Business Leaders in Communications Study, VMA Group (2012): http://cipr.co/XX6J9o

organizations in 2012. Only 15% of respondents said social media skills were "critical" when recruiting to their teams. This is surprising when compared to the fact that three quarters of comms professionals surveyed expect to see an increase in demand for "websites, digital and social media". Almost one in ten "do not see social media as a challenge".

Statistics around the ownership of the digital space raise the possibility that we may be seeing the beginning of a decline in influence for marketing departments as we currently know them. The influence of social media on reputation and brand is well established, and results showed communications departments largely "own" social media.

Communications directors "own" the following:

- 43% corporate advertising – further 15% have indirect remit.
- 34% sponsorship.
- 42% brand and marketing communications.
- 43% corporate social responsibility.
- 43% corporate giving.
- 71% events and publications.

I said corporate communications was a broad term, a fact confirmed by this analysis.

The *Social Media Report* (Nielsen, 2012)[191] reveals social care – customer service via social media – is transforming customer service and has become an immediate imperative for global brands and communications teams.

Customers choose when and where they voice their questions, issues and complaints, blurring the line between marketing and customer service. Brands should consider this evolution and ensure they are ready to react on all channels. Nearly half of US consumers contact brands and service providers directly to voice satisfaction or complaints/questions and one in three social media users say they prefer this method to telephoning.

Enterprise social networks are more than "internal Facebook or Twitter". Altimeter Group defines them as a set of technologies that create business value by connecting the members of an organization through profiles, updates and notifications.

---

[191]State of the media: The social media report, Nielsen (2012): http://cipr.co/VoqAHM

There are many to choose from including Chatter from Salesforce.com, IBM Connections, Jive, Newsgator, SharePoint, Snapcomms, Socialcast and Yammer. I've featured many examples on my blog including how Aviva Investors use Yammer[192] and Coca-Cola Enterprises use Chatter.[193]

According to Altimeter Group, enterprise social network technologies evolve from three scenarios: standalone solution, collaboration and enterprise application add-on and they detail the networks to suit each one.

My research[194] showed that 55% of comms pros who responded felt people expect them to have a "good understanding" of social media. An additional 33% felt they are expected to "know all about" it.

Communications teams are most likely to introduce internal social networks (29%) followed by IT (24%). However, 11% said they didn't know where it came from. Models like Yammer allow employees to sign up using company email; so corporate communicators often have to play "catch-up".

- Social sites communications professionals use personally, multiple choice: Facebook and Twitter (94% each), LinkedIn (91%), Instagram (42%), Pinterest (33%), personal blog (31%), Google+ (25%), other (6%), MySpace (4%).
- Used professionally: Twitter (69%), LinkedIn (40%), Facebook (39%), blog (35%), enterprise social network (23%), none (20%), Google+ (11%), Pinterest (7%), Instagram (5%), other (2%).

Using social technologies

Social technologies are defined by McKinsey & Company[195] as products and services that enable social interactions in the digital realm, allowing people to connect and interact virtually. When used within organizations, they have the potential to raise the productivity of the high-skill knowledge workers that are critical to performance and growth in the 21st century, by 20 to 25%.

---

[192]Do they "like" it., www.allthingsic.com: http://www.allthingsic.com/do-they-like-it/

[193]Chatter that matters, www.allthingsic.com: http://www.allthingsic.com/chatter-that-matters/

[194]Making the business case for enterprise social networks via Altimeter: http://cipr.co/Wwc37D

[195]McKinsey & Company: The social economy: unlocking value and productivity through social technology (July, 2012): http://cipr.co/XRvENe

Using collaborative techniques impacts organizational communication and has many benefits. However, they aren't a magic cure to turn your hierarchical top-down culture into a collaborative, information-sharing organization overnight. They should be approached in the same way as any other channel and be given the same attention, resources and thought.

According to McKinsey, social technologies promise to extend the capabilities of high-skill workers by streamlining communication and collaboration, lowering barriers between functional silos, and even redrawing boundaries to bring in additional knowledge and expertise in "extended networked enterprises".

Does it work? In 2011, 72% of companies surveyed[196] reported using social technologies in their businesses and 90% reported that they are seeing benefits.

McKinsey states: "The benefits of social technologies will likely outweigh the risks for most companies. Organisations that fail to invest in understanding social technologies will be at greater risk of having their business models disrupted by social technologies."

Healthcare specialist Bupa has customers in 190 countries and 52,000 employees and aims to put digital at the heart of the business. It developed BupaLive, a global internal social media platform, which aimed to be "one single place to communicate, collaborate and share". The company introduced it as: LinkedIn = "your career", Facebook = "your social life" and BupaLive = "your work".

Bupa set challenging and measurable business outcomes. These were collaboration across teams/business lines/geographies/time zones, to deliver:

- Searchable employee networks.
- Sharing of knowledge, products, services, best practice.
- Social media capability and coordinated strategy.
- Increased innovation/idea generation.
- Decreased duplication of work/silos.
- Faster communication.
- Rapid integration of new acquisitions.
- Accelerated delivery of Bupa's group-wide corporate strategy.

---

[196]Bughin, Hung Byers and Chui, "How social technologies are extending the organization", *The McKinsey Quarterly* (November 2011)

BupaLive results in numbers:[197] 5,000+ user-generated groups (91% work and 9% social), 85% of desk-based users, 90,000 documents shared, 60,000 comments, 55,000 discussion threads, 12,000 blog posts and 10,000 videos.

I think BupaLive has done well because they took an integrated approach. The site acts as a global internal communications channel and also enables employees to download their smartphone apps and promote them via external social media such as Bupa's Facebook Pages.

The perception of social media as weapons of mass distraction has clearly been overcome, because its leaders have recognized their role as part of the wider business strategy. Incoming CEO Stuart Fletcher was introduced to the organization via a video on BupaLive.

Social business strategist Nick Crawford, who oversaw BupaLive's launch, told me: "Corporate comms teams have a vital role to play in introducing social media within an organisation. Their knowledge and expertise is invaluable to ensuring the best choices are made. They need to work collaboratively with IT and HR and ensure it's not just driven by one function, like IT, as is often the case. Corporate communicators should take the lead as their expertise and knowledge will be critical to success."

Gatwick Airport integrates social media into everything it does. Lindsay Baldwin, head of airport communications, says: "Twitter is used predominantly as a customer service tool to start two-way conversations with customers, across marketing campaigns and internal communication. If we launch a new airline, we use our social media channels to support those as well." The airport uses SoundCloud[198] for its customers by uploading stories for parents to listen to with their children while they wait for their flights.

How can social technologies add value? McKinsey & Company[199] has produced a table detailing 10 ways they can add value in organizational functions within and across enterprises.

My final piece of advice is stop, collaborate and listen. Before you make great strides with social, assess your company's strategy, work with your business, employees and customers to determine what suits your culture and then continue to listen and ask for feedback.

---

[197]Social media from the inside out: http://cipr.co/Vou5Oo: http://cipr.co/14FzUDZ

[198]SoundCloud: Your London airport, Gatwick: http://cipr.co/120wYiv

[199]McKinsey & Company: The social economy (July, 2012): http://cipr.co/XRvENe

Biography

Rachel Miller (@AllThingsIC) is an internal communication and social media strategist. She started her career as a journalist and has worked in internal communication in-house and agency side for companies including BSkyB, L'Oréal, Visa, Tube Lines and London Overground. Rachel was named in *PR Week*'s Top 29 under 29 professional communicators list and is a Kingston internal communications management postgraduate. She is part of the Engage for Success guru group and regularly speaks about, writes and teaches internal communication and social media. Rachel co-founded @theICcrowd, is a CIPR Inside committee member and blogs at www.allthingsic.com.

Chapter 22

Stuart Bruce

Society and the economy are evolving and in today's über-connected world companies and organizations face greater scrutiny than ever with a need to answer to more and more stakeholders beyond just shareholders. The social web provides both opportunities and threats.

CSR, or corporate social responsibility, is a much abused term. According to that fount of all wisdom, Wikipedia, CSR is "a form of corporate self-regulation integrated into a business model". However, it is frequently misunderstood and recently has often been used to refer just to sustainability, which is only one aspect of CSR. In Europe – and the explanation of CSR that I favour – CSR usually means focusing on operating the business in a socially responsible way. In the USA, CSR is often used to refer to corporate philanthropy, where companies donate a certain share of their profits to charitable causes, which may include arts, sports and culture. Corporate citizenship is another useful way of thinking about CSR, as it doesn't just limit itself to philanthropy.

Therefore the definition of CSR can vary for different organizations, geographies and industry sectors. Elements can include environment and sustainability, employment practices, social welfare, diversity, charitable giving, human rights and volunteering. Increasingly some aspects of corporate social responsibility are becoming regulated by legislation, such as taxation policies to penalize polluters and anti-bribery laws.

One driver for the increased importance of CSR is that while national governments find it challenging to regulate multinational enterprises across countries, citizens and consumers don't face the same constraints. The social web makes it easier for anyone with knowledge and expertise to scrutinize the behaviour of companies and publish their criticisms. The social web provides the tools for citizens and consumers to self-organize and rapidly create a tsunami of criticism against companies that they perceive as not behaving responsibly.

An example of this emerged in the UK in the latter half of 2012 when there was a climate of big companies such as Amazon, Google and eBay being criticized for using complex offshore inter-company relationships to avoid paying their fair share of corporation tax. Starbucks was one of the companies criticized. When faced with a rapidly increasing consumer boycott organized on Twitter and Facebook it attempted to deflect criticism by "volunteering" to pay an extra £20 million in tax.

The social web should be integral to CSR

Companies and organizations can use social media in their CSR for far more than just communications and promoting what they are doing. It can and should be a fundamental aspect of how CSR is integrated into the business. Some of the ways that the social web can be used to make CSR more effective and successful include:

- Intelligence: Using online monitoring companies can run an early warning "radar" system to alert them of potential issues such as nascent campaigns by pressure groups.
- Knowledge discovery and sharing: Social media can be used to research new ways of improving corporate behaviour; both by discovering best practice from elsewhere and by improving knowledge management internally so all employees can contribute ideas and highlight problematic activity.
- Crowdsourcing: Innovative ideas for improving a company's corporate social responsibility can be found by tapping into the expertise of stakeholders.

- Reporting and promoting: The most obvious area to use social media is to report, promote and share a company's CSR activity. Social media can transform corporate storytelling by providing powerful publishing platforms for words, pictures, audio and video.
- Partnerships, alliances and community: Social media and social networks make it easier and more effective for brands to partner with NGOs and charities to support and promote common goals.
- Public affairs and lobbying: What constitutes responsible corporate behaviour changes and one factor that affects it is the political climate a company operates in. Therefore it is important to use social media in a public affairs context to monitor opinions, shape conversations and engage with influencers.
- Crisis communications: Companies that don't behave responsibly are more under threat than ever as millions of "citizen journalists" scrutinize their every move and NGOs utilize their online power to campaign against them.
- Engagement: Many companies that use social media for CSR are still focused on broadcast and using social media to share what they are doing. But this misses potentially one of the most powerful ways to use social media, which is to start engaging with people. Once you've established a relationship people are far more likely to be helpful to you, they are more likely to tolerate misdemeanours and less likely to turn into an online lynch mob.

Even before companies start to use the social web proactively to support CSR they should be using it as an intelligence system. One large multinational commissioned a global online audit of both social media and online traditional media to identify the websites, individual influencers and issues that were most likely to have positive or negative impacts on its corporate reputation. As a result it started regular monitoring of environmental forums and identified an increasing amount of conversation about palm oil, enabling it to predict forthcoming campaign activity against it by NGOs on this issue.

By analyzing online conversations a UK-based power generation company looking at potential new sites was able to establish that the local community was not as concerned about potential emissions from the power plant as it was about increased traffic on local roads. As a result the company changed its site plans to make more responsible use of the roads and changed the focus of its communications and lobbying campaign.

Innovative uses of social media for CSR

One of the most powerful uses of social media for CSR is to share ideas and knowledge. A great example of this is Cisco's GETideas.org,[200] which is part of a larger CSR effort. GETideas is a web community that describes itself as an "incubator where education leaders can develop their professional learning networks. Think of this space as a professional idea generator – a place where education leaders can be inspired to make change happen in their school, district, or university. Our goal is to bring people together to exchange ideas toward solving education challenges." It uses blogs, discussion forums and a variety of social media platforms including Twitter, Facebook, LinkedIn, Google+, Pinterest and YouTube.

GE was founded more than 100 years ago by inventor Thomas Edison and today the company continues to innovate. In 2010 it created the Ecomagination Challenge[201] to crowdsource innovative clean energy ideas from stakeholders across the USA. The site has continued to evolve and is now not only a great example of CSR social media, but also of a company that has become a media publishing company in its own right, with a team of professional journalists producing an editorially rich site that has the hallmarks of popular science, engineering and technology magazine sites. GE's latest developments include launching its Healthymagination[202] initiative, where it has created several mobile, tablet (iPhone and iPad only) and Facebook apps to help people manage exercise, diet and live healthier lives.

If CSR is a fundamental part of how a business operates then – just like a company's financial performance – it must be reported. If CSR is about what

---

[200]Cisco GETideas education leaders community: http://cipr.co/Xqd9xE
[201]GE Ecomagination Challenge: http://cipr.co/VYEGIR
[202]GE Healthymagination: http://cipr.co/TOIZIi

affects all stakeholders then it follows that CSR reporting must be directed at all stakeholders. However, groups such as employees and customers aren't necessarily going to be the most avid consumers of a traditional CSR report.

The social web provides a way for companies to be more engaging and interactive in the way they report. One example of this is nikeresponsibility. com[203] which provides an interactive "journey" through Nike's CSR, along with a more detailed "Our Value Chain" that enables stakeholders to drill down into different aspects of Nike's operations. Another emerging trend is companies creating dedicated mobile and tablet apps to improve CSR reporting, such as GE's sustainability report.[204]

In the current climate banks are in the firing line for many people who question their commitment to corporate social responsibility. BBVA's Banca Para Todos or "Banking for All" corporate responsibility blog[205] is an attempt to redress this. BBVA recognized that a glossy, printed CSR report didn't sit well with its sustainability policy and made the switch to digital, which also complemented its existing commitment to social media (bbvasocialmedia. com) with more than 100 initiatives on Facebook, Twitter, YouTube, LinkedIn and blogs.[206]

BBVA wanted its CSR report to be conversational and give stakeholders an opportunity to question it and challenge claims. It did so by dropping both its print and online reports and replacing them with a blog to provide a permanent forum to talk and discuss with stakeholders, analysts, NGOs, academics and ordinary consumers. It deliberately takes a low-key approach using a standard WordPress template and providing links to online forums where related discussions are already taking place.

The blog is a hub for BBVA's other CSR social media channels on YouTube and Twitter, although not Facebook as research indicated that CSR conversation wasn't happening there. The blog gets about 8,000 visits a month from 6,300 unique visitors who read about 2.5 pages each visit, as well as 3,000 subscribers on YouTube with more than 32,000 views.[207]

---

[203]Nike Responsibility: http://cipr.co/XRCTof
[204]GE Ecomagination iPhone/iPad app at iTunes: http://cipr.co/11rUASo
[205]BBVA Banking for All blog: http://cipr.co/VJDKv8
[206]BBVA social media hub: http://cipr.co/XRDCG4
[207]BBVA case study from Digital Communications Awards 2012 (PDF): http://cipr.co/WQOx4Y

The social media trap for bad CSR

Green washing is a term of abuse often levelled at companies that are seen to be using "CSR" to disguise damaging or unethical business practices. BP is one of many companies that has been accused of green washing and in particular was criticized during and after the Gulf of Mexico crisis when its Deepwater Horizon drilling platform spilled millions of gallons of crude oil into the ocean.

BP was criticized for buying relevant keywords and phrases to use Google Adwords to drive web traffic to statements on its website. BP also faced a social media attack from the spoof @BPGlobalPR Twitter account,[208] which amassed more than 100,000 followers in less than a month, compared to less than 10,000 for the official @BP_America account.

The account was set up by a California-based comedian who was annoyed at what he saw as BP's "spin" after the disaster. Some of the spoof tweets included "Catastrophe is a strong word, let's all agree to call it a whoopsie daisy." and "At night the gulf really doesn't look that bad." One reason the spoof account was so successful was that BP's own social media presence was so weak, enabling the spoof account to quickly fill the vacuum. Another was that frequently it was difficult to differentiate between the spoof tweets and some of the equally astounding quotes by BP executives, such as "What the hell did we do to deserve this?" and "The Gulf of Mexico is a very big ocean. The amount of oil and dispersant we are putting into it is tiny in relation to the total water volume", both by BP's then CEO Tony Hayward.[209]

Also in 2010 Nestle provided a classic case study of how to get it wrong. Greenpeace produced a hard-hitting YouTube video parodying the "Take a break" advertising tagline of its hero KitKat brand. The video[210] showed an office worker opening a KitKat, but instead of a chocolate bar he unsuspectingly takes a bite of an orang-utan's finger, as his horrified colleagues look on at the blood dripping down his chin. Nestle responded with threats of legal action and clumsy community management on its Facebook page with

[208] @BPGlobalPR parody Twitter account: http://cipr.co/12vJISb
[209] The Daily Beast, BP's Global PR vs BPGlobalPR blog post: http://cipr.co/VYGeCG
[210] KitKat orang-utan video on Vimeo: http://cipr.co/14UAyif

moderators attacking and threatening consumers. The campaign eventually resulted in victory for Greenpeace, with Nestle capitulating and agreeing to implement a plan to remove palm oil from its supply chain.

Another problem area of CSR is companies attempting to exploit CSR-related issues for publicity and marketing. A prime example of this is Kenco's Fan Forest Facebook app. For every 20,000 "likes" up to 100,000 Kenco donates £500 to buy an "acre of land" through the World Land Trust to protect Rainforest Alliance-certified farms.[211] This isn't CSR and is simply a crude attempt to buy likes and works out at a grand total of £2,500, or less than a penny a like. Kenco will almost certainly have spent more than that on creating and promoting the app. It doesn't instil confidence that it is anything more than a marketing gimmick in that almost two months after launching the app doesn't give any indication of the number of likes or success of the campaign.

New opportunities for CSR social media

It is perhaps no surprise that some of the companies that rank highest for CSR performance and reporting are also some of those demonstrating the most innovation in using social media to enhance and support their CSR programmes. This includes moving rapidly to adopt emerging new social media channels and networks such as image sharing website Pinterest.

Amongst those using Pinterest for CSR are IBM, which has a Pinterest profile that includes pin boards for "Building a Smarter Planet" and "Smarter Cities". Another is GE, which has more than 20 pin boards, many devoted to CSR-related activity such as "Eco Efficient" for "Small #green acts that help our environment in a big way". Pinterest can be used as an attractive "shop window" to share the best CSR imagery and refer people back to your other CSR platforms.

NGOs are also fast to take advantage of new platforms, as Greenpeace's use of Instagram for its Detox "Star in Our Next Video" campaign[212] shows.

[211] *Campaign*, Kenco launches Facebook campaign to save the rainforest: http://cipr.co/14FDVYP
[212] Greenpeace "Star in Our Next Campaign": http://cipr.co/14FEstQ

Greenpeace asked Instagram users to upload photos of themselves wearing plain t-shirts then tag them #detox #peoplepower with a caption saying the name of the fashion brand they want to stop using toxic chemicals. Greenpeace will use the images to make a video using the t-shirts as a canvas for the detox campaign images and text.

As the social web becomes ever more integral to people's lives it will become even more important for companies to start embedding social media into every aspect of their corporate social responsibility. By not doing so not only do they miss out on the opportunities it provides, but also open themselves up to vastly increased risks to their reputation and future survival.

Biography

Stuart Bruce MCIPR (@stuartbruce) is an independent international public relations trainer and consultant specializing in online corporate communications, digital public affairs and corporate social media. Based in the UK he travels to provide PR training and counsel to corporate and government clients in the European Union, Middle East and USA. In 2011, in partnership with the United Nations, Stuart led the world's first global study into FT Global 500 companies using social media for CSR. He was MD of a *PRWeek* Top 150 online PR consultancy, counselling clients such as Unilever, Sony Mobile, PayPal, HSBC and GSK.

Chapter 23

Richard Bailey

We've always been judged by the company we keep. We'll always be judged by our actions. This doesn't change, but there's never been more information publicly available to allow others to judge us on our words, our deeds and the company we keep.

I gained my first job in public relations in 1988 and though I'd been writing about technology for a living, I had not even heard of Tim Berners-Lee. Nor did his invention of the World Wide Web soon after that come to most people's attention until the middle of the next decade.

Back in 1988, wanting to leave publishing and thinking that I knew about the fledgling technology PR sector, I approached a specialist recruitment consultancy. They agreed to speak to the public relations consultancy I said most interested me – Aeberhard and Partners, better known as A Plus – and I secured an interview through this route. An interview with the consultancy founder John Aeberhard (it was then named after him, though it's since been absorbed into one of the global giants) was all it took to secure my break.

Presumably the company followed up with one or more of my referees. But what else could they do to check my credentials? I was not applying for an entry-level position, so a writing test was not appropriate. I'd met some of my new colleagues through my previous role so they knew that I'd been following the sector from the "other side". It was a simple process, mixing luck on my side, and judgement on John Aeberhard's. There was little science to it.

This is a narrative of what's changed in the past 25 years from the perspective of those wanting to make progress in a public relations career.

Some things haven't changed: employers want candidates with experience and expertise, and to choose people they consider the right fit for their organizations.

They may still ask for a CV, though these are fast becoming redundant in the age of LinkedIn and online portfolios, or even ask you to fill out their application form, particularly if they are a large, bureaucratic organization. You will still be interviewed for a job, typically face-to-face.

So what's changed?

You can no longer approach an interview expecting to build a first impression based on a clean slate. Even as you try to impress on a first date, your prospective partner will already have formed an opinion of you based on your online footprint.

It's expected in public relations that you'll be some or all of the following:

1. Networker: so how many followers do you have on Twitter? How many friends on Facebook?
2. Writer: how frequently do you update your blog?
3. Visual storyteller: are you active on YouTube, Instagram, Pinterest?
4. Competitor and a geek: what about your Klout/PeerIndex/Kred scores?
5. Experimenter: what can you tell us about Google+ or another new social network?

A low profile online will prevent you from gaining the first job, while an impressive online presence will recommend you to employers. There's one exception to this: if you've mastered the art of operating undercover like a secret agent, leaving no traces behind you, you'll be even more sought after for your expertise in managing online reputational risk.

We are all negotiating the boundaries between privacy and publicness – but for public relations practitioners it's more than an interesting question. It goes to the heart of what we do. We advise clients and companies on the what, when, how and who of information disclosure – based on our assessment of their own interests, the likely reputational impact and the wider question of public interest.

The biblical saying "physician, heal thyself" could apply to the public relations consultant. The would-be reputation expert should first attend to their own reputation before advising others.

Lies and league tables

Let's put another saying to the test: "he who lives by the sword, dies by the sword".

There were 24 contributors to the first version of *Share This: The Social Media Handbook for PR Professionals* published in 2012. The authors can be assumed to be experts in social media and figures of some standing in the industry, but let's not take this on trust. Let's use some freely available (and free) tools to rank them all objectively.

It took just a few minutes to find the Twitter handles of these experts and to add them to a PeerIndex group. PeerIndex[213] is one of several services that analyzes online influence and calculates an individual score. This gives us a league table ranking of these authors – from one to 24.

So, who tops the premier league, or rather, our Champions League? The energetic Mark Pack is the superstar (on 70/100), followed by our impressive editor Stephen Waddington (66).

If there were no surprises there, then how about third place for Rachel Miller (60)? Her expertise is in internal communication – not typically an area for the technology early adopter – and she's one of only two women in the top ten (league tables and statistics perhaps appealing more to the geeky, competitive male brain).

The scores are dynamic, so these numbers and the relative positions in the rankings will have changed by the time you read this – but you can check out the real-time ranking here.[214]

We can debate the validity of these statistics.

We should challenge the notion that the complexities of influence can be summarized by a single number (I recommend *Share This* contributor Philip Sheldrake's *The Business of Influence* if you want to explore this subject further).

---

[213]PeerIndex: http://cipr.co/yQN4mG

[214]*Share This* contributors group: http://cipr.co/UE9qBU

And yet at university, we assess students out of 100 for most of their work (and I confess we apply a lot of subjectivity in reaching this apparently hard, objective judgement). There's something appealingly quick and easy about numbers and rankings.

It took me just a few minutes. It's not beyond clients to rank potential consultants in such a way, or employers to assess competing job candidates like this. A high score won't be enough in itself to secure you a job or gain you a client, but a low score might mean you don't make it to the shortlist. High or low, you will be expected to know something about metrics if you present yourself as a social media expert.

I used PeerIndex for this table, but Klout scores are more widely known and are becoming something of an industry standard. Like them or loathe them, you will struggle to avoid these numbers.

Welcome to the era of measurement by metrics.

What do I know?

I've already told you that I'm a product of the dark ages. So what do I know of career planning in the age of social media?

Well, when I started a self-coded blog about public relations in 2001, I think that made me the second in the world after Phil Gomes from the US (Ireland's Tom Murphy came third[215]). I changed to a new publishing platform in 2003 and my PR Studies blog then ran for nine years before I retired it in 2012.

I'd not stopped blogging, but blogging had changed. I wanted to put more energy into an online magazine, published using WordPress (www.behindthespin.com). And I, like most others, had stopped leaving comments on blogs because most of our interactions were taking place elsewhere (primarily on Twitter).

As I've been in the same job for the past ten years, I can't claim that blogging has transformed my career. But it has made me much more widely known than I deserve to be and brought me various invitations to speak and to contribute to books such as this one.

Blogging – a personal website – is still the best way to manage your reputation online, since you control what you say and what others see about you.

---

[215]The New PR wiki: http://cipr.co/XXbWow. My initial blog, called The Write Effect, is not listed at it was replaced in 2003 by PR Studies

The discipline of writing with an audience in mind is a valuable one, especially as fewer people go into public relations with a journalism background today, since that avenue has been rapidly closing.

But it's not a quick fix: it will appeal more to the marathon runners than the sprinters among you.

And there are many hazards:

- It's very easy to start a blog, but very hard to keep it going. Think what it says about you if your last blog post was four, or six, or eight weeks ago or more.

  It's very easy to write and publish; it's very hard to edit your own writing. Careless words can cost careers: many of those interviewing you for PR jobs will have journalism backgrounds and for them the technicalities of writing (that's spelling and grammar) matter.

It's a thankless task. You may not gain many visitors, but you will certainly achieve far fewer comments. The only instant gratification to be achieved is in the satisfaction of having communicated your ideas well. **Do as I say.**

In the past ten years that I've been a university lecturer, I've seen many students making a name for themselves and kick-starting their careers through blogging and other forms of social media. Our industry welcomes innovation (and thrives on novelty), so there's an advantage to being first.

Here are some pioneering examples:

Graeme Anthony
A PR graduate who left a job in Manchester in 2010 and announced his arrival in London with a creative, interactive video CV.[216] This attracted widespread attention and led to a job offer from Frank PR, where he now works.

Ben Cotton
Edelman told me they'd been following this Leeds Metropolitan PR graduate for some time before selecting him for their graduate scheme. Now working as a social media manager for an insurance company in Ireland, Ben continues to provide helpful hints for students on his Social Web Thing[217] blog.

---

[216]CV in video: http://cipr.co/VJF9Co
[217]Social Web Thing: http://cipr.co/111rXki8

Stephen Davies

While still a PR student at Sunderland, he was dominating Google searches for what is a very common name in the English-speaking world through his social media presence. He went on to work for Edelman and Frank PR and now works for 33 Digital in London.

Richard Millington

This University of Gloucestershire Marketing graduate forged his own path, becoming a pioneer in the emerging field of online community management chronicled in his Feverbee[218] blog. His book *Buzzing Communities* was published in 2012.

Iliyana Stareva

This Bulgarian International Business graduate turned to public relations and social media for her dissertation at Plymouth University in 2012. Her work reached a wider audience when she summarized the research findings in an infographic.[219] Data visualization and sharing has been a big theme recently (as seen with the emergence of Instagram, Pinterest and infographics).

I'm pleased to have included students from other universities and other courses in this selection (one lesson of social media is that you can know many more people than those you have met), but I'm embarrassed to have listed only one woman, since female PR students massively outnumber males.

It's the same problem I identified earlier with the PeerIndex ranking of *Share This* contributors, where eight of the top 10 were men. I can name many talented and successful female PR graduates, but I can't ascribe their success to being early adopters of social media, so they don't appear here.

That said, at the time of writing, two-thirds of the top-ranked PR students on the *Behind the Spin* #socialstudent ranking were female.[220]

Recruitment as matchmaking

Speaking at a guest lecture at Leeds Metropolitan University in December 2012, PR consultant Helen Standing described the shift from recruitment

---

[218]Feverbee: http://cipr.co/XRGVgz

[219]Impact infographic: http://cipr.co/VJFaWx

[220]Socialstudent ranking: http://cipr.co/XRHNl6

based on advertising of vacancies to a more discreet "matchmaking" service today.

The implications of this are profound. You can't wait for a vacancy to come along; instead, you have to seize opportunities to build your personal profile. If you do this well, then opportunities (jobs, clients, internships or projects) will find you, just as Edelman found out about Ben Cotton before he'd even applied to them.

The best PR consultants gain business based on recommendation (and attract enquiries based on their reputation). Similarly, the best job seekers will come to the attention of employers through their online (and offline) profiles.

Here are some guidelines on to how to develop a strong online profile:

- **Be interesting:** Weber Shandwick's Colin Byrne tells graduates "it's better to know everything about something than something about everything". Your web presence is your opportunity to share your passion for shoes, for Formula One, or for anything else that excites you and a group of like-minded people.
- **Be well-connected:** We're all judged by the company we keep. What do your friends and followers say about you? If you only use Twitter to chat to a close circle of friends, then you're missing out on the potential of an open network.
- **Be easy to find:** Your name is unlikely to be unique, and you may be unlucky enough to share it with a celebrity. But you can still strive to make your name among the first searches within the field of PR. I'm not first among search results for "Richard Bailey", but I dominate search results for "Richard Bailey PR".
- **Tell a consistent story:** We all have multiple identities (we're viewed differently by friends, by family, at work and in public). Can you manage these multiple identities (some use different Twitter accounts and use different social networks for different social purposes)? Or does one aspect of our identity strengthen another? Mark Pack,[221] the social media superstar identified earlier, is a digital PR consultant and a Liberal Democrat activist. Expertise in one field brings him credibility in the other, so he feels no need to separate them.

---

[221]About Mark Pack: http://cipr.co/VoAVDs

- **Be useful:** In a world in which everyone has access to the media (blogs, Twitter etc), it can be very difficult to stand out by being consistently interesting. So another way to create a distinctive online identity is to be useful to others. It's one thing to create great content, but great content has little value until it comes to the attention of others. So there's an emerging role known as "curation". Just as museum curators select and present archaeological finds for others to appreciate, you can become a trusted curator of information in your chosen field. In an early and long-running example, PR academic Karen Russell has been presenting her selection of "The Week's Best for PR students" since March 2007.[222]

Finally, the following sources are highly recommended for those wanting to learn more about the concepts covered in this brief chapter, and for those wanting to know more about how to develop a presence on various social media sites.

- Chris Brogan and Julien Smith (2009) *Trust Agents: Using the Web to Build Influence, Improve Reputation, and Earn Trust*, John Wiley & Sons.
- Louis Halpern and Roy Murphy (2009) *Personal Reputation Management: Making the internet work for you*, Halpern Cowan.
- Antony Mayfield (2010) *Me and My Web Shadow: How to Manage Your Reputation Online*, A & C Black.
- Mark Schaefer (2012) *Return on Influence: The Revolutionary Power of Klout, Social Scoring and Influence Marketing*, McGraw-Hill.
- Victoria Tomlinson (2012) *From Student to Salary with Social Media*, Kindle.

Biography

Richard Bailey MCIPR (@behindthespin) is a public relations educator. He is a senior lecturer at Leeds Metropolitan University where he is course leader for CIPR professional courses, and he also leads executive level courses in traditional and digital media. He edits PR student magazine *Behind the Spin* and has helped guide many graduates into PR careers.

---

[222]The week's best: http://cipr.co/VJFh4D

Chapter 24

THE SOCIAL CEO

Jane Wilson

While the CEOs of the world's largest companies have been quick to grasp the power of social media for their organizations, they are yet to be convinced of the benefits of their own personal use. Here we examine the opportunities for leaders to build and benefit from a social presence and whether this means that the charismatic (and social) CEO is now here to stay.

When Lee Iacocca was given credit for single-handedly turning around the fortunes of US car giant Chrysler in the late 1970s, the cult of the charismatic CEO was born. Since then, a parade of celebrity leaders from GE's Jack Welch to Apple's Steve Jobs have embedded the view that it isn't enough for bosses to be capable managers and administrators relying on a solid senior team and a workforce that delivers. They have to be charismatic, media friendly leaders, prepared to take sole credit when things go well and blame when they don't.

However, the idea that the fortunes of a company are down solely to the CEO is going out of fashion. It creates an unsustainable expectation of the actual impact of any one leader and isn't a true reflection of the personalities of some of the men and women at the top of the world's most successful organizations.

How does this sit with the current trend of encouraging today's leaders to tweet, blog, post and share? With a more intense spotlight on business leaders, is this the right time to be selling even greater scrutiny to your CEO? And should corporate communications directors be nervous? As late as 2010, only one in seven members of the Ipsos Mori Reputation Council[223] of European

---

[223]Ipsos Mori's Reputation Council Insights and Ideas 2010: http://cipr.co/14UGt6s

PR heads reported that their CEO had a blog. Only a small number were keen that their CEO should write an external blog and the main reasons cited were commitment, authenticity and personality.

Social's trending with CEOs

From customer service teams to the public relations department, many of your colleagues may already contribute to the online presence of your organization or the brands you own. But, if the results of the 2012 IBM Global CEO study[224] are reflective of most organizations, then chances are your CEO or MD isn't one of them. The IBM study, which surveyed 1,709 CEOs worldwide, found that just 16% were using social media and only one reported having a blog. Also, a recent study by CEO.com and business intelligence firm DOMO[225] found that while social media is more prominent than ever amongst consumers, amongst Fortune 500 CEOs, only 7.6% are on Facebook, 4% use Twitter and less than 1% use Google+. LinkedIn was found to be the only network where business leaders are slightly ahead of the general public.

However, the IBM study predicts that the percentage of CEOs using social media is likely to grow to 57% within five years, and that social media will become the second most important way of engaging with staff employees and customers after face-to-face engagement. Richard Branson used his own LinkedIn account to respond to the IBM study in a post entitled "Why aren't more business leaders online?".[226] In it, he says that "CEOs have the opportunity to set the bar. By ignoring social networks, they are potentially missing a trick."

But not all leaders are entrepreneurs and certainly not all leaders have Richard Branson's natural talent for communication or his powerful personal brand. In fact, if you work in a FTSE 100 company, there's a 50% chance that your CEO has a finance background[227] and here may be a good reason why

---

[224]IBM Global CEO Study 2012, Leading Through Connections: http://cipr.co/WCc1JD
[225]2012 Fortune 500 Social CEO Index: http://cipr.co/XXeCeJ
[226]Why aren't more business leaders online?: http://cipr.co/X8s43b
[227]Robert Half FTSE 100 Tracker 2011: http://cipr.co/Xqk75A

THE SOCIAL CEO | 219

they have naturally gravitated towards numbers more than words. This is important when deciding whether a CEO writes their own copy and manages their own accounts (preferable if they have the time and talent to do so) or works with one or two trusted advisors to create content that they direct and ultimately sign off on before publication.

Make me social

If your CEO has taken Branson's words to heart and wants a social media presence, he or she will hopefully seek your advice as the communications expert in your organization. Just as there is no single template for the perfect CEO, there is no template for how leaders should engage with social media. So, it's best to start by applying some first principles of Public Relations.

Before a CEO takes the social media plunge, it is important that they understand the context in which their content will appear. If their motivation is to enhance the reputation of the organization that they lead, then what they say and do has to complement what's already happening. Encourage them to talk to those employees who already use social media on behalf of the company, ask for their input and opinion on your social policy and ask them to consider how it would apply to them. Get them to look at the content your organization produces and read the feedback it gets. The potential upside of this exercise is that you may discover an existing platform or vehicle such as a regular blog on the company website that your CEO can use in a less risky and less time-consuming way than, say, daily Twitter updates, personal blogs and LinkedIn activity.

Another contextual element to consider is the regulatory environment in which you operate. For instance, the same rules around market sensitivity apply to a tweet from the CEO as a formal company announcement. And if the CEO really is a social media novice then it is also worth spending some time taking them through the basics. Chapters 1 and 9 of *Share This*[228] are a good starting point.

---

[228]S. Waddington *et al*, *Share This. The Social Media Handbook for PR Professionals*, John Wiley & Sons, 2012, ISBN 978-1-118-40484-3.

All views my own

Once the context has been set, it's time to consider content, audiences, platforms and feedback. CEOs must then ask themselves what aspects of their leadership can be enhanced using social media. Who do they want to influence, why and to what end? If they can't come up with a single business benefit then this might not be the best use of their time.

Help them to prioritize their social media activity by audience. In the same way as you would for your organization, create a simple grid with stakeholder, positioning and platforms/locations, using data to populate the location boxes.

Stakeholder	Positioning	Twitter	LinkedIn	Facebook	Company Website
Employees	We value our employees	X		X	X
Customers	We produce great content	X		X	X
Regulators	We are responsible broadcasters	X	X		X
Advertisers	We are innovative and embrace new technology	X			X
Investors	We have long-term financial growth plans				X

The social media footprint for the CEO of a radio station

This will help a CEO prioritize activity, content and key messages according to the time and resources available to them.

What a CEO says on a blog, on Twitter, in a video, once it is online, has a permanence that can come back to haunt them if they are subsequently proved wrong or change their mind. A social media profile can also be a lightning rod for comment (good and bad). As supporters and detractors seek a public way to engage with the CEO on an issue, there is a risk of being dragged into a public dispute if not properly managed. This can have significant implications for an organization.

The standard disclaimer "all views my own" is fine when an account executive or junior manager comments on an issue, but in today's world where CEOs are so inextricably linked to the organizations they lead, this doesn't wash. CEOs must remember that to the public, their views and those of the organization are considered to be one and the same. They must also remember that the urge to provide an immediate and public fix to a customer service issue highlighted to them on Twitter, for instance, can be a strong but risky one and a policy for dealing with customer complaints that are directed at the CEO should be agreed in advance.

Buy me, trust me, love me

Once a CEO has decided who they want to reach and which platforms are best suited to the audience and the environment, they must then focus on their online persona. Whilst the advice "to thine own self be true" is important, each of us has the very human ability to adapt language, style and presentation to suit an audience. So, unless a CEO decides that they desperately want to use this opportunity to talk about their deep love of topiary or deep sea diving, they should focus their social media persona on the elements of their personality that they bring to their professional life. They should ask themselves "Would I share this information with a group of employees, at a shareholder meeting or an industry event?" If a CEO regularly uses anecdotes from their non-professional life to illustrate speeches and presentations, then these will probably go down well online. If not, then they are likely to jar with the existing reputation that they have in the real world. The number one rule is to be authentic. The number two rule is that authenticity can't be faked and not everyone needs to be cool, funny or controversial.

There are three very broad considerations for a CEO when considering how they want to be perceived – in person and on social media. They are driven by how they want the audience to respond:

Buy me

Using social media activity to promote brands as the personal embodiment of the organization. This is often easiest for entrepreneurs to achieve as they will frequently have a more natural brand affiliation.

Trust me

Using social media activity to position the CEO as an industry authority or for the purpose of promoting a campaign or cause. This is often valuable when there is important legislation pending that could affect a company, or the threat, for instance, of a takeover, where the CEO wants to build a profile as a trusted industry leader.

Love me

Using social media to create a human face for an organization, or to make the CEO themselves more human in the eyes of the public. Useful if a new CEO takes over with a very different personal style and/or strategy that they want to embed quickly as a new way forward for an organization.

The charismatic CEO who takes to social media like a duck to water must remember that the more a CEO hogs the limelight and takes sole credit (and possibly the related salary) when the going is good, so too will they be held responsible when things get tough. And if a CEO strays from the advice of staying authentic and starts to believe their own hype, then good online content can quickly descend into the ranting of the guy at the end of the bar who thinks everyone is listening when in fact the landlord is getting ready to chuck him out.

The final question for CEOs is whether they are prepared to engage. If "All the world's a stage, and all the men and women merely players", then for CEOs the world of social media can be like the infamous Glasgow Empire, where even the brightest stars died with a barbed heckle from the stalls.

With a little preparation, CEOs can decide whether social media engagement is right for them, how and where they will do it, what they will say and how much they will engage in two-way dialogue.

Eight recommendations for the social CEO

1. Listening is important
   Don't just broadcast. Encourage comments if you blog, and use it as an efficient way to respond to feedback. Plan in advance the level of engagement you are comfortable with.
2. Size doesn't always matter
   You don't have to be a FTSE 100 CEO to get heard if you're innovative, entertaining, controversial or informative.

3. Don't bare all

   You're not on Oprah and the world does not need to know every intimate moment of your life – a glimpse, not a guided tour.

4. Be authentic

   Don't be tempted to try to make yourself more "interesting" than you are. You're a CEO for goodness sake. You've got this far without being cool!

5. You can be wrong sometimes

   Once you've tweeted or blogged on a subject, you may change your mind or be proved wrong in future. That's okay now and again. It happens to everyone. Don't try to hide it but do remember to fact check before publishing to minimize this risk.

6. Share the limelight

   Whether it's having guest bloggers on your site or frequent mentions of your colleagues or customers, shine the spotlight on others now and again.

7. Consider the regulatory environment

   Don't share anything you wouldn't be happy seeing on the companies pages of the *Financial Times.*

8. Don't panic when it hits the fan

   If you already have a social media presence, use it as part of your organization's crisis communication activity. Don't shut it down unless there are strong reputational or legal reasons to do so. This is the equivalent of hiding under the blankets until the monster goes away.

Undoubtedly there are risks, but for a CEO who takes the time to listen, engage and build a social media presence, the upsides are huge. People communicate with other people, not companies, and when the man or woman at the top is visible, accessible and engaged, it can reap rewards for any organization.

We'll end with a quote from the original charismatic CEO. When responding on his own website on why he's come out of retirement, Lee Iacocca said (without blushing) "I can't sit on the side-lines when my country needs me". Consider using this when persuading your CEO to get social.

Biography

Jane Wilson (@CEO_CIPR) is the CEO of the CIPR, a Non-Executive Director and business communications expert. With a career in leadership, corporate communications, public affairs and marketing roles she has also gained extensive M&A and change management experience at a senior level within public and private companies. She is a regular blogger, media commentator and conference speaker in the UK and internationally. Her experience spans in-house and agency roles across a range of creative industries.

Chapter 25

Julio Romo

Social media has broken down international barriers and borders. Networks like Facebook, Twitter and Weibo enable us to reach out and listen to conversations overseas. But while these networks are the glue that connects the world today, it is the language, culture and content that shapes how reputations are built and destroyed.

Technology and globalization have brought countries and cultures closer to our front doors. They have made the world a smaller place. Distances that separated us 25 years ago no longer feel that great. And thanks to the internet and mobile phones, today we can connect to people, brands and causes wherever they might be.

Social media has broken down the barrier of distance and time. Have a look at your Facebook or Twitter account and you will see that your friends and those you follow are spread out across the globe. The world today is your marketplace.

According to Martin Albrow and Elizabeth King, globalization[229] is the concept "by which the peoples of the world are incorporated into a single world society". Social media has accelerated globalization.

Social media has empowered people around the world. It has enabled the sharing of comment and collateral in real time. It has fuelled the "Arab Spring", outed corrupt government officials in China and given the world K-pop sensation Psy.

---

[229]Globalisation: Knowledge and Society – Martin Albrow and Elizabeth King: http://cipr.co/WwrMUm

Each of these events has gained notoriety not so much because of the social networks themselves, but because of what people around the world shared on these platforms. It is about people, about individuals and how they identify with content and the conversations that are taking place online. It is also about journalists and bloggers who listen and amplify those conversations. It is this that is challenging public relations.

Social media and globalization

The Chartered Institute of Public Relations describes PR as "the planned and sustained effort to establish and maintain goodwill and mutual understanding between an organisation and its publics". To achieve this "mutual understanding" what is important for PRs are not the networks themselves, but the people on them, their culture, lifestyle and behaviours. Because, while the networks bring people together, it is the PR's skill to understand behaviour, culture and lifestyle that enables organizations to better engage with their audiences.

But what do you need to consider if you want to build your brand or reputation overseas? What are the differences in culture that could stop you in your tracks if you ignore them?

To position your brand, organization or individual internationally there are some essential points to remember. There is no template solution. Above all, the most important point that you need to focus on in international social media is people and what makes them unique in the countries in which you are trying to build a reputation.

Networks by countries

Facebook is the biggest social network in the world. But while it is an "Anglo-Saxon" network, the statistics show that four out of the top five countries with the most active accounts include Brazil, India, Indonesia and Mexico – nations with healthy economic growth figures.

Let it be Facebook, Twitter, Mixi or QQ, always look at the numbers to consider which is the best platform to reach your audiences. Do not just look at the number of users in each country. Consider the penetration rate – the number of active accounts v. the total population or users online today.

Indonesia, for example, has an impressive 50 million active accounts, but a population of 237 million. While in India there are 62 million users, giving Facebook a penetration of just over 5% of 1.2 billion!

China, which blocks international networks, has Weibo, QQ and RenRen. Together these three dominate social media in the country. And international companies with operations in China have not ignored these fast-growing networks.

The CME Group (@CMEGroup), owner of the Dow Jones Industrial Average and Dow Jones Indexes, is one international company that has taken to international social media. CME Group's Executive Director for Corporate Communications, Allan Schoenberg (@AllanSchoenberg), says that the company took to Facebook five years ago "as an experiment". They found that customers were talking about them, the exchange and what was happening in the marketplace.

The company now has a presence on Twitter, Google+, LinkedIn and even Pinterest. With Asia being a target market, the group decided to set itself up on China's micro-blogging service Weibo, a network with over 360 million registered users that is seen as a hybrid of Facebook and Twitter. The attraction to Weibo for CME Group was that this social network gave it access to "roughly 36.5 million active users daily", an identified group of which were interested in the financial markets.

Since it set up its Weibo account in November 2011, CME Group has built a strong presence in the country, reaching out to over 24,000 individuals, with 17.9% of its followers in the southern economic heartland of Guangzhou, while followers from Beijing and Shanghai represent 8.1 and 7.4% respectively.

At the same time, rather than take to YouTube to reach stakeholders in China, CME Group set up two channels on China's popular YouKu video sharing site. The company uses one channel to promote corporate videos and the other to share twice-daily market commentary videos.

The move to use popular local social networks was made not just because of the Chinese shift ban of Western social networking sites, but because it made sense to have a presence on the networks in which its target audiences were spending their time.

Language and culture

Social networks are just that, networks. They are a hub for people, who speak different languages and dialects, and whose cultures shape their individual behaviour.

Such has been the adoption of Twitter in the Arab world that the micro-blogging giant decided to release an Arabic interface.[230] Since this release, and according to Dubai School of Government's influential Arab Social Media Report,[231] Arabic is now "the fastest growing language ever on Twitter".

The same report confirms that while "English and Arabic are the dominant languages in the Arab region," tweets in Arabic almost doubled those in English by March 2012 (62.1% and 32.6% respectively). Tweets made in Arabic in the United Arab Emirates showed the greatest jump, from 17% in March 2011 to 26% in 2012.

The same survey found that in Gulf Cooperation Countries social media has helped to enforce national identities. Eighty five per cent of people in Egypt, 83% in Bahrain and 78 and 73% respectively in Saudi Arabia and the UAE said that social networking has made them feel they have stronger social links with fellow citizens.

While your audience might understand English, never rely on this fact. After all, if your audience mother tongue is Arabic, Farsi, Bahasa Melayu or Indonesian, then why not communicate in their own language? After all, international public relations is about engagement on their terms and in their language.

And do not consider using translation tools. Language is individual and technology-based translators can create embarrassment for you and your brand. And with the speed of retweets, that dodgy translation can trend and create issues where there should have been none.

Take Westfield Stratford City Shopping Centre, which, during the London 2012 Olympics, displayed huge banners in Arabic to welcome visitors from around the world. The words on the signs were completely incoherent. Speaking to the BBC, a spokesperson for the Council of Arab-British Understanding

---

[230]Twitter Now Available in Arabic, Farsi, Hebrew and Urdu – Twitter Blog: http://cipr.co/XqrvOy
[231]Arab Social Media Report – Dubai School of Government: http://cipr.co/11Pn9Ia

said, "It beggars belief they cannot even write 'welcome' in Arabic. What will our Olympic guests be thinking? It is cringeworthy."[232]

Above all, make sure that your market engagement is led by a person that can speak the language in the country in which you are managing the outreach. Native speakers understand that cultural understanding can add value and safeguard you from mistakes.

But language is not the only point to bear in mind when planning social communications initiatives. Japan, for example, has adopted Twitter to the extent that over 14% of the world's tweets were in Japanese[233] in October 2011. That is impressive. One of the reasons for Twitter's popularity in Japan is because culturally Japanese people prefer to remain anonymous online, something that Facebook has not been able to offer because of its real name policy.

But of course, it isn't just about language, but also about culture and lifestyle. For example, the weekend in some countries in The Gulf and Middle East is on Friday and Saturday. But not all: in Saudi Arabia it's on Thursday and Friday. And never forget national holidays and festivals, which are based on religion or days of national significance.

Desktop v. mobile

In April 2010 the self-proclaimed "Queen of the Net" Mary Meeker, formerly with Morgan Stanley (@MorganStanley) and now at Venture Capital Firm Kleiner Perkins Caufield & Byers (@kpcb), predicted in her 2010 Internet Trends Report that within the following five years "more users will connect to the Internet over mobile devices than desktop PCs". Meeker gave the date of 2014 for when the majority of the world would be using a mobile device to access the internet.

According to recent data from the International Telecommunications Union[234] though, some countries already have a majority of people accessing the internet via mobile broadband subscriptions compared to fixed wired subscriptions.

---

[232]London 2012: Westfield Arabic Banners "Incoherent" – BBC News: http://cipr.co/121jKkY
[233]39% Of All Tweets Are In English, But Arabic Now Fastest-Growing Language On Twitter
[234]Mediabistro.com: http://cipr.co/14UPb4C)

Knowing how people access the internet and social networking sites is essential.

Country	Fixed (Wired) Broadband Subscriptions per 100 Inhabitants 2011	Active Mobile Broadband Subscriptions per 100 Inhabitants 2011
BRIC Nations		
Brazil	8.6	20.9
Russia	12.2	47.9
India	1.0	1.9
China	11.6	9.5
CIVEST Nations		
Colombia	6.9	3.7
Indonesia	1.1	22.2
Vietnam	4.3	18.0
Egypt	2.2	21.0
Turkey	10.3	8.8
South Africa	1.8	19.8

How people access the internet

Data from the International Telecommunications Union and UNESCO'S Broadband Commission for Digital Development *The State of Broadband 2012 Report*.[235]

Would you develop a campaign designed to be activated on desktops when the majority of your target audience in Brazil, Russia and Indonesia accesses the internet through iPhones or Android devices? You wouldn't.

The reliance of mobile broadband is one reason why apps like Instagram are so popular in countries in Asia, says Jon Russell in The Next Web blog.[236]

Social networks like Facebook, Twitter and Google+ have mobile apps available in multiple languages for international markets. But mobile instant messaging apps are already crossing the divide to desktop.

---

[235]International Telecommunications Union: http://cipr.co/11PnXwB

[236]International Telecommunications Union and UNESCO'S Broadband Commission for Digital Development: http://cipr.co/WRos2E

Japanese instant messaging app Line has gained over 70 million users since it first launched in June 2011. With over 32 million accounts in Japan alone, the application, which also allows users to send each other images, video, audio media messages and make free VoIP calls, has gained a 40% penetration in its home market.

So popular has Line become in Japan that the country's Prime Minister's Office has set up an account, which will be used to provide essential information in the event of an emergency or disaster. And knowing that so many Japanese nationals use Line on their mobiles, it is a move that signals how the government is reaching out to citizens.

The move to establish itself a presence in English on social networking sites is new for Japan's government.

On 3 March 2011, Japan was shaken by the magnitude 9.0 Tōhoku earthquake. The resulting tsunami caused devastation across the northeastern seaboard of Japan.

Before the quake, Japan's government communications had been focused on internal conversations. This changed after the quake, when research identified that the reputation of "Brand Japan" had been damaged. There was a clear need for a communications team that focused on engaging with international influencers overseas. Immediately, a Global Communications Department within the Prime Minister's Office was set up.

Led by Noriyuki Shikata (@NoriShikata) the brief was to address global issues and "overcome reputational damage" following the quake, as well as regain Japan's credibility, especially as a manufacturing base and investment destination. Two weeks later the department set up a Twitter account in English for the Prime Minister's Office of Japan (@JPN_PMO). This was followed by the creation of a dedicated website in English for the Prime Minister's Office and account on Facebook and Weibo.

Immediately, the new Global Communications Department started to be followed on Twitter by journalists and media outlets that it was targeting. Its presence on these platforms also enabled it to be fleet of foot and identify sentiment, data that enabled it to know the view of the international stakeholders it wanted to engage with.

The social media that join the world together is highlighting the differences between us. Professional communicators must understand these. More than ever before PRs have to understand people. There is no excuse for dragnet communications campaigns that ignore what people are like, the beliefs that they have and the tools that they use to share the opinions.

To be successful in international social media there is a prerequisite to be forensic. To localize your communications. People appreciate being understood, and with sufficient commitment they will reward you with the mutual understanding that you work for.

Speaking to *Forbes* magazine *Economist* Global Correspondent Vijay V. Vaitheeswaran reminds us that, initially, most corporations were caught out by the explosion of social media. However, "through trial and error many are now doing better. They must, as the future belongs to firms that can best harness the global trend toward open, networked and user-driven approaches to innovation."[237]

Biography

Julio Romo MCIPR (@twofourseven) is an International PR, Social Media Consultant and Digital Strategist. He has over 15 years' experience working with clients in the UK, mainland Europe, The Gulf and Asia, advising and delivering strategic training to governments, financial services institutions, telecom companies and sports personalities. He speaks at conferences and comments on how digital and social is changing the face of business and communications. You can reach him through his blog at www.twofourseven. co.uk.

---

[237]Suvarnabhumi Airport in Thailand tops Instagram's list of most photographed places in 2012 – The Next Web: http://cipr.co/XXkjt2

Part VI

Business Change and Opportunities for the Public Relations Industry

Chapter 26

Jed Hallam

Here we do not examine the importance of social business, or even its implications, but instead look at the critical stages to laying the foundations of a social business. From creating new job roles and setting up working groups, to changing culture and encouraging mistakes – becoming a social business won't happen overnight, but following these key stages will help to start the ball rolling.

Over the last few years the concept of "social business" has entered the zeitgeist – a combination of the rise in technology (leading to an increasingly demanding consumer) and an appetite for agility within businesses has led to this. What was initially seen as a communications tool for public relations and marketing practitioners in 2005 is now becoming an area of interest to the entire business, from the CEO to the IT department – this change has had an impact on everyone.

Then add the fact that the new generation of business leaders is "digitally native" (i.e. they've never experienced life without an internet connection) and it's easy to see that the future of business will be neither offline nor online – it will be integrated. I've discussed this extensively in the past, mainly in my book *The Social Media Manifesto*[238] (Palgrave Macmillan, 2012), but a question that is repeatedly asked of me is: But how do we respond to this?

So, my purpose is not to explain the impact or rationale of social business, but instead to look at the two major challenges that businesses face in starting to incorporate social technology into their organization. However, before we

---

[238]J. Hallam, *The Social Media Manifesto*, Palgrave Macmillan, 2012, ISBN 1137271418

do this, it's important to recognize two overlying trends – convergence and complexity. These are, fundamentally, the two themes that cause the greatest issue for businesses looking to change, and within both there are organizational and cultural challenges.

Convergence

I think I may have twisted Henry Jenkins's definition beyond the limits of its original incarnation, but in my mind convergence is the increasing integration between online and offline – and the next generation certainly doesn't see the boundaries between the two, they just don't make that distinction. The increasing access to always-on internet (primarily through mobile) now means that there's never been a smaller gap between online and offline – from Apple's iMessage to FourSquare deals – the social web has become ubiquitous in our offline lives.

This has two major impacts on the way in which an organization operates: externally and internally. Externally means that your customers expect to always have a point of contact – in the same way that it's annoying when the local Post Office closes at 5pm (well before you've inevitably left work) or when a washing machine breaks down the evening before a wedding – it'd be incredibly powerful for a customer service team to help fix the problem that very evening, rather than waiting for a plumber to visit a few days later.

The challenge is around creating an "always-on" culture that doesn't fatigue your employees – ensuring that "flexi-time" is actually flexible, so that when an employee is spending an entire Sunday speaking to someone influential on behalf of your business, they're compensated accordingly. In the same way, if your customer care team is helping someone to fix a product or explain a part of a service in the middle of the night, then this has a massive impact on the relationship with your consumer – and it should be recognized and encouraged.

This convergence has to be reflected in the organization too – with social technology and insight being built into the business. It is no longer acceptable to have a "digital strategy" when consumers no longer separate the two. A business isn't viewed by a consumer as multiple departments and third-party agencies – it's seen as a single brand, and we should endeavour to convey this – our employees shouldn't be putting forward a mixed brand message, and this is inevitable when "digital" is separated from business strategy.

There are two key steps to take when trying to build a single brand message:

1. Integrate online and offline strategy – creating a truly integrated strategy, and
2. Ensure that your internal communications messaging is clear. The same brand message should reach the human resources department as the message that reaches the marketing team.

Complexity

With the rise in technology we're also seeing a massive influx of data – data that has, so far (apart from a few exceptions), been kept within the marketing function of many organizations. Sentiment, share of voice, spread of messaging, complaints, queries – all of this data is usually circulated within the marketing department in a beautifully designed PowerPoint document at the end of each month.

However, what if this was circulated around the entire organization? What if different departments could ask for different sets of data to be collected? What about market data? Competitor data? Information from influencers on potential product or service developments? How can we use data to become more intelligent and responsive – across the whole organization? The obvious problem that this throws up is the sheer volume of data. Big Data.

The challenge with this new data is the complexity that surrounds it. How do we utilize the information in the most efficient way, without misinterpreting it? The major challenge at the heart of this issue is the quality of data – sentiment being the best example of the somewhat shaky quality of data that the social web throws up. With automated analysis of sentiment come error rates – sometimes as high as 60% – which is not reliable enough to base business decisions on. The key is to manually track data over long periods of time, conducting a balance of micro and macro analysis, and trying to spot emerging trends.

In *The Social Media Manifesto*, I suggest that this should be the responsibility of a new role within the organization – the Chief Data Officer. This position would look to pull social data into the organization, review and weight that data accordingly, then collate it with other business data, feeding it into the rest of the organization as appropriate.

On top of this external social data, there is also the internal social data that should be recognized and understood. Traditionally, businesses have "brand guardians": people within the organization that are responsible for shaping brand perception and reputation. The social web has blown this apart, and now within a couple of minutes a disgruntled employee could have published content that spreads the globe – overriding any "positive spin" that may have been built.

Many organizations have responded to this by issuing totalitarian "social media guidelines", but a more social way of approaching this issue would be to improve internal communications using social media, giving every employee an understanding of how your organization treats social technology, and understanding where the pockets of influence sit within your organization (outside of hierarchical structures). Combine this with your organization's external networks (say, if an analyst has a personal friendship with an influential journalist) and you can begin to build a bigger picture of your organization's "influence eco-system".

Overriding this complexity isn't easy, however, setting up an internal working group that bridges the whole organization should help to begin to overcome the silos that exist within traditional business structures. In time, this working group can meet less and less frequently as the responsibility for social dissipates across the organization – eventually leading to it being an inherent part of everyone's roles and responsibilities. This type of cultural shift is incredibly important, but it won't happen overnight.

Becoming a social business takes time and, more importantly, leadership. While individual departments can push their thinking forwards, it remains siloed, and (eventually) causes more problems when your organization is trying to create the single brand impressions that are so valuable to consumers. With strong leadership and a thorough understanding of the implications of what social business actually means and entails, the whole business can work together to help create that sort of culture.

As promised at the start of this chapter, I believe that there are five key steps to becoming a social business. While they are by no means the entire process, they are five stages and should begin to prepare your organization for becoming more social and innovative.

1. Appoint someone within the organization to understand the data – the job title doesn't matter, but the responsibility does. Understanding the validity of different types of social data and the impact its insights have is incredibly important – and moving that data between departments. As Craig Mundie, head of research and strategy at Microsoft, said in a recent *Economist* article:

"data are becoming the new raw material of business: an economic input almost on a par with capital and labour".[239] This data shouldn't be overlooked or assigned to a graduate or intern.

2. Create a working group across the business with a senior member of staff from each department involved. This will allow the social data collected to be fed into the appropriate departments and used as efficiently as possible. This needs to be led by a senior member of the leadership team and, ideally, involve the entire c-suite – this ensures that the transition is being taken seriously, and that its impact is being measured based on business results, rather than meaningless "vanity" metrics such as "buzz". This team should have regular (weekly) meetings to assess the progress of each department, share best practice, and help to then produce a case study for communicating this process to the rest of the business.

3. It's important that everyone within the organization understands that in a converged world, "social media" is not the responsibility of a single person. It is everyone's responsibility and your consumers expect your organization to behave that way. As part of the working group's responsibilities, communicating to the wider organization is key. If your business is to create a single brand impression, then providing every member of the organization with an understanding of "the vision" (I hate myself for writing that phrase, rest assured) is part of that process. It also allows employees outside of the working group to contribute ideas – always remember that innovation doesn't come from a job title, it comes from experience and secondary knowledge.

4. Allow people to make mistakes – an organization that is scared of failure won't break any new ground or become innovative – but provide a framework (think Google's 20% time). Innovation isn't limited to a single department. While this tends to conjure images of bean bags in reception and all-business paintballing, it shouldn't be viewed as an activity to appease Generation Y – it's an important culture to create that facilitates ideas, engendering innovation, rather than encouraging people to wear novelty t-shirts and high-five each other every morning. Innovation is an integral part of any business that wants to sustain itself and grow beyond the first three years – encourage your employees to listen to your consumers (using social technology) and not be afraid to make suggestions and you'll have the whole organization thinking about the future of your business, not just the CEO.

---

[239]Data, data everywhere, Kenneth Cukier, *Economist*, 27 February 2010

5. Create an open framework for using your network – both inside and outside of the organization. Influence doesn't spread from one department or one consumer group – it's everywhere. So learn to listen to it, and use it appropriately. This is not intended to be a Big Brother exercise – far from it – instead this is about understanding the power of your employees, giving them access to your consumers (and potential new consumers) and helping them to spread the brand message. This works in a number of stages: (1) understanding how your employees communicate with each other outside of the hierarchical structure of the business, and (2) understanding how they communicate with those outside of the organization (this sounds more difficult than it is – it could be a simple Facebook application that allows you to view the secondary and tertiary networks of your business).

Becoming a social business isn't limited to having a Twitter account (just take a walk around Burberry's Regent St store), and it's certainly not limited to having "buzz" around your products and services (just ask the O2 social media customer service team). It's about true integration with your consumers; it's about producing better products and services, and being more reactive to the needs of your consumers. Becoming a social business isn't a short-term process, but it will certainly reap long-term rewards. From becoming more engaged with your employees, to over-delivering on product and service development – and all this combines to drive down costs and drive up profit.

Biography

Jed Hallam (@jedhallam) is the Head of Social Strategy at Mindshare, and author of the best-selling *Social Media Manifesto*. Amongst Jed's clients are Three, first direct, and Mazda. Prior to joining Mindshare, he was the Social Director at VCCP, working on O2, Coca-Cola, Unilever, and McDonalds. Jed helped to launch and build Wolfstar Consultancy (one of the UK's first social media consultancies) where, in his capacity of Head of Innovation, he worked with global clients such as GlaxoSmithKline, Discovery Channel, PayPal, and Sony Ericsson. Jed is recognized as one of the most influential marketing bloggers in the world by AdAge, and he regularly speaks at conferences around the world on social business strategy. He has been awarded many PR and Marketing awards, as well as contributing numerous essays to popular marketing books.

Chapter 27

Katy Howell

As the potential value of social media reaches the boardroom, the big question looms large: can social media drive sales? This chapter explores ways in which to monetize conversations and connections, detailing best practice and latest innovations in social commerce.

There are many ways in which to evaluate results from social media, but none as sharp or as pleasing to the board as increasing sales. It seems obvious, then, that at least some part of your social media programme directly drives purchases. This is social commerce.

Back in 2010, Facebook founder, Mark Zuckerberg, saw the opportunity. He said: "If I had to guess, social commerce is next to blow up." Since then all the tech providers, app developers, platforms and social networks are investing in turning chatter into money.

Defining social commerce

The term social commerce isn't new. In fact, it was used by Yahoo! in November 2005. The phrase social commerce is now well established and can be briefly described as transactions resulting from social media.

Brands, businesses and entrepreneurs that are experimenting in social selling are learning quickly how social media is both a driver and contributor to sales.

There are doubters though. A Forrester Research analyst was quoted as saying that trading on Facebook is "like trying to sell stuff to people while they're hanging out with their friends at the bar". On the face of it, that seems like a sensible conclusion. After all, the thinking goes, we spend time on our networks to be with friends – not really to shop.

IBM's 2012 Black Friday[240] report reveals how poorly social estates performed in delivering last click to sale. The analysis suggests that Facebook, Twitter, LinkedIn, and YouTube generated 0.34% of all online sales on Black Friday, down 35% from 2011.

Yet there are documented successes, indicating significant promise and growth potential. Evidence that tells us that Black Friday aside, we should not dismiss the sales opportunity so fast:

- When a user posts on their news feed that they have bought a ticket, Ticketmaster gains an additional $5.30 from socially connected friends wanting to attend the same event.
- Fab.com reports a 15% conversion rate[241] from traffic generated through discovery in news feeds and shares in social media.
- Play.com attributes £2 million of sales to Facebook, with engaged fans spending 24% more than those that didn't come from the social network.

There is confidence in the future success of social commerce. Booz & Co research[242] estimates that social commerce sales will total $30 billion worldwide by 2015. Analysis of customers' purchase journeys reveals the value social has in contributing to the sale – 71% of consumers[243] are more likely to purchase based on social media referrals. People connect, discuss, review and rate products and services. It appears that when you look beyond last click data, social media is increasingly essential to purchase decisions.

Technology continues to evolve, making selling through social easier, but technology is not the whole story. In truth, social selling is more complex. It is much more akin to real-world shopping where understanding behaviours

---

is the key to unlocking sales. Because when you understand your audience, you can design your social activity to sell and influence purchase.

There are four social shopping behaviours that inform your social commerce approach:

IMPULSIVE PURCHASES	INFLUENCED TO BUY	COLLABORATIVE PURCHASES	BUYING EVERYWHERE
Direct sales	Talk numbers	Crowd sourcing	Multichannel
Discounts	Share results	Co-creation	Integration
Discovery	Activate advocacy	Business intelligence	Attribution

©immediatefuture

Impulsive purchases: harnessing the spontaneous buyer

Social media is not the natural home of shopping. When people want to buy, they don't go to their social networks; they go to search, retail stores, review sites and to the shops with specific intentions.

Many of the original Facebook storefronts launched by Gap, Old Navy and Gamestop are now closed. ASOS too launched a Facebook store in January 2011 that closed a year or so later. Most withdrew due to poor sales. People don't quite trust transacting within Facebook just yet; nor do they tend to return to pages once they've "liked" them. Social stores that replicated the whole catalogue often performed much slower. Not a great experience.

Still, this doesn't prove that social networks don't have value as sales channels. It is more likely that businesses haven't yet identified the right way to approach consumers on social platforms.

What is apparent is that people will buy on social through impulse. A report from Ryan Partnership[244] suggests 22% of those who follow retailers

---

[244]Retailers' Social Media Efforts Seen Driving Product Trials, Impulse Buys: http://cipr.co/11PChW1

have been influenced to make an unplanned purchase, and 15% report having spent more as a consequence. Interestingly, the least influential in driving unplanned purchases were search engines (5%).

Get the timing, proposition and mechanics right and businesses can tap into impulse purchases. There are three ways to motivate a spontaneous purchase:

1. Direct links unlock sales

Facebook rather leads the charge on driving sales to sites outside of the network. By tapping into news streams it is proven to deliver significant returns. According to Burberry, last year 29.1% of site traffic was from Facebook.

But Facebook has competition. The jewellery and accessories e-tailer Boticca claims that integrated "Pinterest buttons" on its website assist around 10% of sales and bring 86% of visits from new customers. Twitter, too, is not to be outdone. For Zappos an order shared on Twitter generates $33.66 in sales: 45 times that of a Pin.[245]

Facebook realizes the value of the impulse purchase and is looking at ways to harness the opportunity. It is currently allowing US consumers to purchase gifts for friends – tapping into events such as birthdays. Already proving to be successful, it is likely to roll out in the UK in 2013.

Timeliness and frequency are crucial for success. By focusing on the posts, tweets and Pins that deliver the traffic and conversions, you can optimize this process.

2. Discounts and flash deals to motivate and drive immediacy

It seems obvious that discounts in social media are likely to increase sales. It offers instant gratification for the buyer. Almost a third of Europeans connect with retailers for deals, coupons, promotions and flash sales.[246]

On Google+, brands are increasingly delivering results with discounts and flash sales. Fashion brands lead the way with Top Man, New Look, Very,

[245]Pinpointing Social Media Value: Zappos – One Tweet is Worth 45 Pins . . . : http://cipr.co/VJQClc

[246]Deal with It! Discounts Drive Brand Love on Social Media: http://cipr.co/XXqcGN

Boden, Uniqlo and H&M all gathering momentum on the platform and driving traffic through discounts and offers. In fact, H&M claims[247] to have increased click through rates by 22% as a result of activity on Google+.

The American Express Sync programme allows cardholders to match their cards to Twitter, Foursquare or Facebook accounts, select from a list of offers and digitally add them to their credit cards – a clever mechanism that allows automatic redemption for simplicity and rewards sharing in social media.

Promotions often deliver an immediate ROI too. They are simple to deploy using apps, coupons, hashtags and pop-up stores for flash sales. However, they still need to be used judiciously or they can undermine your brand, impair relationship building and erode your profit margin.

3. Discovery to inspire spontaneous purchase

Amazon is deft at using links to inspire impulse purchases. Its recommendation engine is the cornerstone of its success. It now has "Pages" for brands to use in aiding the discovery of new products, allowing businesses to create customized destinations and posts to promote products and mirror the success of Facebook Pages.

Facebook is experimenting with "Collections", a Pinterest-style feature that allows users to create wish lists through "Want" or "Collect" buttons. And you can't blame them for copying the well-known pinboard when a report suggests that 70% of Pinterest users are inspired to purchase (compared to just 21% on Facebook).[248]

YouTube, too, is getting in on the act. Homebase has a store on the video channel that allows people to explore images and click on products that take you through to relevant pages on the ecommerce site.

What is clear is that by being in the right place at the right time with a relevant story and link, businesses can drive visits and impact sales. You don't need to make the transaction within the network, just inspire and motivate your customer to make that impulse purchase.

---

[247]H&M Uses Google+ to Deliver Engaging Exclusive Content: http://cipr.co/XqAcII

[248]Pinterest vs. Facebook: Which Social Sharing Site Wins at Shopping Engagement?: http://cipr.co/12iF3ms

Influencing to buy – social proof

It is simply human nature that we assume that other people possess more knowledge and reflect the correct behaviour. We look for this social proof in choosing what products or services to buy, often looking to our peers and those whom we perceive to be an authority:

1. Wisdom of the crowd

In making a judgement we often believe that there is a collective wisdom from groups of people. We are as likely to consider product reviews from strangers as from close friends. For example, "Trends" on the Twitter sidebar encourages users to join more conversations and make new connections.

2. Expertise and fame

Credible experts from journalists to academics have always given sales a boost. We trust those in a position of authority. But they are not the only people to have influence. So, too, are the famous. Celebrities have legions of followers and a single product suggestion or endorsement can have immediate impact.

3. Exclusivity and scarcity

If something is exclusive it is premium and thus desirable. When launching, Pinterest didn't just beta test. You had to ask for an invitation. The consequence was that everyone wanted one.

By understanding these behaviours you can consider ways in which to motivate purchase and increase sales:

- Talk numbers

  Tell people how many shares, likes, views or pins your products get. Some retailers even display numbers of sales or subscribers couched as most successful, bestselling or sold out.
- Share results

  Testimonials, recommendations and referrals trigger sales. In fact, a leading white goods manufacturer has shown that reviews increase purchase 2.5 times.

■ Activate advocacy

Offering exclusives to the most influential experts, celebrity endorsement or rewarding super fans. Not only does this validate purchase decisions but it creates aspiration that motivates sales.

You ultimately want to positively influence the sale. This means that activity requires testing with various calls to action and then measuring, rigorously.

Collaborative purchases

Businesses are turning attention to the commercial opportunities within communities. It requires a more transparent approach, but the rewards can be high. Customers invest time, ideas and much more, making sales more likely and loyalty higher.

This approach is often referred to as crowdsourcing, although differing interpretations can include business intelligence (insight from customer social behaviours), collaboration and co-creation.

From Groupon to LivingSocial, many are experimenting with collaboration as a trigger for sales. And not all models are proving successful.

GiffGaff is a well-documented example of success. With only 25 staff, its customers drive the business and provide customer support, shaping product offerings, and even marketing materials. Benefits are passed on – £1 million was passed on to the community in 2011.

Barclaycard US has launched Barclaycard Ring, a social network credit card. Driven by the influence of an online community, the card offers a low interest rate, reduced fees and an opportunity for card members to shape and share in the product's financial success. Members have visibility of financial profit and loss statements. These brands are prepared to empower their customers.

When thinking about using this technique for social commerce you need to remember:

■ Collaboration and community needs to be guided and supported to get the best results.
■ You will need to be transparent and share results and outcomes.
■ You need a long-term strategy and plan that will grow with your community.

- It is an exchange of values that makes this work and benefits cannot be one-sided.
- Success will take time and realizing results from a community can be a long game.

Buying everywhere: social across the consumer touch points

Social is not always a sole driver for sales, but instead it "contributes" to purchase. Reviews, recommendations and social connections all support the sale. Businesses with a more sophisticated approach to social commerce lift the lid on the sales cycle; look beyond last click data; and examine the opportunities for social to accelerate, confirm and decide a purchase.

1. Integrate across the channels

Social media is leaky. It doesn't stay in the confines of the social networks, but slips out across customer touch points. Consumers tweet in stores, share online purchases and upload real-world pictures of products and brands. Social media is multichannel.

Smart social commerce evaluates all these channels to look at where and how social media has impact. The key is in isolating the social connections that contribute to the sale. How do email and social enhance purchases? Where can mobile strategies and social capture buyers on the move? How can social in-store increase spend?

The most obvious social integration is in connecting the social graph to your website. Currently only available from Facebook, there are rumours that Twitter is planning a mobile-friendly version. Using "Facebook Connect" and "Connect with Twitter" makes it easier for visitors to log in. There are benefits for business too. For instance, Facebook log-ins are nine times more likely to engage with those sites' social features and share content with friends.[249] Of course, there is a downside, as brands using open graph are not gaining proprietary data.

---

[249]Facebook-Connected Users 9x More Likely To Engage With, Share From E-Commerce Sites: http://cipr.co/WTerSy

Social commerce integration throws up one further complication: the need to unify cross-functional teams to maintain a consistent customer experience. After all, you don't want your store prices to contradict your online charges without a clear rationale – or social complaints may rise.

2. Attribution across the funnel

In many cases the sales driver on a website is measured by the last click to result in a sale. The problem with this way of measuring is that it doesn't account for the way people purchase. As we said earlier, when in buying mode, social is not always the primary destination.

More businesses are beginning to attribute social impact across the sales pipeline (or purchase funnel). Social has already changed the way people shop and therefore the pipeline.

©immediatefuture

Often, social media is shown to have impact in instigating the sale and contributing to the purchase decision rather than converting the sale.

Google's own study of purchase behaviour, Zero Moment Of Truth,[250] suggests that people consult 10.4 different sources before making a purchase. Many of those sources originate in the social space: comments from purchase experiences (second moment of truth) as reviews, recommendations and referrals.

By understanding how social media can be attributed to the sale, businesses can identify how to maximize the commercial opportunity and fine tune social commerce to deliver ROI.

If social media is to succeed in the boardroom, it has to be attributable to sales: whether it is directly driving the transaction or a major contributor to the purchase journey. Either way, as communications professionals our role is to understand buying behaviours and the role that social plays in making sales. This requires a mix of capabilities from understanding buyer psychology to crunching numbers for sales attribution. As we said at the start of the chapter, social commerce is complex, but as it is also results driven, it is enormously satisfying.

Biography

Katy Howell (@katyhowell) is CEO of social media consultancy, immediate future. She helps brands like Sony, Indesit, Diageo, Staples, BBC, HSBC and JD Williams adopt, integrate and deploy social media. With over eight years' social media experience and 25 years in marketing, she is a recognized authority in social communications: speaking at events around the world and training for the IDM, CIPR and CIM.

She advises companies, creating robust, measurable social media strategies. From social business to community management, she works alongside a team of consultants at immediate future to support initiatives, or builds client capabilities with training and mentoring.

---

[250]The Zero Moment of Truth: http://cipr.co/XqAkry

Chapter 28

Gemma Griffiths

This chapter looks at how to make a case for social media to C-level executives. It also examines ways to create and execute a change management programme that will influence employees to ensure that they are fully on-board an organization's social media train.

It is no secret that social media has fundamentally changed the way businesses operate. For some the integration has been easy; for others it has been a struggle.

As those who have successfully adopted social media will know, to get a workforce interested and active in social media, organizations must do a lot more than create a social media policy and run ad hoc training sessions on Twitter, LinkedIn and Facebook.

Organizations must change mindsets and will often have to adapt the existing company culture to be more open, transparent and flexible. This requires an effective and extensive change management programme.

Change management and transformation processes used to be a discipline for people implementing change at large-scale corporate companies. Now it is fast becoming a skill public relations professionals need to effectively get a team, department or an entire organization to embrace social media.

Using change management principles to increase social media adoption

The basic premise of change management is to influence people to alter their behaviour – a practice familiar to most public relations professionals – and adopt new practices, tools and ways of working.

According to Kurt Lewin, a psychologist known for his organizational behaviour theory, to deploy a change management programme effectively, organizations need to "unfreeze" old attitudes, values and beliefs; "change" and then "refreeze" new attitudes, values and beliefs.[251]

This all sounds straightforward. However, many companies struggle to complete such programmes. According to comprehensive research conducted by Dr John Kotter, a former professor at the Harvard Business School, author and consultant, "70% of all major change efforts in organizations fail".[252]

Failure can be a result of a whole host of problems, not least the inability to take a holistic approach and roll out change at all levels of an organization, ranging from individual to departmental and company level.

In the 1990s Dr Kotter wrote a book called *Leading Change* that many leaders still use and reference to this day. The book outlines the following eight simple principles of human and organizational behaviour.[253] The principles apply in all manner of organizations whether it is producing Fast Moving Consumer Goods (FMCG) or providing a consultancy service.

- Establishing a sense of urgency
- Creating the guiding coalition
- Developing a vision and strategy
- Communicating the change vision
- Empowering broad-based action
- Generating short-term wins
- Consolidating gains and producing more change
- Anchoring new approaches in the culture.

It is useful to apply Dr Kotter's principles when implementing a change management programme for social media adoption.

---

[251]Unfreeze, Change, Freeze: http://cipr.co/Yd2pU5

[252]Change Steps: http://cipr.co/XSrUuS

[253]Kotter International Principles: http://cipr.co/XSrUuS

- **Make sure the social media strategy addresses a fundamental business need.** Highlighting the business problem makes it easy for people to support a new strategy. Wanting to use and be present on social media because a competitor is isn't a worthy reason for engagement.
- **Commit to realistic timelines.** Different people will have different reactions to the proposed change programme; inspiring and motivating people to get on-board may take longer with some than others. Similarly, some employees may require more training than their colleagues. All of this needs to be taken into consideration.
- **Set up your taskforce.** Identify early adopters from all tiers within an organization – senior executives, middle management and junior staff – and make them part of processes from the beginning. They will help to influence their peers' opinion of the programme.
- **Communicate the vision in one sentence.** Painting a clear picture of the future will help motivate employees to take part in the transition process. It is a lot easier for them to help a change agent or team achieve their mission if they know what it is.
- **Don't make it a "top-down" approach.** Get buy-in from members of the taskforce and anyone of any level with an interest in social media. The change programme needs to be shaped by people who are interested in the subject and willing to help drive the programme forward. Existing champions of social media respond well to someone dictating the programme and are likely to lose interest in the project shortly after it has been introduced.
- **Ensure detractors are involved in the transition process.** All feedback should be welcome including negative feedback. By involving detractors in the process there is a chance an agent can convert them from a detractor to an advocate. If they don't, at least the agent will understand their concerns and be better armed to address their negative influence.
- **Tailor communication.** An organizational change management programme will affect some employees more than others. An agent or team should create and communicate different messages for different audiences – a classic PR principle.
- **Remove organizational barriers and confront troublesome employees.** Barriers to change come in many forms. For example, some change agents find they need to work with the IT department to allow certain sites to be accessed and software to be installed. Other agents find people can be their biggest challenge. Both problems need to be addressed head on and resolved to ensure limitations to the project are as small as possible.

- **Showcase visible support.** People talk to each other and are influenced by each other. Every person that supports the change is progress. Ask the employees who support the programme to voice their support by creating a post for your company intranet or internal blog.
- **Take baby steps.** Adopt an agile approach. Don't overwhelm employees with change. Launch or integrate one component at a time. Solicit feedback and allow that feedback to influence the change programme and how future components of the project are rolled out. This will show employees that the agent or team is taking their feedback on board and will make them feel part of the transition process.
- **Repetition is key.** Repeating the vision and keeping people up to date with progress of the project is integral to ensuring everyone stays engaged with the project. If the project is going well, resist the urge to take it easy. Effective change management requires relentless repetition and constant communication right up until the end of the programme.
- **Make the change part of the organization's DNA.** The transition process needs to be embedded in the culture. Employees need to see that the organization is taking, and will continue to take, the social media project seriously.
- **Accept it will be hard.** Change is difficult and some take to it easier than others. Change agents have to understand this and help people along the journey. Praise them for good progress and continuously hold their hands to ensure everyone gets to the next milestone.
- **Celebrate success.** Once everyone crosses the finish line then everyone should do a lap of honour, together. Celebrating as a team or organization will help everyone understand that they played a part in making a difference.

Departments that must be influenced

In addition to the above, anyone attempting to integrate social media into an organization usually has to influence the legal and HR departments. The very nature of these professions means that they are used to fixed boundaries and discipline.

A change agent's role is to outline the opportunities and risks involved with social media and encourage the respective departments to create new policies that are flexible enough to allow employees freedom when it comes to social media but strict enough to ensure that anyone who intentionally brings the company into disrepute will face the appropriate disciplinary process. There is a fine balance to be had.

Making a case for social media

If a change management programme is successful then an organization is likely to reap the benefits of social media. But how does a change agent get C-level executives to understand the advantages of social media and give them the green light, and sometimes budget, needed for the change management programme in the first place?

Just like the change management programme itself, the case needs to be planned, robust, strategic and well executed. According to Tim Creasey, Chief Development Officer at Prosci, an organization that describes itself as "the world leader in research and content creation in the field of Change Management", if you are not talking about achieving results when putting your case forward, then you are having the wrong conversation.

C-level executives always respond to figures, so a natural assumption would be to gather the necessary metrics. However, it is impossible to predict the return on investment of social media before a company has effectively and whole-heartedly engaged. A change agent can talk about the cost savings but it cannot accurately predict how social media will impact the bottom line.

Therefore, the case should be inextricably connected to organizational success and focus more on strategic goals than financial benefits. Strategic reasons for getting involved with social media include improving relationships with stakeholders as well as improving search engine rankings and reducing customer service costs (particularly important if the organization in question is a service organization).

A taste of what is to come

Getting buy-in from a line manager and gaining the approval to conduct a small-scale trial should definitely form part of a business case for social media.

Firstly, it is useful to define the purpose of engaging with social media and who the target audience is. Next, conduct research into where the target groups hang out and how they behave online. Pause and listen to the tone and the topic of conversation for a while before starting to directly engage.

It is worth making sure you measure the trial effectively (see Chapter 30) and collect all the necessary data and insight. This allows you to focus on tangible results and helps you showcase outcomes when you are looking to present a case for how the project may scale.

Reporting back on sentiment analysis, engagement activities and brand recognition should all be of interest to a chief marketing officer (CMO) or a chief executive (CEO) who understands and values public relations and an organization's reputation.

Remember to keep it simple. Meaningless stats and fancy charts are likely to irritate executives who deal with numbers on a daily basis and are more interested in the bottom line than how many followers an organization has on Twitter.

If a CEO is interested in the popularity numbers then it is important to remind them that the organization is investing in social media for the long-term gain. Short-term wins, such as the number of Twitter followers or Facebook likes, should not be how the company measures engagement with social media.

A trial will give senior executives a taste of what type of results engagement may reap and will demonstrate that the change agent or team is committed to the cause and is knowledgeable on the subject matter.

Statistics for the boss

Whilst it is difficult to provide management with figures about the financial benefits of engaging with social media, it is possible to provide them with statistics that will help executives understand the importance and benefits of engagement.

According to a recent report by Social Media Examiner,[254] 85% of marketers say the top benefit of social media marketing is increased exposure, followed by increasing website traffic (69%) and providing marketplace

---

[254] Social Media Marketing Industry Report 2012: http://cipr.co/TPKLZB

insight (65%). Furthermore, over half of marketers who have been using social media for three years state that it has helped improve sales.

Finally, a recent whitepaper from Sysomos[255] revealed that 83% of business-to-business leaders communicated that they are using social media and 66% have been doing so for more than a year. Finally, 89% believe social media will increase in value for their company over the next year and 58% expect the increase to be significant.

Change is inevitable

Everyone knows that those who embrace and respond well to change achieve competitive advantage. Social media presents a wealth of opportunities for companies and half-heartedly playing around on Twitter does not count as a successful social media strategy.

Those serious about reaping the rewards need to commit to the change programme and make sure the seats are full on their social media train.

Biography

Gemma Griffiths (@gemgriff) is managing director of public relations consultancy The Crowd &I. Throughout her career Gemma has crafted and executed PR campaigns for a wide range of clients including Motorola, Adobe and LG, Wikimedia UK (local organization behind Wikipedia in the UK) and start-up companies with disruptive technologies such as Rebtel (mobile VoIP) and iZettle (mobile payments). Gemma runs the informal social media training workshops for the CIPR throughout the summer and is a presenter on the live web show, CIPR TV.

---

[255]Sysomos Social Media Business Case: http://cipr.co/VGtrmf

Chapter 29

Philip Sheldrake

The world has changed since the dominant "Excellence model" of public relations emerged more than two decades ago. Does our use of social media and related information technologies require a new model?

A model is a thing used as an example to follow or imitate, a simplified description of a system or process. At least that's how the *Oxford English Dictionary* describes it.

I want to describe a new way of looking at the world of public relations, and practising it; a new model prompted by the continuing developments in social media and related technologies, and their widespread adoption.

In "Real-time Public Relations", Chapter 17 of this book's predecessor, *Share This*, I concluded that "the real-time social Web leads us, then, to the Excellence model of public relations: Grunig's fourth model of two-way, symmetrical communication fostering mutually beneficial relationships between an organisation and its publics".[256]

So is that it? Is the fourth model sufficient? I think not, but a chapter on real-time PR wasn't the place to go on to debate the merits of a new model. This chapter is.

---

[256]S. Waddington *et al.*, *Share This. The Social Media Handbook for PR Professionals*, John Wiley & Sons, 2012, ISBN 978-1-118-40484-3

Grunig's 4th

The two-way symmetrical model of PR, James Grunig's fourth model, "uses communication to negotiate with the public, resolve conflict and promote mutual understanding and respect between the organisation and its stakeholders".[257]

This description shares much in common with my definition of PR: the planned and sustained effort to influence opinion and behaviour, and to be influenced similarly, in order to build mutual understanding and goodwill.[258]

Despite the similarity, my definition avoids two words: communication and public. It does so to focus on the outcome of the profession rather than presume to scope the methods employed, and I hope you'll agree this turns out to be more than semantics as we crack on with that new model.

Let's construct a model, carte blanche. Can we describe the situation we find ourselves in without falling back too heavily on old verbs rammed with preconceptions?

Some definitions

Let's start with some nouns and brief definitions. First we have "organization" as there isn't much sense to this topic without it, and then descriptions of parties that surround it:

- **Organization** – an organized group of people with a particular purpose.
- **Stakeholder** – a person or organization with an interest or concern in our organization or something our organization is involved in.
- **Competitor** – an organization with objectives that clash with our own either directly (e.g. fly with us not them) or indirectly (e.g. don't fly, video conference instead).

---

[257]J. Grunig *et al.*, *Managing Public Relations*, Harcourt, 1984, ISBN 0030583373
[258]Public Relations Defined – The Anatomy of a Candidate Definition, Philip Sheldrake: http://cipr.co/zLcv62

Taking a step down into "stakeholder" we find the normal array:

- **Customer** – a person or organization that buys goods or services (where "buys" includes paying with one's attention or time, and includes "consumer").
- **Prospect** – a person or organization regarded as a potential customer.
- **Client** – a person or organization under the care of another.
- **Partner** – a person or company of importance to an organization in achieving its objectives.
- **Citizen** – a legally recognized subject or national of a state or commonwealth with rightful interest or concern in the workings of that nation or state.
- **Employee** – a person employed for wages or salary (taken to include their dependants, and also retired employees still financially reliant upon the organization's ongoing success).
- **Shareholder** – an owner of shares in a for-profit organization (taken to include those with other financial holdings or investments contingent upon the organization's financial success).

We'll assume that some citizens represent the environment and non-human sentient beings by proxy.

You might say that the definition of stakeholder here could include competitors, but we'll adopt the common distinction between the two.

No organization is an island. Rather, it must interact with all those parties around it in order to pursue and achieve its objectives, and the nature of its interactions is or should be defined and governed by its motivation and objectives and the strategies formed to achieve its objectives.

Mapping the interactions

Now we can begin to map out the interactions, defined as:

Interaction – reciprocal action or influence.

We have four primary types of interactions:

1. The interactions between our organization and stakeholders.
2. The interactions between our stakeholders with respect to us.
3. The interactions between our competitors and stakeholders.
4. The interactions between stakeholders with respect to our competitors.

I refer to these as primary interactions because one could also look at the interaction between an organization and its competitors in, for example, so-called coopetition (cooperative competition), or trade association activities. One could also look at the interactions of its stakeholders with the competition's stakeholders, such as those between football fans of opposing teams. I found, however, that, while these may be important interactions, they didn't have a material impact on this rethink.

Mapping the influence flows

We can break down interaction (reciprocal action) into action one way and action the other way. Or indeed the influence one way and the influence the other way, where the verb influence is defined as:

> Influence – to have an effect on the character, development, or behaviour of someone or something.

In other words, you have been influenced when you think in a way you wouldn't otherwise have thought, or do something you wouldn't otherwise have done.

This gives us six primary influence flows:

1. Our organization's influence with stakeholders.
2. Our stakeholders' influence with each other with respect to us.
3. Our stakeholders' influence with our organization.
4. Our competitors' influence with stakeholders.
5. Stakeholders' influence with each other with respect to our competitors.
6. Stakeholders' influence with our competitors.

Figure 29.1 shows these flows. For simplicity, I have lumped all stakeholders in the middle but of course our organization and our competitors may not share a universal set of stakeholders.

Moreover, an organization is just a collection of stakeholders, but an organization can persist beyond the lifespan of any group of individuals and is generally considered to have its own identity. Actually, perhaps most pertinently, a diagram consisting of nothing more than a load of little circles representing a bunch of individual stakeholders isn't quite so useful in communicating the model!

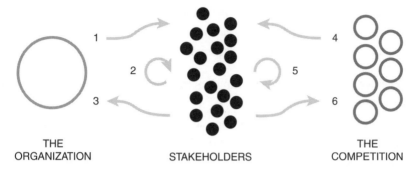

THE ORGANIZATION   STAKEHOLDERS   THE COMPETITION

Figure 29.1: The six influence flows

It's probably too simplistic but not too far off the mark to consider the historic focus of marketing and PR practice as being predominantly on the first influence flow (our influence with our stakeholders), with a bit of the third in the form of the internal circulation of news clippings for example, and eliciting information with marketing research to improve one's understanding of consumer preferences, attitudes, and behaviours (as long as you systematically ensure that these have an influence).

Sometimes we also try to infer a third flow (our stakeholders' influence with us) from implicit data such as sales volume or growth – "it's not selling as fast as we'd expected, there must be something they don't like."

Should a competitor have great success with its first flow (the competitor's first flow is our fourth) then one might conduct some ad hoc research to find out how it acted upon stakeholders.

This traditional emphasis was probably down to a combination of what appeared to work at the time, what was expected at the time, and what was possible within the systematic and budget constraints of your typical marketing and PR operation.

The second flow and the internet

Grunig's first three PR models focus on the first influence flow, our influence with our stakeholders. Even where the two-way symmetrical model for PR is adopted for the fourth model, the emphasis remains on treating the first and third influence flows equally. Or does it? What about the second flow (our stakeholders' influence with each other in respect to us)?

Grunig continues to support the validity of the two-way symmetrical model in the digital age and in *Paradigms of Global Public Relations in the Age of Digitalization*,[259] he specifically responds to quotes from two books:

- "The Web has changed everything", according to Brian Solis and Deirdre Breakenridge;[260] and;
- ". . . it is hard to avoid making the claim that 'the internet changes every-thing' . . . for public relations the unavoidable conclusion is that nothing will ever be the same again", David Phillips and Philip Young.[261]

Phillips and Young continue:

> "[The] Excellence [study] characterizes the vector of communication as being between an organisation and its publics, and is concerned with the balance – the symmetry – of this transaction. The bold claim that emerges from the arguments put forward for 'the new PR' is that the fundamental vector of communication that shapes reputation and an organisation's relationship with its stakeholders has flipped through 90 degrees. Now, the truly significant discourse is that which surrounds an organisation, product or service, a conversation that is enabled and given form and substance by the interlinked, aggregated messages that emerge from internet mediated social networks."

Grunig responds to the claims the internet changes everything: "I do not believe digital media change the public relations theory needed to guide prac-tice, especially our generic principles of public relations. Rather, the new media facilitate the application of the principles and, in the future, will make it difficult for practitioners around the world not to use the principles."

And to the claim by Phillips and Young that things have "flipped through 90 degrees":

> ". . . I do not believe that the 'internet society' or the 'new PR' challenges the Excellence paradigm, as Phillips and Young argued in these two

---

[259]Grunig, Global Public Relations in the Age of Digitalization: http://cipr.co/12BwPWS

[260]B. Solis and D. Breakenridge, *Putting the Public Back in Public Relations*, FT Press, 2009, ISBN 0137150695

[261]D. Phillips and P. Young, *Online Public Relations*, Kogan Page, 2009, ISBN 0749449683

passages. They seem to believe that 'an organisation and its publics' are distinct from 'internet-mediated social networks'. Instead, I believe that an organisation and its publics now are embedded in internet-mediated social networks but that public relations is still about an organisation's relationships with its publics.

Organisations do not need relationships with individuals who are not members of their publics even though these people might be actively communicating with and building relationships with each other. Organisations simply do not have the time or resources to cultivate relationships with everyone – only with individuals or groups who have stakes in organisations because of consequences that publics or organisations have or might have on each other."

First, "internet-mediated" communication isn't just a new media form in my opinion. It has unprecedented emergent behaviour, a scientific term used to describe how very many relatively simple interactions (e.g. blogging, tweeting, sharing) can give rise to complex systems – systems that exhibit one or more properties as a whole that aren't manifest for smaller parts or individual components. Weather is complex. The stock market is complex. A city's transport system is complex.

By definition, then, this behaviour cannot be attributed to one or a set of relationships with one or a set of stakeholders. It is the combination of the whole that itself exerts influence.

Second, instead of saying that "organisations do not need relationships with individuals who are not members of their publics", we can say that organizations will find it advantageous to maintain awareness of all Six Influence Flows regardless of the genesis or properties of the influence that flows therein. Organizations can prepare for the expected and unexpected emergence of influences that might warrant attention, because perhaps they represent reputational risk, or an opportunity for organizational learning, or a positive sentiment that can be harnessed in constructive ways.

A new stakeholder

Perhaps we have also found a new stakeholder, an individual who did not know she was a stakeholder until . . . hang on there, look, she just shared that link. And she also added a little comment. Atoms of influence from a so-called netizen.

Netizens are not "online publics" in the normal "digital PR" context; such groups are simply the usual stakeholders with internet access. Rather, netizens are stakeholders because they are online and because they are willing to act in ways that represent their moral compass so to speak – their feelings for what is right and wrong, or good and bad. Or perhaps they act simply on what makes them happy or sad, excited or chillaxed. The netizen is a most complex being whose responses boil down to a synaptic-like mouse click, or not. And given that humans are unchanged, some act apparently rationally, others have no regard for logical discourse whatsoever and the majority lie somewhere in between.

And there are many many millions of them.

So instead of Grunig saying "organisations simply do not have the time or resources to cultivate relationships with everyone", we can say that organizations will find it advantageous to wield information technologies to "relate" to the use (both directly and programmatically) of information technologies by others (see Chapter 33 on Big Data.)

The ramifications

There is influence in everything an organization does. And sometimes in what it does not do. The Six Influence Flows permeate the entirety of organizational life. Our concern has therefore widened beyond the PR department, or internal comms, or investor relations, or public affairs, or marketing, or customer service – as if these functions can still be considered separate. Our concern includes procurement, and HR, and production, and R&D, and, well, everything.

Organizations have invested significant sums in recent decades on IT systems tracking the flows of time, money and materials. Now they can wield social information technologies and define new policies and process to lend similar gravitas to the flows of influence under the direction of professionals who really get influence, mutual understanding and goodwill. Ah, could that be you then?

Social business

This model is part and parcel of social business, or at least it is if you define social business as I do:

> Social business – To adapt the way in which an organization delivers its mission and pursues its vision by designing the organization around influence flows, connecting: its people, partners, customers and other stakeholders; its data, information and knowledge in and all around it; more openly, productively and profitably with the application of social web, Big Data and related information technologies.

A new model of PR?

So is the Six Influence Flows a new public relations model, and is this the new vista of the public relations professional? Or will the focus of public relations remain on communicating directly with publics, on the 1st and 3rd flows, leaving the wider picture to a new breed of "influence professional"?

Adapted from *The Business of Influence: Reframing Marketing and PR for the Digital Age*, John Wiley & Sons, 2011.

Biography

Philip Sheldrake (@sheldrake) is the author of *The Business of Influence: Reframing Marketing and PR for the Digital Age*, John Wiley & Sons, 2011, and chapters of the CIM's *The Marketing Century*, John Wiley & Sons, 2011, and the CIPR's *Share This*, John Wiley & Sons, 2012. His ebook *Attenzi – A Social Business Story* was published May 2013 at attenzi.com. He is a Chartered Engineer, Managing Partner of Euler Partners and Board Director of Intellect. He co-founded the CIPR Social Media Panel and advises the Association for the Measurement and Evaluation of Communications (AMEC). He blogs at philipsheldrake.com.

Part VII

Future Proofing the Public Relations Industry

Chapter 30

METRICS THAT MATTER

Richard Bagnall

Social media measurement should not be an afterthought left solely to software platforms auto-generating fancy graphs and charts. Done properly it should be tailored to your organization's objectives, with emphasis on what has changed as a result of your work.

Output, outtake and outcomes. Three words that most PR practitioners should be familiar with but to which may not have given much thought. Yet in the understanding of these three simple words lie the challenges and the opportunities that the PR industry faces when looking to measure its effect successfully and credibly in both traditional and social media measurement.

Let's begin with looking at each of them in turn. AMEC, the International Association for the Measurement and Evaluation of Communications, which does so much to promote education and better understanding in communications measurement, has created an online glossary of terms used in PR and social media measurement. AMEC defines each of these terms as:

AMEC's standard definitions of output, outtake and outcome

Output

"The material and activity that the PR professional generates such as a press release, email, events etc. as well as the ensuing media coverage

(Continued)

---

that is generated. Outputs will also include proactive communication by an organisation on its *owned media* channels and properties."

Outtake

"What an audience now understands having been exposed to content about an organisation or a brand. Outtake occurs before an outcome, although some pundits ignore outtake and just discuss *outputs* and *outcomes*."

Outcome

"Something that has happened as the result of a campaign. In *public relations* this would typically be defined as a *measurable* change in awareness, knowledge, attitude, opinion, behaviour or *reputation* metrics."

Put simply, outputs are the things and content that we create and distribute as well as the content that others write about us. Outtakes are what our audiences now think having been exposed to our outputs and outcomes are what the audience has done as a result of exposure to our work. Before seeing an output, our audience was likely to have been unaware, once they have seen the content they become aware, and then once aware, they move to the last stage, the desired outcome itself (see Figure 30.1).

In the old world of traditional media relations, media analysis and media evaluation usually only went as far as measuring the outputs – the press cuttings and sometimes the video and audio clips (although more often just the transcripts of these or even a summary alone) – generated from campaigns.

No matter how sophisticated the analysis technique that was used, how clever its scoring system, algorithm or index, it couldn't hope to measure anything beyond the content itself. The effect that content had on its audience's thoughts (outtakes), or the effect that it had on its audience's actions (outcomes) were in all but the fewest cases not measured, the reason for this

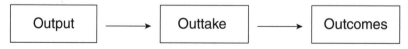

Figure 30.1: We need to move from measuring our outputs to measuring the effects on our target audiences via outtakes and outcomes

being normally put down to cost. Cost was an issue because to measure out-takes – changes in thoughts – and outcomes – changes in actions – would have involved costly market research.

Gaining an accurate understanding of the outtakes and outcomes would also have necessitated complex econometric modelling (or market mix modelling) which was beyond most PR budgets or handled in different marketing silos from the communications team.

Let's focus on the metrics that matter . . .

Here lies the problem. No organization measures its success on output metrics alone. Instead they focus on the metrics that matter – the outcomes. The sales, the voluntary donations, the client retention, the like for like uplifts, the share price, the attendees at an event – all of these things are the numbers that organizations obsess about. Any organization that is succeeding in its outcome metrics isn't going to worry if its outputs aren't quite what they had planned. It's as irrelevant to an organization how many press releases were written or how many articles ended up in print as whether the staff turned up to work a minute or two late or took an extra lunch hour. What really matters to all organizations isn't the outputs but the outcomes – what has happened as a result of all of the organization's efforts. If a sales team is smashing its targets does it matter that they arrive occasionally a few minutes late for work?

Organizations focus on outcome metrics, and so too should the PR executive in today's world of traditional and social media communications. Many PRs, when confronted with the challenge of measuring social media, sign up to an online listening tool in the mistaken belief that running some pretty charts from it counts as measurement.

There are a couple of problems with this. One problem is that these charts tend to focus on counting just the "output" metrics from the social media content and are not tailored to any organization's objectives. Facebook likes, Twitter retweets, follows, number of pieces of content, etc. are all too often positioned as measurement when in fact they may not be telling you anything meaningful at all.

The other problem is that many of these tools have incorporated their own made-up and proprietary scores to try to help identify "influence", "reach" and "engagement". None of these scores and indexes agree with each other or provide consistent, accurate or meaningful data. Even the basic metrics that they all try to capture consistently never agree with each other. Even simple things like volume of content differs wildly across providers owing to the different methods that they use to source the content, the accuracy of their spam filters, the quality of their search algorithms and their licensing agreements with the different social media channels.

. . . Not just count what's easy to capture

We need to be wary of focusing on counting what is easy to count, rather than measuring what matters. The good news is that to move beyond the basic metrics, to measuring what matters, is to follow the process that all high-performing communications teams have always done.

A simple, credible approach

Start with your organization's current goals and objectives. From here map your PR team's social media goals and craft measurable objectives to support those of your organization. Remember that all objectives must be "SMART" – Specific, Measurable, Achievable, Realistic and Time bound. Focusing on supporting your organization's outcome objectives will ensure that you drive the right behaviours in your social media efforts.

Every time you establish an objective, ask yourself up to three times why it matters to you. For example, if you find yourself setting an objective of increasing retweets, ask yourself why this matters. What is it that you really want from retweets? What will they achieve? More awareness? Better exposure? Better understanding of one of your organization's messages? And if so, amongst which particular audience? Asking yourself why a number of times will really help you to understand your true objectives and how best to measure them.

Another useful technique to focus on to bring credible metrics to your social media work is to map what you're doing against the well-known marketing funnel. In Figure 30.2 I have listed on the right the familiar stages of

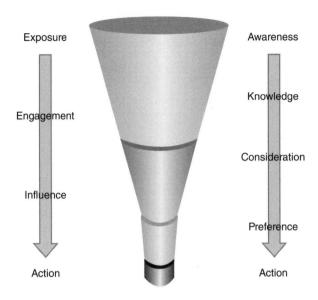

Figure 30.2: A suggestion for how social media metrics can be mapped to the marketing funnel

the funnel that organizations have been using for decades. To the left I have listed how the funnel might look from a social media perspective.

The challenge now is to think about each of these stages from your organization's perspective and shape some relevant metrics into each.

A non-exhaustive list of suggestions could include:

Exposure metrics
    OTS / impressions / eyeballs
    Brand mentions
    Share of conversation
    Messages
    Tone
    Search rank
    Click-throughs

(Continued)

Engagement metrics
 Comments/posts ratio
 Number of links
 @ mentions / RTs / RT %
 Bookmarks / likes / votes
 Pins
 Shares and Likes
 Subscribers
 URL visits
 Awareness
 Resolution rate

Influence
 Ratings
 Reviews
 Likelihood to recommend
 Net promoter score

Action
 Footfall
 Purchase / donations
 Website visits and downloads
 Coupon redemption
 Endorsement

A non-exhaustive list of potential metrics that could be used to measure each stage of the process. Tailoring these to your objectives is crucial.

What you will see is that as we work our way through the different stages, the metrics by and large change from output metrics through to outtake metrics and finally the metrics that all organizations want to see – the outcome metrics.

The important thing to do in each case is to think about these stages from the perspective of your own campaign. Not all of the metrics suggested here will be relevant to you and there may be others that you should include that are not in the list. By working through your objectives, and fitting them against each of the social media funnel stages, you should be able to come up with a tailored list that is appropriate for the needs of your organization.

For additional help, support and ideas on how you can frame relevant metrics to the work that your organization is undertaking, refer to AMEC's website. Suggested scorecards and frameworks are all available for download.[262]

A single number to measure social media does not, and will never, exist.

This is the key point about social media measurement – there isn't and won't ever be a single metric that can measure your effect in the space (as frustrating as that might be). The way to measure with success is to design your own suite of relevant and appropriate metrics that are shaped to each campaign's objectives. And if these objectives are aligned to your organization's objectives and KPIs then you will be in a great place to really prove the value of your work.

To summarize, here are some tips and key points to remember when measuring social media.

1. Don't start by selecting a social media monitoring tool and then expecting it to measure your effect in a meaningful manner. Begin by setting your goals and objectives, from these set your strategy and tactics, and only then consider which tool or service would be most appropriate to help you with your measurement.
2. Use tools appropriately. Remember that they are exactly that – just tools to help you, not a panacea or one-size-fits-all approach to measuring your success.
3. Don't forget that some of the metrics that you may have relied on for years are potentially no longer relevant. Volume of content, impressions/OTS and AVEs in particular are three that are becoming less and less easy to justify with any real meaning in reporting. Move further down the "funnel" and look to measure engagement and outcomes instead.

---

[262]AMEC's social media measurement resource page: http://cipr.co/WLaTTX

4. There isn't a single number that can measure social media now, never has been and nor will one ever be invented. The sooner we all as an industry accept this, the better.

5. Finally, don't forget that social media measurement needs more than just charts, numbers and infographics to be meaningful. It needs relevancy, insight and context, all assets that humans not software bring to the equation. Use the tools, but tailor the data that they provide appropriately. When reporting, speak to your organization's goals and objectives to be successful.

Biography

Richard Bagnall MCIPR (@richardbagnall) ran Metrica for 15 years before selling it to Exponent Private Equity, who merged it with Durrants and Gorkana to form the Gorkana Group. After three and a half years, with Gorkana Group integrating the evaluation business and building it to become one of the world's largest specialist communications measurement companies, Richard left to pursue other opportunities within the industry. Richard chairs AMEC's social media measurement group, is a member of the CIPR social media panel and is also a member of the Cabinet Office's Evaluation Council.

Chapter 31

Drew Benvie

What's the next Twitter? What's the next Facebook? These are some of the most frequently asked questions in digital communications back offices. The answer is not a site or social network. It is a movement called the Quantified Self.

The Quantified Self movement is a way of applying the social web, apps and consumer technology for personal health and productivity. It enables brands to listen not just to what we say online, but what we do.

Quantified Self manifests itself in the form of systems like Nike+, Sleep Cycle, Fitbit, Lift, Drive to Improve and more.

Quantified Self will allow brands to engage and listen at a whole new level. Whether it's knowing what your customers are doing, as opposed to saying, how to engage a workforce or how to attract people to your brand, it is a movement for digital practitioners to dive into while it is on the rise.

The rapid rise of Quantified Self

We are far more likely to share information about ourselves online now than we were 10 years ago. Social media has done this to us.

For the advocates amongst us, the usefulness of social media far outweighs any negatives that the social media era has brought. That's not to say that security and privacy issues are not important. Speak to the parents of any trashed house after a "Facebook party" and I'm sure they will have a different view to the one being laid out here. But when properly managed, social media has proven to be a powerful force for change and enablement, not just for socializing and sharing information.

It is this platform that has enabled the Quantified Self movement to flourish today. The concept of recording information about your movements, weight, diet and sleep patterns then sharing it online would never have stuck had we not been trained by the billion people movement now on Facebook and half a billion on Twitter and Google+.

The term Quantified Self was first coined by *Wired* magazine editors, Gary Wolf and Kevin Kelly, in 2007. In internet years, this was a pretty long time ago that the movement started. Even still, Quantified Self for many is not a natural behaviour to embrace. So for brands and individuals, what is the opportunity?

The sentient world

Industry analyst Jeremiah Owyang of Altimeter Group spoke at Le Web London, the major digital industry event, in the summer of 2012.[263] The subject of his talk was a concept he terms The Sentient World.[264]

Jeremiah's idea was simple. The connections between us that social media has facilitated have started to emerge between connected objects that have both smart sensors and web connections. These objects might include a fridge that connects to your online groceries account and orders milk when you're running low, children's pyjamas that alert you when your baby falls ill in the night, or billboard advertising that is as tailored to you as the adverts that follow you around on the web because they saw what you last looked at in John Lewis.

The opportunity for brands, as Owyang put it, is threefold:

1. If everything around us emits data, how will we interpret this data and make use of it? If you don't begin doing this now, your competitors will.

---

[263]Jeremiah Owyang: Le Web keynote 2012 covering Altimeter research themes: http://cipr.co/WVDDuA

[264]Altimeter: The key to faster than real time? Anticipation. Presentation with Jeremiah Owyang: http://cipr.co/XhRxXO

2. How will your customers and consumers begin to interact differently in their day-to-day lives now that everything is connected? This is more about understanding future consumer digital trends and applying that understanding to your marketing and business strategy.
3. How can companies take advantage of a self-sufficient world?

Clearly the opportunities for brands facing the rise of Quantified Self, from the perspectives of understanding a new level of data deluge, unpicking new consumer behaviours and creating new business concepts in a self-sufficient world, all revolve around specifics. It's important therefore to look at the current major Quantified Self concepts, products and technologies shaping the movement.

Quantified Self in action

The emergence of new technologies is building at breakneck speed. Here is an overview of the major technologies that paint the picture of the Quantified Self space.

Body monitors:
- Fitbit – A suite of devices including accelerometers and altimeters that track calories burned, steps taken, stairs climbed and sleep patterns.
- Nike FuelBand – A wrist device which tracks steps taken, calories burned and Nike's own "fuel" measurement.
- Bodymedia/Ki Fit – A device which straps to the upper part of the arm and tracks steps taken, sleep efficiency and calories burned.

Sleep:
- Zeo – A headband device which straps to the head and tracks sleep time and variations of sleep including light, deep and REM sleep.
- Sleep Cycle – An iPhone app that tracks sleep based on your movement in bed, which has reached #1 paid app in the App Store in nine countries according to App Store data.

Mood:

- Mappiness – An iPhone app developed by the London School of Economics which lets users track their mood throughout the day recording where they are, who they are with and what they are doing.
- Moodscope – A web-based application for measuring, tracking and sharing your mood.

Cardio/fitness/weight:

- RunKeeper – A mobile app for iPhone and Android that tracks distance, duration, speed and calories consumed.
- Nike+ Running – A mobile app created by Nike which tracks running distance, duration, speed and calories consumed.
- Endomondo – A sports community based on real-time GPS tracking of running and cycling.
- Withings Blood Pressure Monitor – A device for tracking blood pressure that connects to the iPhone and produces historical data graphs.
- Azumio Heart Rate Monitor – An iPhone app which uses the phone's camera flash to determine your heart rate.
- Withings scales – Wi-Fi enabled bathroom scales which send a user's weight to an online database so they can track their weight progression over time.

Diet and nutrition:

- The Eatery – An iPhone app that lets you take photos of your food where the wider community rates the health of it.
- Waterlogged – An iPhone app that allows you to record your daily water consumption, producing historical data graphs on your water drinking habits.
- NHS Drinks Tracker – An iPhone app created by the British National Health Service which allows you to add your alcohol consumption by the unit and alerts you when it goes over the recommended daily amount.
- Calorie Counter – An iPhone app with a calorie database of over 1.5 million foods, allowing you to track your calorie consumption using historical data graphs.

Cognitive:

- Lumosity – A website and iPhone app where a user plays scientific games designed to improve brain speed, attention, memory, problem solving and flexibility. Users can then chart their cognitive performance improvement.

Productivity:

- RescueTime – A desktop app time tracking and management tool which tracks which web programs you use the most.
- 42Goals – A goal-tracking web app that allows users to track, chart, annotate and evaluate many different goals in one place.
- Lift – An iPhone app that helps you create good habits of your choice. The community element around it gives you "props" when you continue with the habit.

Down to business

In my office at Hotwire and 33 Digital, we started experimenting with some of the above technologies in 2010/2011, and more seriously at the beginning of 2012. We invested in some of the higher end equipment being used, begged, borrowed and stole some of the beta invites to the newest of the new web apps and services, and we learnt a hell of a lot about comms consultancy as well as innovation. It all boiled down, once again, to Jeremiah Owyang's three principles:

Data: we could see there is a need to capture and analyze consumer data for brands in a way they are not yet able to, and use this for brand management as well as research and insights.

Business innovation: we began advising clients more practically about new business concepts, products and services that could be brought to market that could take advantage of the Quantified Self space.

Consumers: most important of all, we could see first hand how to tap into a new kind of self-tracking, always-on consumer behaviour trend.

Outside of the comms consultancy bag, we also ate our own dog food when it came to digital health. A small number of us were seeing health benefits from our use of these technologies. The benefits included improved productivity, diet and health. So we decided to offer all global staff access so some of the entry-level Quantified Self consumer technology. We rolled out FitBits to all staff in the summer of 2012 and gave employees access to an online leader board and forum where they could compete and exchange tips.

It's early days for us but the results have blown us away. Such a small change can create such a big impact on mood, health and wellbeing.

The employer brand

In addition to the business development opportunities brought about by Quantified Self, opportunities and responsibilities are arising which affect the employer brand.

There are clear concerns by many about devices which track your personal data and then store it somewhere before analyzing that data then sharing it back to you and/or with the world. This is the backbone of Quantified Self.

So, from a personal perspective, you may think Quantified Self is intrusive, you may worry about your personal data and, were it to be tracked and analyzed, where it would be stored. By whom would it be used? Or you might be more liberal and embrace the benefits that could be experienced through the apps and gadgets available to you.

You may, if you are a progressive sort, disregard your personal views and consider the implications of the fact that this is a rapidly-growing trend and the opportunities outweigh the potential risks.

Either way, the brand should consider the following points:

- Employees: how can you foster wellbeing, bring about improved productivity and increase ongoing learning and development through integrating the available technologies into the day-to-day, in a safe and secure environment?
- Protection: your staff are using your company smartphone to log their runs, track their sleep and analyze their diets already. It's the employer's responsibility to ensure you are on top of the implications of who owns the data and how it is being used.

What's next? Why us?

Taking all the progress to date into account and the various opportunities that will emerge for brands, you might be thinking, why is this important for the PR profession? And what should you do about this to seize the opportunity?

Quantified Self meetups are emerging across the world. The types that attend them are from all walks of life. In business, they come from different sectors and work in all sorts of disciplines. But there's the same early adopter mentality that I last saw when social media first began to make an impact on the communications industry. And you see some of the same faces that I saw back then – some of the earliest bloggers who can now see the impact that Quantified Self could have on businesses and how their role in forging the path could be an important one.

Above all else, I feel the communications industry has evolved beyond recognition at the hands of social media over the last five years. The agency landscape looks entirely different. Skill sets for the consultant have changed. The media landscape for brands is completely different. For me, the communications professional simply has to be at the crest of the Quantified Self wave as it breaks; there is no other way. The impact that will be felt by brands from the new data deluge, new consumer behaviours, new business concepts and the responsibilities of the employer brand will be too great to ignore.

Biography

Drew (@DrewB) is a seasoned agency CEO and digital and social media PR specialist. Drew was named the UK's #1 most respected individual in *New Media Age*'s 2011 Reputation Online survey, one of *PR Week* magazine's 29 under 29, a regular feature in the *PR Power Book* and he wrote the Wikipedia page on social media in 2006. He runs UK and global digital and social media campaigns for brands including Red Bull, Pearson, Microsoft, the BBC, Evernote, Premier Inn and Sage.

Chapter 32

NETWORK TOPOLOGY

NETWORK TOPOLOGY

Andrew Bruce Smith

The study of network structures (or topologies) has exploded over the last decade, covering everything from computers to power stations, neurons and genes. However, the scrutiny of human social networks will have the biggest impact on public relations.

Malcolm Gladwell's book *The Tipping Point*, first published in 2000, was an attempt to understand how (and why) certain messages and behaviours spread successfully through an audience. He introduced notions such as connectors, mavens and salespeople to the lexicon of influence. He also outlined his "Law Of The Few" – the idea that "the success of any kind of social epidemic is heavily dependent on the involvement of people with a particular and rare set of social gifts".[265]

In other words, a small number of influential people (relative to the overall size of the audience concerned) were the gatekeepers to the success or failure for a message or product. This view appeared to be supported with the publication in 2003 of Edward Keller and Jonathan Berry's book *The Influentials*.[266]

However, the idea of "opinion leaders" who influence a wider audience is hardly new.

The two-step theory of communication popularized by Elihu Katz and Paul Lazarsfeld[267] back in the 1940s and 50s posited that mass media information

---

[265]M. Gladwell, *The Tipping Point*, Back Bay Books, 2002, ISBN 0316346624

[266]E. Keller and J. Berry, *The Influentials*, Free Press, 2003, ISBN 0743227298

[267]Wikipedia, Two Step Flow of Communication: http://cipr.co/VLvsxx

is channelled to the "masses" through opinion leadership. The people with most access to media, and having a more literate understanding of media content, explain and diffuse the content to others.

For those working in public relations over the last few decades, this view has provided an intellectual underpinning for their work. Namely, by seeking to influence the media, i.e. journalists, a PR professional has the most effective means of reaching (and hopefully influencing) opinion formers and their publics.

However, more recent research into the general area of the structure and function of social networks has begun to cast doubt upon this notion of influentials. For example, Gladwell's book made much reference to Stanley Milgram's now (in)famous Six Degrees of Separation experiment. As the Wikipedia entry on Gladwell's book points out:

> "Milgram distributed letters to 160 students in Nebraska, with instructions that they be sent to a stockbroker in Boston (not personally known to them) by passing the letters to anyone else that they believed to be socially closer to the target. The study found that it took an average of six links to deliver each letter. Of particular interest to Gladwell was the finding that just three friends of the stockbroker provided the final link for half of the letters that arrived successfully. This gave rise to Gladwell's theory that certain types of people are key to the dissemination of information."[268]

However in 2003, Duncan Watts, a network theory physicist at Columbia University, repeated the Milgram study by using a website to recruit 61,000 people to send messages to 18 targets worldwide. According to Wikipedia:

> "He successfully reproduced Milgram's results (the average length of the chain was approximately six links). However, when he examined the pathways taken, he found that 'hubs' (highly connected people) were not crucial. Only 5 per cent of the email messages had passed through one of the hubs. This casts doubt on Gladwell's assertion that

---

[268]Wikipedia, *The Tipping Point*: http://cipr.co/VSfebq

specific types of people are responsible for bringing about large levels of change. Watts pointed out that if it were as simple as finding the individuals that can disseminate information prior to a marketing campaign, agencies would presumably have a far higher success rate than they do. He also stated that Gladwell's theory does not square with much of his research into human social dynamics performed in the last 10 years."[269]

Helpfully, Nicholas Christakis and James Fowler's book *Connected*[270] (first published in 2010) provides an excellent round-up of Watts's research as well as many other studies into the structure and function of social networks. One of the key findings in the book is that the structure of a network may be more important than the nodes (human beings) contained within it. According to Christakis and Fowler: "Whether influential people can exercise influence at all may depend entirely on the precise structure of the network in which they find themselves, something over which they have limited control. As we have seen, some networks permit wide-reaching cascades and others do not."[271] Thus, the study of network structure (or topology) has come centre stage in the study of social network dynamics while the rise of online social networks has also opened up far broader data sets to examine. This has been further aided by the emergence of inexpensive tools to allow the examination of the structure of relationships within these networks. As a result, ground-breaking social network research in recent years has begun to uncover fundamental rules that govern both the formation and operation of social networks – both on- and offline.

Such rules have far-reaching implications for communications professionals. For example, the dissemination of influence and information may rest more heavily upon the structure of a network than was previously thought possible. Although the ability to exploit these insights practically has been limited up to now, that is set to change. In particular, the structure of networks on the web and within social media can now be analyzed fruitfully and utilized for communication purposes. We'll now look at three specific examples

---

[269]Ibid

[270]N. Christakis and J. Fowler, *Connected*, Harper Press, 2010, ISBN 000734743X

[271]Ibid

of network topologies (or graphs) that have huge potential importance to PR professionals: the link graph, the social graph and the economic graph.

The link graph

Google's ubiquitous search engine attempts to deliver the most relevant web content results relative to the keyword term used by the searcher. The original Google algorithm used the metaphor of academic citation to determine the role that connections (i.e. weblinks) from different pages and sites should have determining search results. Over time, this has given rise to notions of trust and authority in relation to specific pages and sites. For example, a site such as www.bbc.co.uk would have a generically high trust rating. But it would not necessarily be authoritative on every subject.

With recent changes to Google's algorithm (known as the Penguin and Panda updates, designed to demote pages which relied upon low quality content and spamming tactics), high placement in Google's search results rests even more heavily on gaining links from high trust and high authority sites. Ironically, it means that one of the key skills required in search engine optimization (SEO) today is the ability to identify where those nodes of trust and authority exist – and to be able to build relationships with the right individuals behind those sites and pages in order to earn the right to gain a link or reference.

Fortunately for the PR community, low-cost tools exist to help make this process easier. One of the most popular is Majestic SEO's Site Explorer.[272] In simple terms, this tool makes use of what is claimed to be "the largest commercially available link index on the planet".[273]

By analyzing trillions of link connections, Majestic SEO allows pages and sites to be assessed on two key metrics – citation flow and trust flow. According to the firm, flow metrics are produced by studying how various metrics alter as they flow through the link graph. This technique provides an indication of how sites compare for trust and authority within the context of the web overall. In other words, the Majestic SEO tool analyzes the network topol-

---

[272]Majestic SEO website: http://cipr.co/Y8mTN1
[273]Majestic SEO website, About: http://cipr.co/12xr5Jn

ogy or link structure of the web to determine where authority and trust resides within the network relative to specific keywords (and, by definition, user intent).

PR practitioners seeking to better understand the potential network topology for the most effective dissemination of a message via the web can use the tool to identify which pages and/or sites are best placed to provide the highest degree of trust and authority. In some cases this may simply confirm that relevant media sites may carry the highest degrees of trust and authority. Or that other, perhaps less intuitive, places may be more worthy of targeting. The point being that the use of network topology analysis (in this case of the structure of the web) provides a way of planning, researching and developing more effective strategies for maximizing the impact of a particular message with a particular audience.

The social graph

According to Wikipedia: "The social graph in the internet context is a sociogram, a graph that depicts personal relations of internet users." It has been referred to as "the global mapping of everybody and how they're related". The term was popularized at the Facebook f8 conference in 2007[274] and the wide adoption of this particular social network is probably the most visible form of the social graph in an online environment.

The term "social graph" has thus become common currency in the world of social media and PR. However, few practical examples have so far emerged of how analyses and understanding of the social graph (or at least, those segments of the social graph that represent a defined audience) can be exploited to deliver more effective and efficient communications programmes.

However, Fowler and Christakis offer an interesting perspective on the kinds of techniques that could be deployed (but borrowed from other fields).

One example cited is how to create an efficient and effective immunization programme: "Understanding networks can lead to still other innovative, non-obvious strategies. Randomly immunizing a population to prevent the spread

---

[274]Wikipedia, Social Graph: http://cipr.co/X2gC8j

of infection typically requires that 80 to 100 per cent of the population be immunised. A more efficient alternative is to target the hubs of the network, namely those people at the centre of the network or those with the most contacts."[275]

But, as highlighted by Duncan Watts earlier in this chapter, what if you have no insight into the actual structure of the ties of the audience you are targeting? Fowler and Christakis's response is a creative alternative – "a strategy that allows us to exploit a property of networks even if we cannot see the whole structure". As they explain: "Acquaintances have more links and are more central to the network than are the randomly chosen people who name them. The reason is that people with many links are more likely to be nominated as acquaintances than are people with few. In fact, the same level of protection can be achieved by immunising roughly 30 per cent of the people identified by this method than would otherwise be obtained if we immunised 99 per cent of the population at random".[276]

How does this relate to public relations? Imagine you wish to target an audience of 100,000 people on Twitter. Targeting all 100,000 directly may be impractical, as would attempting to analyze the relationships between all 100,000. But what if you could randomly select a smaller number of the audience and identify who are the most commonly followed members of that audience?

An inexpensive tool such as Followerwonk[277] would allow you to do just that. By targeting your message to the most central members of any particular audience, you may more efficiently and effectively increase the chances that your message will reach the whole audience.

The economic graph and beyond

In December 2012, LinkedIn CEO Jeff Weiner declared in a blog post: "Our ultimate dream is to develop the world's first economic graph. In other words,

---

[275]N. Christakis and J. Fowler, *Connected*, Harper Press, 2010, ISBN: 000734743X
[276]Ibid
[277]Followerwonk website: http://cipr.co/wAAcdw

we want to digitally map the global economy, identifying the connections between people, jobs, skills, companies, and professional knowledge – and spot in real time the trends pointing to economic opportunities."[278]

This is an ambitious vision and the implications of such an economic graph would be enormous. Not least for the world of reputation management and public relations.

Without getting too carried away, it is worth a note of caution from Fowler and Christakis:

> "Some recent work has clarified the specific circumstances whereby influential individuals are apt to be able to exercise their influence. It turns out that influential people are not enough: the population must also contain influenceable people and it may be that the speed of diffusion of an innovation (or message) is more dependent on the properties of the latter group than the former. The key point however, is that networks with particular features and topologies are more prone to cascades, that both types of people are required for cascades to take place, and that understanding the shape of the network is crucial to understanding both naturally occurring and artificially induced cascades."[279]

There is no question that advances in social network dynamics and network topology are providing insights that PR professionals could only have dreamed of in the past. More importantly, it points to moving PR away from old models of communication to looking at new ways of better understanding the complex network of relationships that underpin any public or audience. Those PR practitioners that have the ability to understand the structure of these social networks and the way in which network structures impact on the success or otherwise of message dissemination must surely be better placed to succeed than those that don't.

Perhaps the long-term goal of public relations will be the successful engineering of artificially induced cascades of message distribution and behaviour

---

[278]J. Weiner, LinkedIn blog: http://cipr.co/WllqFH
[279]N. Christakis and J. Fowler, *Connected*, Harper Press, 2010, ISBN: 000734743X

change. In which case the understanding of social network structures may become a core skill requirement for the PR practitioner in the 21st century.

Biography

Andrew Bruce Smith (@andismit) is managing director of Escherman, a specialist online PR, SEO and analytics consultancy. Smith has been a consistent PR innovator, being among the first UK practitioners to exploit email (1991), the World Wide Web (1994) and Twitter (2007). Described as the "de facto godfather of PR blogging", he is a regular speaker and media commentator on the integration of PR with social media, search optimization and analytics.

Chapter 33

THE PUBLIC RELATIONS POWER OF "BIG DATA"

Simon Collister

According to IBM 90% of the world's data has been created in the past two years, due to social media's rapid growth.[280] *This chapter argues "Big Data" has practical applications for PR and can secure a future for the industry.*

Public relations, according to the CIPR, involves "the planned and sustained effort to establish and maintain [. . .] mutual understanding between an organization and its publics".[281] The context within which these relationships must be established and managed, however, is highly fluid.

As PR academic Anne Gregory points out "society is changing: new issues and trends arise, some of them very quickly."[282] For PR practitioners, being able to identify and track such trends, recognize their potential impact and adapt communication strategies accordingly is a daily challenge. This challenge is made all the more complex by our contemporary networked society where the proliferation of social technology, an increased willingness to share information and the empowerment of individuals is transforming political, economic, social and technological environments faster than ever before.

---

[280]Bringing Big Data to the Enterprises, IBM: http://cipr.co/14JLnlP

[281]It's important to note there are literally hundreds of different definitions of PR, although many of these consider the management of relationships between organizations and their specific publics as a central function

[282]The Context of Public Relations, Exploring Public Relations: http://cipr.co/11x7tKD

This chapter will suggest that the ever-increasing flow of information driven by socially networked individuals – increasingly referred to as "Big Data" – is both the catalyst for such breakneck dynamism as well as a potential solution to help PR practitioners manage this rapidly changing organizational environment. The chapter will give an overview of Big Data and how it presents PR practitioners with strategic and practical opportunities, using a case study of Big Data analysis within the Financial Ombudsman Service. It concludes by arguing that, if adopted and applied pragmatically, Big Data could potentially establish PR as a lead function within organizations and the wider communications, marketing and management sectors, thus helping secure a prosperous future for the industry.

What is Big Data?

Our starting point for this exploration of "Big Data" and its impact on PR must be with a definition of the term. The most fruitful approach, perhaps, is to break down the concept and tackle each of the term's component parts one at a time. However, rather than deal with the individual terms in order, I will initially address the issue of "data," as this will help us comprehend why the scale of Big Data is so significant.

Firstly, then, what exactly do we mean by "data"? Technically, big "data" can include website traffic, search engine marketing performance data, online polls, online product reviews, tweets, photos and videos uploaded or shared via social networks, CRM databases, purchase transaction databases, GPS signals from our mobile phones – ultimately anything that contains information which may be useful when combined with other data sources. For our purposes, it is perhaps better to refine our understanding of data to specify the freely and publicly available textual data generated through social media that more and more of us are sharing each day, via an ever-increasing number of social channels and platforms. This, arguably, offers the most immediate potential and practical uses for PR.

Then there's the issue of size. Big Data is, well, "big". But how big? There are a number of ways to deal with this. Firstly we can attempt to address the sheer scale of Big Data through numbers. According to technology and consulting company, IBM, each day the socially networked public generates 2.5

trillion bytes of data. That's 2.5 exabytes. Not megabytes, or gigabytes or tera-bytes – not even petabytes, but exabytes![283] But, while this gives us an idea of raw size it is not necessarily a helpful way to address the issue.

To provide a more comprehensible understanding (and to root the notion of Big Data firmly in the realm of social media), the Canadian social media analytics company, Sysomos,[284] claims that its software collects more than 16 million posts *every hour* from social media sources, such as blogs, forums, Twitter, Facebook, YouTube, Flickr, LinkedIn and others.

This interpretation, while helping us get to grips with "Big Data" at a literal level, needs further refinement if we want to recognize fully Big Data's stra-tegic and practical potential for PR. As Danah Boyd and Kate Crawford have observed, the term "Big Data" is misleading as the real value it offers is not primarily in its size or type of data, but "from the patterns that can be derived by making connections between pieces of data, about an individual, about individuals in relation to others, about groups of people, or simply about the structure of information itself".[285] To put it more succinctly, while we may have access to increasingly vast amounts of information through the rise of social media, it is the ability to gather, analyze and interpret this data that brings about ground-breaking opportunities for PR practitioners.

Big Data and text mining applied to PR

With the inexorable rise of data available for analysis, PR practitioners must understand how it can be analyzed – or "mined" – to find the vital insights that will yield competitive advantage. Data mining, or more specifically text mining, is a process that allows the analysis of a diverse range of public and proprietary information, such as tweets, product reviews and even individual purchase histories.

At text mining's core is usually high-powered analytical technology that enables users to make connections and spot patterns in the vast amount of data that is simply not possible through manual analysis due to the sheer scale

---

[283]Bringing Big Data to the Enterprises; IBM: http://cipr.co/14JLnlP

[284]Sysomos Products; Sysomos: http://cipr.co/Y8mLgz

[285]6 Provocations for Big Data; Danah Boyd and Kate Crawford: http://cipr.co/Xzx3da

of resources and human effort this would require. This allows analysts to not only identify emerging issues or trends relevant to organizations but also begin to predict potential future events. Text mining of Big Data can help us identify the elusive "unknown unknowns" that former US Defense Secretary, Donald Rumsfeld, so eloquently described and in theory develop an appropriate response. An example of how text mining of Big Data has helped deliver PR outcomes for a national UK organization might help illustrate its potential benefits.

Case study: Financial Ombudsman Service

Early in 2012 the Financial Ombudsman Service, the UK's independent organization set up to resolve complaints between consumers and financial businesses, briefed the global conversation agency, We Are Social, to undertake a strategic social media project. The project had three primary objectives which were to help the ombudsman service:

1. Use social media to engage directly with stakeholders and consumers.
2. Manage its brand reputation by monitoring and responding to mentions of the ombudsman service brand.
3. Identify and manage "unknown conversations" relevant to the ombudsman service's work.

This case study focuses on the third objective as it offers the best example of how text mining analysis can be applied to big sets of social media data for PR purposes.

The business goal for identifying conversations about financial services and providers unknown to the ombudsman service was to enable the organization to add value through social media engagement. By being able to spot and resolve potential consumer problems before they became more serious and complex complaints requiring greater resources to resolve, the ombudsman service ultimately hoped to minimize its case workload and potentially reduce costs. Secondarily, this activity would help strategic business and communications planning by spotting and potentially predicting emerging consumer finance issues and trends.

This was a complex challenge that involved human as well as automated text analysis and insight and was achieved as follows. Initially, We Are Social worked closely with the ombudsman service to identify a set of "base terms" corresponding to the ombudsman service's main areas of focus, such as bank, insurance and mortgage, and other key words and phrases used by consumers when discussing finance products or providers online. These included "credit rating", overdraft, "over limit", etc. Using these terms, searches of social media data were undertaken using the analytics platform Sysomos Map.[286] This generated a high volume of conversations with low levels of accuracy, as the search terms identified general finance discussions that were irrelevant to the ombudsman service.

To increase the accuracy of results, additional text mining techniques were applied to the search, including:

- Proximity constraints: ensuring that Sysomos Map only looked for conversations with a maximum of ten words between the base term and other key words.
- Personalization: use of personal pronouns in genuine complaints, such as "My pension was missold" or "I was overcharged" identified through manual analysis of natural language patterns.
- Everyday expressions: use of emotive language and colloquial terms likely to be used in potential consumer complaints identified through further manual analysis of relevant conversations, e.g. "nightmare!", "get a resolution", "what can I do?", etc.

This helped identify a much smaller volume of conversations (e.g. 1,500 discussions over a six-month period, rather than several thousand) with much higher levels of accuracy and relevance. As a consequence, We Are Social and the ombudsman service were able to distinguish specific

(Continued)

---

[286]Sysomos MAP; Sysomos: http://cipr.co/Z9WFk2

problems and potential complaints from general financial discussions. The analysis also uncovered three main types of conversations:

1. General complaints
2. Specific questions or advice
3. Highly emotive rants.

This enabled We Are Social and the ombudsman service to work out a strategic engagement plan with a tailored approach to the different types of conversations identified. The analysis also helped predict likely changes in conversation volumes over time, which meant the ombudsman service could help adequately plan its resourcing of future conversation engagement.

Limitations of Big Data

Despite the increased analytical power of software and technology being adopted in text mining Big Data, this technologically determinist approach cannot adequately deal with the complexities of interpersonal communication. For example, one of the biggest challenges software technology faces is how to interpret the highly nuanced and individualistic use of language. Automated analysis can rarely identify and process human traits such as sarcasm or irony with any accuracy; similar problems are encountered in sentiment analysis. While many commercially available technology products may claim to provide 80% reliability in their automated analyses, the experience of many PR professionals engaging in social media research suggests this is an over-statement.

A further potential restriction is the language used by an organization's stakeholders or publics within a globally networked environment. Although English is the internet's most widely used language, Chinese and other globally dominant languages, such as Spanish and Portuguese, are nearly as popular. This can cause problems for analytical technologies which can only function with English texts. This limitation is further exacerbated by the significant presence of non-Latin languages, such as Chinese and Arabic, online. One obvious solution for these challenges is to replace automated analysis with human oversight. Given the volume and complexity of Big Data, however, any manual analysis will have to balance using a limited data set capable of human interpretation or potentially spending vast sums of money hiring, training and maintaining substantial teams of highly-qualified analysts – a luxury not many organizations or PR agencies can yet afford.

While the incorporation of human insight can offer a potential solution to the linguistic challenges of Big Data analysis facing PR professionals, this presumes the skill set of PR practitioners is evolving to meet the need of a Big Data-driven communications environment. Unfortunately, evidence from studies into the changing skill sets of PR professionals belies this assumption. Research carried out during 2012[287] indicates that while UK practitioners are adapting their skill sets to the rise of social media technology, this change is not necessarily as rapid as it could be and may lead to the industry falling behind other, more data-driven industries such as advertising, management and specialist social media consultancies.

Such a shift in terms of PR skills, however, is not enough to fully deliver a renewed industry capable of engaging with Big Data-driven public relations. Without buy-in from senior practitioners and support from industry bodies, such as the CIPR and PRCA, the contemporary and possibly future reality of PR and Big Data may represent a further limitation to the strategic and creative contribution the sector might make to wider marketing and communication strategies. The consultant and author Martin Thomas ascribes PR's reluctance to embrace the strategic potential offered by opportunities such as Big Data to historically-driven traits like intellectual laziness, lack of confidence and executional fixation. The results have arguably been that PR has prioritized media relations over the development of strategic and creative insights designed to ensure the long-term viability of the PR function within organizations.[288]

---

[287]Recruiting for PR 2.0; Sarah Williams, Jennifer Challenor and Simon Collister: http://cipr.co/12Le7MC

[288]PR & Planning; Martin Thomas: http://cipr.co/XzKRRm

Conclusions and future directions

But it needn't be like this. While some of the potential applications of Big Data to PR might seem daunting (or fanciful) to some, forward-thinking organizations are already adapting and utilizing Big Data in some way. To help illustrate this, perhaps it might be helpful to go back and restate our understanding of Big Data and sketch out how it might be applied tactically and strategically by PR practitioners.

Firstly, Big Data is arguably not a distinct, uniform concept but rather a way of understanding the proliferation of publicly available data and the ways in which analysis can be used to develop strategic and tactical insights for organizations. Some of these approaches include using Big Data insights to:

- Identify new types of value-driven audiences or communities based on self-expression and the type of things they're saying, doing or buying in real time.
- Identify and predict longer-term changes in audience or stakeholder attitudes or behaviours.
- Identify, analyze and even predict internal and external events likely to impact on an organization, such as operational crises or consumer dissatisfaction.
- Devise more creative and strategic responses to communications objectives.
- Craft more targeted messages and create more relevant content in the format most appropriate to the audience.
- Evaluate the impact of communications campaigns more effectively and across a broader range of organizational metrics.

In all instances, however, these opportunities will bring about new practical and theoretical approaches for PR practitioners. In order to adapt successfully it is crucial for practitioners to recognize Big Data's limitations and approach analysis and organizational application with a set of realistic and workable objectives. Done right the results offer the PR profession significant short- and longer-term opportunities.

For example, Martin Thomas suggests data-driven PR practice can help the discipline gain greater recognition and respect from clients and thus improve influence among senior management. Such status, in turn, can help strengthen PR's position both within client organizations and also with regard to other marketing and management industry competitors, such as advertising, SEO and management consultancies (all of which claim to be operating to the same organizational objectives). The ultimate result is that data-driven communications can help generate increased reputation, revenue and greater profit margins. Such tangible benefits, it should be clear, point to a successful, increasingly strategic and thus long-term future for PR.

Given the potential outcomes of Big Data it's no surprise that the World Economic Forum this year categorized data as a commercial asset in the contemporary knowledge economy. To ensure PR secures a future for itself as a strategic business function in this networked era, it is going to be vital for practitioners to tap into these assets and make the most of them in establishing, maintaining and even predicting likely changes in the mutual understanding between organizations and their publics.

Biography

Simon Collister is a senior lecturer at University of the Arts, London. He is currently conducting PhD research at Royal Holloway, University of London's New Political Communication Unit on the mediation of power in networked communication environments. Before entering academia, Simon worked for a number of global communications consultancies, planning and implementing research-led campaigns for a range of public, voluntary, and private sector organizations.

INDEX